CHRONICLES OF BRITISH BUSINESS IN ASIA
1850-1960

Chronicles of British Business in Asia 1850-1960

A bibliography of printed company histories with short accounts of the concerns

LIONEL CARTER
Former Librarian, Centre of South Asian Studies, University of Cambridge

MANOHAR
2002

First published 2002

ISBN 81-7304-470-8

Published by
Ajay Kumar Jain for
Manohar Publishers & Distributors
4753/23 Ansari Road, Daryaganj
New Delhi 110 002

Printed at
Lordson Publishers Pvt Ltd
Delhi 110 007

To the memory of my mother,
Marjorie Ellen Carter

Contents

Introduction

This volume seeks to provide a comprehensive list of available printed histories of British companies operating in Asia during the last century of British imperialism. The starting date of 1850 was chosen because many of the businesses in this final phase of British rule originated in the third quarter of the nineteenth century. At the other end of the period most of the firms included were, by 1960, having to come to terms with a vastly changed world. Many were taken over – some by nationals or governments of the countries in which they operated. Others altered direction. Relatively few actually closed down. The dates 1850 and 1960 have not, however, been interpreted in a rigid sense. A business must have been operating during these years to be included in the volume. But where it was founded before 1850, the origins and early years are described. Similarly I have often gone beyond 1960 in order to bring a history to its logical conclusion.

The list is confined to printed histories. The act of printing (even where publication was private) does indicate a wish to place the history 'on the record' and to achieve this by at least a measure of circulation. The histories vary greatly in quality and value. They range from volumes commissioned by the firms themselves (often prepared by a retired member of staff) through to completely independent surveys by academic historians of high standing. In between, there are coffee-table works written by professional writers. Often these are of great interest but lack annotation or any indication of the available sources which have been used. In order to make the present list as comprehensive as possible, I have included histories of firms which appear as articles in journals or as chapters in collected volumes. I have also listed biographies of individuals where a person was so closely bound up with a firm that his story amounts in fact to the history of the firm at a particular period (for example, Sir Marcus Samuel of Shell (**721**)). I have not gone so far, however, as to include references to entries in *Who was Who* or similar biographical dictionaries.[1]

In compiling the list, I have avoided the question of whether the companies in question were registered locally or in London. For example, for much of their existence HSBC (**106**) and Jardine Matheson (**307**) were registered in Hong Kong and had their head offices there while a business like the Chartered Bank (**102**) was registered and operated from London right from the beginning. It is sometimes claimed that the locally registered companies were more truly Asian as their capital was denominated in the local currencies and their entrepreneurs understood better the needs of their customers. Be this as it may, my test for inclusion has simply been the empirical one that the eligible companies had an actual physical presence in some part of Asia and that they were run by British people. Occasionally, as with concerns like Unilever (**724**) or the Imperial Ottoman Bank (**405**), it may be open to argument whether the concerns were British ones but in such cases I have explained, in the individual entries, my reasons for inclusion.

Particular problems arise in connection with British multinational and similar companies which form the subject matter of Chapter 7. It would clearly be wrong to include British companies simply because they traded with Asia through a local agency house. On the other hand inclusion is justified in the case of those British companies which established local subsidiaries, networks, branches or factories. Such inclusion can, however, only take place if the appropriate history of the company covers these Asian experiences in an informative way. Regrettably some companies have had to be excluded as their histories do not discuss the Asian side of their operations. Similarly in a number of cases (for example Imperial Chemical Industries (**711**) and Unilever) only some of the available histories are listed here. The excluded ones have been judged unsuitable for present purposes. There is a clear overlap between some of the big businesses described in Chapter 1 on the entire Asian region and the multinationals in Chapter 7. In general it may be said that for the firms in Chapter 1, Asia formed a large part, if not the central part, of their business. On the other hand for the multinationals Asia was generally only a part (and sometimes a rather insignificant part) of their worldwide activities.[2]

Transportation, in particular shipping, provides the material for a substantial proportion of this work. It seemed essential to include the shipping companies as they played such a major role in nineteenth and twentieth century inter-Asian trade and in binding the Asian economy with the rest of the world. Indeed the operations of these companies lay at the core of the last phase of the British imperial experience. The problem however was that there are so many eligible shipping companies that to have included all with printed histories would have seriously unbalanced the volume. I finally decided to include those companies in the main text where Asia was central to their operations. Histories of companies not principally serving Asian ports have been listed in Appendix 1.[3]

In contrast to the shipping companies, histories of Asian railway companies have not been included in the main text. In actual fact there are very few such histories which fall within the scope of this volume. I found that the only eligible items related to Indian railway companies. Here the position is complicated because these companies came under considerable governmental supervision and control from a fairly early stage.[4] After 1879 (when it acquired the East Indian Railway) the Indian government began a policy of taking over the ownership of the companies while leaving management in private hands. From 1925, the government went further and assumed direct management of the lines it owned. Moreover, to make the picture more complicated, from 1869 government itself began constructing its own railway lines.[5] In Appendix 2 I give details of the few histories which relate to Indian railway companies that began life as public companies run by British people and which had their own boards of directors.

In order to make the bibliography comprehensive, it has been necessary to trespass into parts of North Africa. It would not have been possible to prepare a meaningful guide on the 'histories' of British companies in the Middle East without including Egypt and the Sudan. By 1900 the British had effectively taken control of the two countries and were to turn them into one of their main spheres of influence in the region. It is hardly surprising, therefore, that British-owned companies set-down firmer roots in Egypt and the Sudan than was possible in Iran, Iraq or the French-influenced states of Lebanon and Syria.

* * *

Each entry includes a brief account of the origins of a particular firm and the main developments in its history. This seemed desirable because so many of these concerns which were once household names, both in Britain and the East, are now forgotten. I have not been able to consult manuscript material (and in many cases this no longer exists) and the accounts I give are mainly drawn from the histories which are cited. (I have in a few cases corrected obvious errors revealed by secondary sources.) This does mean that I have not been able to bring some accounts of firms up to 1960 where the company histories end their narratives before that date.[6]

Thacker's Indian Directory for 1899 has thirty-six pages devoted to 'Merchants, Agents, Joint-Stock Companies, Trading Firms, &c.' in the

Calcutta region. This suggests that there were more than five hundred eligible businesses in Eastern India alone at that time. Consequently, while I believe that the present volume provides a representative selection of British firms and a sense of commercial life as it existed, it cannot claim to be a general survey.[7] Few of the many failures achieved a historical study. The 'company histories' are in the main success stories. We are fortunate that so many key British businesses in Asia had their histories written but there are regrettably a few notable omissions. Sadly no account of the Eastern Bank – so important in the Middle East – seems to have been produced and many of its records no longer exist.[8] For China there appears to be no history for the important agency house of Dents;[9] for India we lack histories of Killick Nixon, Forbes and Company and Jardine Skinner amongst others; in South-East Asia I have found no history for Symes, Barlows or Hendersons; in the Middle East we lack a proper history of the famous concern of Lynch Brothers[10] while in Persia, the history of Lloyd Scott seems not to have been chronicled.

Many of the businesses described here started life from quite humble beginnings as typical mid-Victorian small businesses. Perhaps, as with James Killick (**109**), there was a need for a sailor in retirement to find a living on land. In the case of William Strang Steel (**616**), who had already worked for others in the East for almost twenty years, the idea appears to have been to set-up a Rangoon business which could then be run from London on his return to Britain (which occurred three years later). Often the concerns faced a real crisis when the first or second generation of founders died or retired. This was certainly the position with the shipping concern which took the name of Gellatly, Hankey and Company (**104**). There the effective managing director of the business put together a partnership to keep the firm going when the previous owner died without an heir. Management of some of the tea companies (for example the Jorehaut Tea Company (**515**)) stayed within the family for generations but the experience of Deacon and Company (**302**) was that none of the descendants of its founders wished to remain as managers. (One may add here in parenthesis one's amazement that Deacons should have survived at all when it had compradores abscond with a large part of the funds in 1908 and 1934, was run by a managing-partner who arranged for half the firm's capital to be siphoned off as dividends in the early 1920s, and then was decimated by the Japanese during the second world war.) Many of the Calcutta agency houses (such as Balmer Lawrie (**504**)) had passed beyond being mere family concerns by the start of the twentieth century and were already sizeable institutions in their own right. The banks, of course, were large concerns from the beginning but they were to face their own serious problems from the late nineteenth century depressions and the recurring depreciation in the value of their silver.

More than one author of the company histories has commented to the effect that whatever one's views of determinism as a historical force, for British companies in Asia in the last century, the existence of the right men in the right place and at the right time was absolutely crucial for their survival and growth. It is certainly a striking fact that the East seemed to claim the attention of some of the most able British entrepreneurs of the period. Men like the first Sir John Ellerman (**103**) (perhaps the ablest of them all and certainly the richest), the first Lord Inchcape (**108**), Sir Paul and Sir Edward Benthall of Birds of Calcutta (**506**), Lord Cadman of Anglo-Persian Oil (**402**), Sir Ernest Cassel behind the schemes for the National Banks of Egypt (**407**) and Turkey (**408**) not to mention Turkish Petroleum (**409**), Sir John Hay of Guthries (**607**), Sir Thomas Jackson of HSBC, Arthur Lampard of Harrisons and Crosfield (**608**), Sir Marcus Samuel of Shell, Sir Thomas Sutherland of P. & O. (**113**), John Samuel Swire of Butterfield and Swire (**309**) and Robert I. Watson of Burmah Oil (**606**) – the list could be considerably extended.

A major theme running through these histories concerns the extent to which the various entrepreneurs foresaw the fundamental changes which national independence and other political developments would bring and the ways in which they took appropriate action to deal with these changes. For example, the directors of the Williamson Magor tea company in India (**526**) realised early in the 1960s that the participation of a key Indian on their board was crucial for the future of their business. Their wise assessment undoubtedly helps to account for the survival of the group as one of the world's largest private tea producers. Key personnel in the Imperial Bank of Persia (**404**) as well as the British Political Resident in the Gulf were realising throughout the 1940s that the Bank had no future in Persia. By 1952 it had been transformed into virtually a new bank and its strategy of concentrating on other Middle Eastern countries, particularly the Gulf states, gave it a run of almost three decades before it was totally integrated within the structure of HSBC. Some of the companies chose to relocate elsewhere in the British Commonwealth. The Borneo Company (**603**), for example, decided to move many of its assets to Canada. Other companies chose less politically developed parts of the Commonwealth. Finlays (**508**) were to move into Kenya as early as 1926 and set-up tea estates in that country. However there were to be problems when independence finally reached these areas. A number of the firms in this volume completely changed the nature of their activities.[11] Quite a few were to end up with a heavy emphasis on chemicals including Burmah Oil, Harrisons and Crosfield, Parrys (**517**) and the British end of Andrew Yule and Company (**527**).

Not the least fascinating part of this bibliographical project has been to watch the historical jigsaw for the end-game being put together as I worked. Grindlays (**511**), having survived in tact within ANZ Bank, was acquired by Standard Chartered (included in the volume). James Finlay was taken over by its largest shareholder, Swires (also included in this volume). Harrisons and Crosfield, having become Elementis, was in merger discussions. Most remarkably of all, Burmah Castrol was taken over by BP Amoco – a company which, in part, Burmah had created 91 years before (see **402**).

* * *

It would not have been possible to have undertaken this project without access to the rich resources of the British Library in London and I have incurred many debts there. My first is to the staff of the Humanities Reading Rooms who have always been most willing and helpful. Then I would like to acknowledge the suggestions and valuable assistance received from the staff (past and present) of the Oriental and India Office Collections (many of them former colleagues from my India Office Library days). I would particularly like to mention in this connection: Ian Baxter, Richard Bingle, David Blake, the late Barry Bloomfield, Paul Carter, Andrew Cook, Anthony Farrington, Jill Geber, Cynthia Goodwin, Patricia Herbert, Patricia Kattenhorn, Margaret Makepeace, Martin Moir, Michael O'Keefe, Salim Quraishi, Timothy Thomas, Graham Shaw, Hedley Sutton and Penelope Tuson.

Another library which holds unique materials that were central to my work is the British Library of Political and Economic Science at the London School of Economics. I am most grateful to the staff there for their patience in the face of persistent enquiry. At the Library of the School of Oriental and African Studies in London I was much helped by Helen Cordell and Ramesh Dogra. I would also like to thank the enquiry staffs of the Guildhall Library and the National Maritime Museum Library for their assistance.

In Cambridge I owe a particular debt for help received from Catherine Ansorge (Librarian of the Faculty of Oriental Studies) and her staff. At Cambridge University Library valuable suggestions and comments were made by Geoffrey Roper and Heather Bleaney of the Islamic Bibliography Unit. I would also like to thank the staff in the Reading and West Rooms and on the Periodicals Desk for their unfailing helpfulness.

I wish to record my gratitude to the Archivist of the Flintshire Record Office at Hawarden for help with the Gillanders Arbuthnot entry. The history and papers of Gillanders form a part of the Gladstone Collection at Hawarden. The Librarian of the Merseyside Maritime Museum has given me valuable assistance with respect of materials held in the Museum. I also wish to acknowledge help received on the Standard Life Assurance Company from Professor Michael Moss, Archivist of the University of Glasgow, and Kate Hutcheson, Archivist of Standard Life.

Finally I should like to thank Theon Wilkinson for drawing my attention to a number of important histories; Barbara Burton for very kindly reading through the text at an early stage and commenting on it; my former colleagues at the Cambridge South Asian Studies Centre; and Ram Advani, K.K. Aziz, Sanjoy Bhattacharya, Sangeeta Chawla, Sonia Holmes, Kathleen Kazer, Jayne Ringrose and Anne Thompson for wise counsel and many kindnesses. None of the persons mentioned above bears any responsibility for the facts and judgements presented in the volume.

Unless indicated otherwise at the end of an entry, all material cited in this bibliography is to be found in the collections of the British Library, London. Cross-references are given in bold type.

Harrow, May 2002 LIONEL CARTER

NOTES

1. Two of the most important biographical dictionaries for recent British business history are: David J. Jeremy (Ed.), *Dictionary of business biography: a biographical dictionary of business leaders active in Britain in the period 1860-1980.* (5 vols.) London: Butterworths, 1984-6; Anthony Slaven and Sydney Checkland (Eds.), *Dictionary of Scottish business biography (1860-1960).* (2 vols.) Aberdeen: Aberdeen University Press, 1986-90.
2. I have found the following three bibliographies particularly helpful in identifying eligible multinationals for this volume: Francis Goodall, *A bibliography of British business histories.* Aldershot: Gower, 1987. (Business history series; no.3.); Francis Goodall, Terry Gourvish and Steven Tolliday, *International bibliography of business history.* London: Routledge, 1997; Stephanie Zarach, *British business history: a bibliography.* (2nd ed.) Basingstoke, Macmillan, 1994.
3. Key works on the British shipping companies, their sources and histories are: P. Mathias and A.W. Pearsall (Eds.), *Shipping: a survey of historical records.* Newton Abbot: David and Charles, 1971; K.J. Smith, Christopher

T. Watts and Michael J. Watts, *Records of merchant shipping and seamen.* Kew: Public Record Office, 1998. (PRO readers' guides; no. 20.) Mention should also be made of the article by Francis E. Hyde on 'British shipping companies in East and South-East Asia, 1860-1939' in C.D. Cowan (Ed.), *The economic development of South-East Asia.* London: Allen & Unwin, 1964, pp. 27-47.

4. The account of government control over Indian railways given here is taken from the article on 'Railways' by John M. Hurd in Dharma Kumar (Ed.) with Meghnad Desai, *The Cambridge Economic History of India, Vol. 2: c. 1757–c. 1970.* Cambridge: Cambridge University Press, 1983, pp. 737-61. Perhaps the best source for information on the pre-independence Indian railway companies is: J.N Westwood, *Railways of India.* Newton Abbot: David and Charles, 1974.
5. The famous North-Western Railway, which was eventually to run to the Khyber, was an example of one of these State-founded railway companies.
6. A volume which has been invaluable in providing accounts of the last days of British businesses in India is: Stephanie Jones, *Merchants of the Raj: British managing agency houses in Calcutta yesterday and today.* Basingstoke: Macmillan, 1992.
7. The best available general survey is: R.P.T. Davenport-Hines and Geoffrey Jones (Eds.), *British business in Asia since 1860.* Cambridge: Cambridge University Press, 1989. There is also an important general study of the origins and development of many of the agency houses in this bibliography in Stanley Chapman, *Merchant enterprise in Britain: from the industrial revolution to World War I.* Cambridge: Cambridge University Press, 1992. (Chapter 4 'The agency houses: trade to India and the Far East' is particularly relevant.) See also Professor Chapman's *The rise of merchant banking.* London: Allen & Unwin, 1984.
8. See: Rodney Wilson, 'Financial development of the Arab Gulf: the Eastern Bank experience 1917-50.' *Business history* (London). Vol. 29, Part 2 (April 1987), pp. 178-98. Unfortunately Wilson's account is not sufficiently general to allow an entry for the Bank to be included in the present volume.
9. See, however, the entry for the British North Borneo Chartered Company (**605**) for an account of Sir Alfred Dent's involvement in the early development of that company.
10. See, however, the entry for the Euphrates and Tigris Steam Navigation Company (**403**) which describes Lynch Brothers' role in the running of the company.
11. Professor Geoffrey Jones has used the expression 'reinvention of themselves' to cover these twentieth century changes of activity by British firms with overseas interests. See his *Merchants to multinationals: British trading companies in the nineteenth and twentieth centuries.* Oxford: Oxford University Press, 2000. The history of Harrisons and Crosfield is certainly a remarkable example of such changes of direction. Starting as tea and coffee merchants, the firm moved into plantations (particularly rubber plantations) around 1900. It then diversified in many directions including into building supplies. Eventually it was to end life as a chemical firm with a specialism in rubber-based technology.

CHAPTER 1

Histories relating to Asia in general

101. BRITISH INDIA STEAM NAVIGATION COMPANY

The famous Calcutta agency house of Mackinnon Mackenzie was set-up in 1847 (*see under* Inchcape and Company **(108)**) and soon became involved in chartering ships to send cargoes to Britain and Australia. However in order to establish a viable shipping line of its own it was necessary to obtain contracts from government for the carriage of mail. When Sir William Mackinnon secured the contract to carry mail between Calcutta and Rangoon in 1856, he felt able to establish the Calcutta and Burmah Steam Navigation Company. The early years of the new concern were to prove difficult. One of the first vessels was almost immediately requisitioned by the Government of India to move troops during the Indian Mutiny. Then an attempt to run a service between Calcutta and Madras failed, while in 1859 a vessel was lost at sea. (Between 1856 and 1866 eleven of thirty-one ships were wrecked.) In many ways the year 1862 was critical for the company. That year Sir William was on the point of obtaining contracts which would allow further services to be run from Calcutta to Singapore and Malacca and from Calcutta to Bombay, Karachi, the Persian Gulf and Basra. Accordingly the Calcutta and Burmah company was transformed into the British India Steam Navigation Company with a capital of £400,000 registered in Scotland. It had nine vessels at work; six being built; and two chartered.

It must be stressed that the British India company started life as a coastal shipping concern. Operations centred on India, Burma and the Gulf and exports included rice, teak and jute. Many Indian labourers were carried as deck passengers while in 1869 British India began transporting pilgrims to Jeddah. The company was much involved in the movement of troops and of course mail. It was very anxious not to antagonise the larger P. & O. company **(113)** which ran fast 'Home Line' services to Britain. British India was to act as a feeder operation for these services. By 1868 inter-change arrangements between P. & O. and British India ships were in existence at Aden, while the following year the two companies negotiated a written agreement which standardised certain of their freight charges. British India also undertook not to oppose the P. & O's profitable Bombay-China opium trade or to otherwise interfere with P. & O's interests.

The opening of the Suez Canal completely altered Mackinnon's conception of the British India concern as 'Home Line' services now made much more sense. Even so he did not directly challenge P. & O. when British India began regular sailings in 1872 from London to the Persian Gulf calling at Karachi. A London-Calcutta route was added in 1876. Mackinnon chose to turn his attention particularly to the development of East Africa and shipping services thereto. An Aden-Zanzibar service began in 1872 to be followed in 1890 by a London-Zanzibar service by way of Aden and Mombassa. In 1881 a regular U.K.-Queensland service was begun with a mail subsidy but this did not last long. When Mackinnon died in 1893, the British India fleet amounted to 87 vessels and was a major force in world shipping.

Mackinnon was followed by the man who was later to become the first Lord Inchcape. Inchcape did not in fact takeover the chairmanship of British India until 1913 but he effectively ran the company from 1893 until his death in 1932. The economic environment he faced was much harsher and more competitive than in Mackinnon's time but Inchcape possessed qualities of toughness and diplomacy which allowed him to further expand the concern. By the beginning of the first world war British India had become the world's largest shipping line while in 1922 (despite war losses) it possessed 158 ships.

Inchcape's way of working was to come to agreements with competitors and also takeover operators as opportunity allowed. In 1902 he was much involved in the work of the Colombo Shipping Conference which laid down routes, spheres of influence and freight rates for the participating companies. In the 1920s Inchcape made generous agreements with the Morarjee family who owned the Indian Scindia shipping concern. In 1910 Inchcape acquired the Bombay-Hedjaz Company (Shah Line) and two years later took over the Apcar Line which carried Chinese immigrants and cargoes to Singapore as well as having a significant presence in Japanese ports. In 1913 British India took over the Australian Currie Line while in 1928 it acquired the Arakan Flotilla Company which operated on the rivers of Upper Burma. The most spectacular development in these years, however, was the merger of British India with P. & O. in 1913. As we have seen, there had been a great deal of co-operation between the two companies and at first it appeared that P. & O. had taken over British India. However Lord Inchcape became chairman of P. & O. in 1914 (in addition to his chairmanship of British India) and he allowed British India to continue operations very much as before. In fact British India was not finally integrated into P. & O. until 1971 and remained autonomous until then.

British India vessels played a crucial role in both world wars although of course many of the usual passenger services had to be reduced or discontinued during the hostilities. In addition the company set aside nine ships for use in the League of Nations sanctions against Italy in 1935. British India lost about 20 per cent of its ships during the first world war and about 50 per cent in the second. After Indian independence in 1947 the firm was not granted a licence to operate coastal shipping services where an Indian shipping concern was able to do so. This meant that only the Bombay-Basra coastal service survived. The firm saw its future in running medium-sized vessels which allowed greatest flexibility. On the occasion of its centenary in 1956, British India was carrying 280,000 passengers a year and nearly three and a half million tons of cargo. However in 1957 the line moved its management to London. Thereafter the decline in passenger traffic was extremely rapid and in 1969 the last British India ship on the East Africa service was sold. The same year all regular P. & O. group passenger services to the Far East were withdrawn.

See also Peninsular and Oriental Steam Navigation Company **(113)** *for related material on the history of the British India Steam Navigation Company after 1913.*

BI: the British India Steam Navigation Company Limited. By W.A. Laxon and F.W. Perry. Kendal: World Ship Society, 1994. 256p., ill.
[National Maritime Museum Library.]

B.I. centenary 1856-1956. By George Blake. London: Collins, 1956. 272p., ill. Index.

'British India steamers and the trade of the Persian Gulf, 1862-1914.' By Stephanie Jones. ***The great circle: journal of the Australian Association for Maritime History*** (Sydney), Vol. 7, No. 1 (April 1985), pp. 23-44.

Merchant adventurers 1914-1918. By F.A. Hook. London: A.& C. Black, 1920. viii, 319p., ill. Index.
[A history of the P. & O., British India and Associated Lines during the first world war.]

'Scottish overseas enterprise and the lure of London: the Mackinnon Shipping Group, 1847-1893.' By J.F. Munro. ***Scottish economic and social history*** (Glasgow), Vol. 8 (1988), pp. 73-87.

Trade and shipping: Lord Inchcape 1852-1932. By Stephanie Jones. Manchester: Manchester University Press, 1989. xiii, 222p. Bibliog. Index.

Valiant voyaging: a short history of the British India Steam Navigation Company in the second world war 1939-1945. By Hilary St. George Saunders. London: Faber and Faber, 1948. 216p., ill. Index.

102. CHARTERED BANK OF INDIA, AUSTRALIA AND CHINA

The Chartered Bank of India, Australia and China was granted its Royal Charter in 1853 largely through the efforts of James Wilson who had earlier founded *The Economist.* However it took some time for the bank to become operational as a block of the shareholders felt it was unwise to proceed in the difficult circumstances of the Crimean War (1853-6). It was not until 1858 that the British Treasury granted the bank the certificate that allowed it to commence business. The Chartered Bank had the right to issue banknotes. Those of its offices which did so were termed branches; the other offices were called agencies.

It soon became clear that the bank's activities would be unwelcome in Australia so attention was directed towards Asia. Agencies were opened in Bombay and Calcutta during 1858 with branches in Shanghai and Hong Kong in 1858 and 1859 and an agency in Singapore in 1859. (It became a branch in 1861.) The bank had begun operations at a fortunate time when the Eastern economies were expanding but in Bombay the bank's agent adopted an imprudent policy which tied up his capital in the wrong sort of business. Attempts to call the money in during 1865 were to result ultimately in £45,000 being written off. This led the head office in London to adopt the conservative and cautious policy for which the bank became renowned. Advances on the security of shares were in general not allowed until the end of the century. Financing was short and medium term and strongly centred on commodity trading. Before 1900 the bank's branches were almost all located at the major Asian ports.

The Chartered Bank's cautious policy was soon tested and it survived the 1866 banking crisis well. In Calcutta the bank particularly suffered from the panic caused by the failure of the Commercial Bank but reserves were brought in from Rangoon and Bombay and the crisis passed. In China there were some minor losses following the collapse of several important business houses. In Singapore the bank had a very difficult time but pulled through with the support of the Chinese community.

Perhaps the key event in the Chartered Bank's history was the appointment of J.H. Gwyther as London manager in 1871. When Gwyther retired as chairman of the bank in 1904 he could look back on a transformation in which the bank had moved from being a small and struggling Eastern exchange bank to become a powerful and respected international institution with an extensive branch network throughout eastern and southern Asia. Gwyther was greatly assisted by T.H. Whitehead, manager at Hong Kong for almost twenty years, who was an effective match for Sir Thomas Jackson of HSBC **(106)**. It was Gwyther who brought the bank through the silver crises at the end of the century. In 1885 he recalled almost all the allotted capital from the East and branches thereafter had to make do with local deposits for local funds. With a cautious exchange policy and avoidance of forward contracts, Gwyther's move effectively minimised exposure to silver. Gwyther was very doubtful of China's ability to absorb capital productively and he avoided the railway and government funding schemes of the China Consortium. It was a policy the bank came rather to regret by the time of the first world war.

Some of the Chartered Bank's most successful offices were in those countries where it had been one of the first of the western banks. The bank opened in Rangoon as early as 1862 and soon moved into a commanding position in Burma. In Singapore the Chartered Bank was the most popular bank in the country by 1880. The bank opened an agency in Batavia in 1863 and by the mid-1870s had become the leading bank in the city. On the other hand it found competition very intense in the remainder of Indonesia. The bank opened an agency in Yokohama in 1880 but for the first ten years found it difficult to make any headway against HSBC. The same was true of Siam where HSBC had opened an office in 1888. There was little new trade for the Chartered Bank when it arrived in 1894. Around the turn of the century the bank made a deliberate decision to become a prime contributor in the development of Malaya. Offices had already been opened in Penang in 1875 and Kuala Lumpur in 1888. Now agencies were opened at Klang (1909), Seremban (1910), Malacca (1911), and Ipoh (1912). The move inland was matched in India with the opening of agencies in Amritsar and Delhi (1910 and 1911).

The Chartered Bank was extremely active during the first world war and financed a vast quantity of war materiel as well as the commodities with which it was more usually involved. It also had to contend with the effects, in the last years of the war, of the collapse of many Indian banks. The most notable of the failures was the Indian Specie Bank which threatened a great decline in the price of silver and the Chartered Bank became involved in measures to prevent this happening. The inter-war years were difficult ones for the bank because of the collapse in the prices of all the commodities which it financed. It was to face disturbances in Amritsar, Shanghai, Canton, Hong Kong, Indonesia and Siam. In addition the bank's premises suffered from the effects of serious floods and earthquakes. All was not on the dark side, however. During the inter-war years the Chartered Bank opened further agencies in India, Malaya, Sarawak and Manchuria. In 1927 it secured control of the P. & O. Banking Corporation. The Corporation had nine branches of its own across Asia and also had control of the Allahabad Bank with a branch network in India.

In 1942, as a consequence of the Japanese War, the Chartered Bank found itself without any branches east of Calcutta with the exception of Chungking. However it remained in business and there was never any doubt as to its stability and viability. The post-hostilities planning it undertook during the war enabled it to return very rapidly to eastern Asia. By 1948 it had re-opened all its pre-war establishments as well as new branches in Cochin, Chittagong, Sarawak and Sabah. During 1959 the bank purchased the Eastern Bank which strengthened its position in India and gave it a presence in the Persian Gulf. In the post-war years the bank had to come to terms with the independence of many Asian countries and in some its branches were to be nationalised. For example the Allahabad Bank in India was taken over in 1969. Similarly the Irano-British Bank was nationalised in 1979. (The Chartered Bank had established this bank during 1959 in conjunction with a group of Iranian investors.) At the beginning of 1970 the Chartered Bank merged with the Standard Bank to form the Standard and Chartered Banking Group.

Realms of silver: one hundred years of banking in the East. By Compton Mackenzie. London: Routledge & Kegan Paul, 1954. xiv, 338p., ill.

A story brought up to date. Standard Chartered Bank. New enlarged edition. London: The Bank, 1983. 99p., ill.

[A reprint of ***Realms of silver*** and an earlier edition of ***A story brought up to date*** formed Vols. 1 and 4 of ***A history of the Standard Chartered Bank*** published by the Bank in 1980. Vol. 2 of the ***History*** dealt with the first hundred years of the Standard Bank of South Africa and Vol. 3 with bankers in West Africa.]

103. ELLERMAN LINES

For all but its last fourteen years the Ellerman Shipping Lines were under the control of two generations of the Ellerman family. Both father and son had the same name – Sir John Reeves Ellerman. Ellerman senior (1862-1933) was himself of German-Lutheran stock. His father had moved from Hamburg to Hull around 1850 and had set-up as a corn merchant and shipbroker. The young Sir John trained as an accountant and moved to London where at the early age of 24 he opened his own practice in Moorgate. He soon became involved in company promotion and learnt the value of investment trusts. His move into shipowning came about by chance but in many respects it was the logical development of his career. By the end of the nineteenth century the British shipping industry was highly fragmented and was becoming uncompetitive compared with its foreign rivals. There was a need for a consolidator and for someone who could implement effective accounting measures and cost control.

Early in January 1892 Frederick Leyland collapsed and died on Blackfriars Station in London. Leyland was the owner of the Leyland Shipping Line which mainly traded with America. Within a year a syndicate consisting of Ellerman, Christopher Furness and Henry O'Hagan acquired the Leyland Line. Furness was appointed chairman but did not long survive in that position and Ellerman took over. There were considerable doubts as to whether Ellerman could make the Leyland Line profitable but in fact he turned it into a spectacular success. Between 1892 and 1901 annual dividends averaged 11 per cent. In 1901 Ellerman sold the concern to J.P. Morgan's International Mercantile Marine while buying back some 20 ships for his own future operations which were to take place within a new venture called the Ellerman Line.

The arrangement with Morgan included a stipulation that Ellerman would not compete on Atlantic routes. Consequently, as Ellerman himself put it to a journalist: 'The Leyland deal deprived me of the Atlantic trade so I've turned to the East and hope to do equally well out of it.' (It should be mentioned here that Ellerman was also to turn to South Africa and to Latin America.) Ellerman made his move East through the takeover of a considerable number of established shipping lines. In 1901 itself he acquired the Papayanni Line (8 ships); the Hall Line (11 ships); the City Line (15 ships); and Westcott and Laurance (9 ships). In 1908 Ellerman took over Bucknalls (44 ships) while in 1916 he acquired the Wilson Line (68 ships). (Brief details of the previous histories of these lines are given at the end of this entry.) Ellerman's method of business was to keep the acquired lines running as separate entities. He retained the existing managements which were further stimulated by competition within the group. Ellerman worked to obtain the closest possible degree of control over the companies. He generally issued himself with a large number of 'management shares' and almost invariably held all or most of the ordinary and preference capital.

Ellerman soon set to work extending his eastern services. By 1905, jointly with the Clan Line, he was operating a service from the British west coast to Malabar. That year his ships became part of a joint service carrying jute between Calcutta and Latin America. With the Strick Line, Ellermans also inaugurated a monthly service to Marmagoa. At the end of the year about five Ellerman ships were transferred to the Glen Line **(105)** when that concern met financial difficulties. This involved Ellerman in Far Eastern trade but earnings were disappointing and he withdrew in 1908. At that point, however, the Bucknalls purchase allowed the development of Persian Gulf trade and Ellerman entered into an agreement with the Strick Line to share the cargoes equally. In 1906 Ellerman won the right for his ships to serve Madras and Pondicherry.

All told the Ellerman concerns lost about a hundred ships in the first world war but the war stimulated trade and Ellerman made the most of this. In 1915 he started a New York-Bombay service in addition to a USA-Calcutta operation. The following year his ships began running from Canada to the Mediterranean, India, Ceylon and the East Indies. In 1915 Bucknalls began a new service from the Far East to Britain with additional cargoes taken on at Colombo and the Malabar Coast. The same year Ellerman acquired rights over the German Diekmanns Mills in Rangoon and the Arracan Company (another rice-milling and trading concern). The shipping conference allowed him to take the milled rice in his own ships to Madras and Colombo where they were further loaded with cargoes for Britain.

Ellerman continued with similar developments in the years after 1919 although the period was obviously one of increasing difficulty for him. In 1920 he began a weekly service from Jaffa for the transport of oranges. In 1921 a regular service from Middlesbrough and northern Europe was begun which ran to Malaya, Hong Kong, Shanghai, Japan and north China returning via the Philippines and Colombo to London. In 1925 Ellerman purchased Lacey and Cannan, a Shanghai agency house with offices elsewhere in China. The extent of Ellerman's losses during the great depression is not known. When he died in 1933 Ellerman was the richest man in Britain with a fortune of between £37 million and £40 million although this had been made in a number of areas besides shipping.

The second baronet (1909-73) was not of the same calibre as his father but he was a competent businessman who left much of the running of the concerns to his managers. He adopted a conservative approach and left the structure of the conglomerate as it was but he did innovate and modernise. The Ellerman Lines lost about 95 ships in the second world war which was a very large proportion of the total fleet. However there was rapid re-building and purchasing after the war so that by the early 1950s the concern owned some 129 ships. The story up to 1960 is largely one of Ellermans pulling out of the South Asia trade. In 1949 the Hull-India service was ended and in 1950 the concern decided to concentrate on South African passenger services in preference to Indian ones. In 1961 Ellermans withdrew the United States-India services. Between 1950 and 1960, however, the line ran a jute service from the new Chalna Port in East Pakistan to Dundee. Legal developments in Burma made it impossible to operate the rice mills and Ellermans left the country altogether. However in 1961 the line began new direct shipping services to ports in Sabah and Sarawak.

Ellermans took up containerisation as early as 1964 although it was left out when the largest shipping groups formed Overseas Containers Limited. So together with the Ben Line **(114)**, Harrisons and others, Ellermans formed its own consortium with the name of 'Associated Container Transport'. Eventually container services were started to Australia and the Far East with a refrigerated operation from the Pacific to the United States. In 1972, just before the second baronet died, Ellermans was converted into a charitable trust and the concern was restructured. This meant the ending of the separate lines. Instead Ellermans was organised in divisions such as shipping and travel and leisure. In 1984 there was a management buy-out of the concern and in 1987 Trafalgar House (owners of the Cunard Line) acquired Ellermans for £24.1 million.

Brief histories of the shipping lines taken over by the first Sir John Ellerman are given below:

Bucknalls

Henry Bucknall and Sons was founded in London around 1740. The firm traded in cork and had its own house in Lisbon. At some point in the mid-nineteenth century Bucknalls acquired a fleet of four or five ships to carry its business cargoes. The ships were tramped quite often to Indian and Burmese ports. In 1890 the separate company of Bucknall Brothers was set-up to manage the shipping side of the business with Edward Lloyd as the manager. The following year Lloyd established a shipping line – the British and Colonial Steam Navigation Company. His big success was to win the contract to serve President Kruger's Transvaal Railway at its port of Delagoa Bay. In 1894 Lloyd established a service between New York and Calcutta followed by a New York-Bombay service. These American operations were run by the new Bucentaur Steamship Company. In 1900 all Bucknall shipping interests were combined in the 'Bucknall Steamship Lines'. Three years later a service was established to the Persian Gulf and between 1899 and 1902 some twenty new ships were acquired. This proved to be over-expansion given the depressed freight levels of the time and also the Boer War which affected the line very badly. When Ellerman acquired Bucknalls in 1908 the business was close to bankruptcy.

City Line (George Smith and Sons)

George Smith of Ayrshire and his two sons set-up their business in 1826. They were warehousemen and merchants. In 1840 they bought their first ship which they arranged to be sailed to Calcutta. The fleet had expanded to twelve vessels by 1855 and the Smiths were running (jointly with another line) a regular monthly service to Calcutta. In the 1860s a regular service to Bombay was started and this soon began to call at Karachi en route. Between 1870 and 1890 the Smiths acquired 20 steamers and added Australia and the Far East to their destinations. The City Line was floated as a public company in 1892.

Hall Line (Robert Alexander and Company)

In 1853 Robert Alexander was sent to Liverpool by his father to help with the family shipping business which was being established in the port. Fifteen years later he formed his own firm, the 'Sun Shipping Company', and acquired the *Haddon Hall* – first of the famous *Hall* vessels. Sailings were to Australia at first but Alexander soon came to consider Bombay as one of his principal destinations. In 1879-80 a regular service was begun to Karachi when Alexander obtained the contract to supply British coal to the North-Western Railway. This ended in 1898. Alexander had a fleet of fifteen steamers in 1890 but for some years around this date the firm was not very profitable and dividends were passed. The Sun Shipping Company was liquidated in 1899 and replaced by the Hall Line Limited. By the end of the century the line was facing managerial problems because of Alexander's ill health.

Papayanni Line

Georges Michael Papayanni was a Greek merchant who settled in London in 1832, moving to Liverpool in 1844. He became naturalised in 1852. Papayanni bought his own ships to control freight costs. With his brother and a Turkish friend the firm expanded and acquired its first steamer in 1855. By the 1880s the Papayanni Line was the leading British shipping firm serving the Mediterranean from Greece to Turkey and Syria. However by the turn of the century it had inadequate capital to replace its ageing vessels.

Westcott and Laurance

William George Westcott was a ship's captain sailing to the Mediterranean for the Black Sea and Levant Steam Navigation Company. In 1865 the company became insolvent but Westcott was persuaded to continue on his own. He went into partnership with Robert Simpson Houseden and although they only owned one ship at first, they built up an important business through very skilled chartering. Destinations included Greece, Turkey, the Black Sea and Danube ports, Malta and Alexandria. In 1871 Houseden died and Westcott entered into a new partnership with Charles James Laurance. The line gradually expanded in the years up to 1901.

Wilson Line

Thomas Wilson of Hull set-up in business in 1822 bringing iron ore over from Sweden for use in the Sheffield foundries. He bought his first ship in the late 1820s. In 1841, when all his partners had retired, he formed Thomas Wilson, Sons and Company. At this point he owned nine steamers; won the UK-Norway and Sweden mail contract; and started a Hull-United States service. By the 1870s services were running to the far Baltic, Constantinople, the Black Sea and Colombo, Madras and Calcutta. In 1875 Wilson decided to enter the Atlantic trade seriously and cut-down his Indian operations retaining only a service to Bombay and the west coast of India. In fact Wilsons increasingly concentrated on the Baltic, the Mediterranean and the Atlantic. By the early twentieth century the firm owned around a hundred ships. It seems likely that Wilsons decided to sell their shipping interests in 1916 because of the high replacement cost of their wartime losses and also their doubts as to the future of the Baltic and Russian trades.

Ellerman Lines. By John Clarkson and Roy Fenton. Preston: John & Marion Clarkson, 1993. (Ships in focus.) 72p., ill. Index.
[Mainly photographs of ships with captions but begins with a one-page history of 'The Ellerman achievement'.]

Ellerman Lines. By Duncan Haws. Hereford: TCL Publications, 1989. (Merchant fleets, no.16.) 203p., ill.
[Cambridge University Library.]

Ellermans: a wealth of shipping. By James Taylor. London: Wilton House Gentry, 1976. 320p., ill. Index.

Rise and progress of the City Line. By Captain John Smith. Glasgow: John Smith and Son, 1908. xi, 225p., ill. Index.

The Westcotts and their times. By Ian D. Merry. London: National Maritime Museum, 1977. (Maritime monographs and reports; no. 25, 1977.) x, 147p., ill.
[National Maritime Museum Library.]

Wilson Line: the history and fleet of Thos. Wilson, Sons & Co. and Ellerman's Wilson Line Ltd. By John Harrower. Gravesend: World Ship Society, 1998. 216p., ill. Index.
[National Maritime Museum Library.]

Wilson Line of Hull 1831 to 1981: the rise and fall of an empire. By Arthur G. Credland and Michael Thompson. Beverley: Hutton, 1994. 143p., ill.
[National Maritime Museum Library.]

104. GELLATLY, HANKEY AND COMPANY

The firm was established in 1862 but is able to trace its origins back to around 1796 when a Scot, Duncan Dunbar, set-up as a dealer in wines and spirits in Limehouse. Dunbar turned to supplying beer to the British overseas and bought ships for the purpose. Eventually he sold his brewery to Taylor, Walker and decided to concentrate on the shipping business. His son carried on the firm and set-up shipyards at Moulmein in Burma and Howrah in India. However the younger Dunbar died without heirs and it was Edward Gellatly, effectively the general manager, who organised a partnership to keep the concern going.

The partnership prospered and by the 1890s there were branch offices in Manchester, Liverpool, Glasgow, Antwerp, Hamburg, Marseilles, Jeddah and Suakin (Sudan). Until the 1920s Gellatlys owned its own ships and ran regular shipping services to Asia using these and other firms' vessels. It also acted as managing agent for the Mogul Steamship Company (1883-1922). The Mogul Company ran triangular services from Britain to Australia and then on to the Far East. Later the company was to run services from Britain to the Far East and from there to the eastern United States.

Gellatlys, however, did far more than simply run these shipping lines. The firm's strength was in ship management work for other owners, agency work, brokerage, insurance and general trading. From the 1860s it was agent for the British India Steam Navigation Company **(101)** and it ensured that that company made steady earnings by employing its ships to the best advantage in the tramp cargo trades and by making profitable short-term time charters. Subsequently Gellatlys were agents for the Shaw Savill and Albion Line, the Allan Line and Wilsons of Hull as well as for a number of leading French shipping concerns. The list of agencies was to greatly expand after 1918.

In the twentieth century Gellatlys became particularly involved in the Middle East. It was in the mid-1880s that the firm started business in Suakin and Jeddah. At that time it arranged the transport of pilgrims across the Red Sea to Mecca and probably handled supplies for the British Army in its operations against the Mahdists. Gellatlys remained in Suakin when the town was besieged in 1888. In 1905 the firm opened an office in Port Sudan although the quays of the new port were not completed until 1908. A further branch was opened in Khartoum in 1911. Gellatlys handled all types of goods needed for Sudan's economic development for example, railway materials, coal, coke and items for the construction of dams. The firm engaged in cotton procurement becoming agents for Peel and Company of Manchester, the largest exporters of cotton from Egypt.

After the first world war Gellatlys further diversified in the Sudan. It started-up in engineering and formed the Red Sea Stevedoring Company and the Sudan Warehousing Company. Refrigeration plant was handled through the firm's 'Sudan Shipping and General Stores'. Agencies were secured for activities as diverse as selling Morris cars and soap-making. In the late 1920s further branches of the company were opened in Wad Medani and El Obeid. Gellatlys took over in 1931 the agency for the Ethiopian Motor Transport Company. This concern was building a road link between Ethiopia and the Sudan but the project foundered on the Italian invasion of Ethiopia. Gellatlys were involved in a big development thrust in the Sudan at the close of the second world war and benefited from the huge post-war boom in cotton. The company opened a branch in Cairo in 1945 but this was closed at the time of the Suez invasion in 1956.

As far as Arabia was concerned, Gellatlys' office in Jeddah was looked after by local staff during the first world war. After the war was over, Gellatlys were faced with much inter-Arab feuding and consequent disruption. The firm became particularly involved in banking in Saudi Arabia and extended loans to Ibn Saud in the first years of his rule when he was faced with budgetary difficulties. (These banking activities were taken over by the British Bank of the Middle East **(404)** in 1955.) Gellatlys helped provide plant for water supplies and supplied cars, silver coinage and even furnishings for the royal palace. Once the country became rich from oil revenues, it provided finance for merchants selling consumer goods and also played an important part in supporting the country's general economic development. The firm opened an office in the Yemen after the first world war. Gellatlys became a part of the Inchcape Group **(108)** in 1984.

Gellatly's 1862-1962: a short history of the firm. By George Blake. London: Blackie and Son Ltd., 1962. 178p., ill. Index.

105. GLEN AND SHIRE LINES

The Glen Line was founded in 1869 by James McGregor, a partner in the shipbroking firm of Alan C. Gow and Company. The line's first steamer made its maiden voyage to China from London in 1871. By 1882 Glen were operating fifteen steamers to the Far East. The ships were noted for their speed. However from the mid-1880s there were signs that the company was not keeping up with the competition. It was hit by a declining tea trade and suffered from a rather staid and inflexible management. By 1911 the Glen Line was in difficulties and it was taken over by one of the constituents of Lord Kylsant's Royal Mail Shipping Group.

The Shire Line was set-up in 1861 by Captain David Jenkins. Initially it provided services to the Caribbean but in the mid-1860s the Shire Line started services to the Far East. Its first steamer sailed from the U.K. to the Straits, Hong Kong and Yokohama in 1872. Like the Glen Line, Shire built fast steamers in the 1870s and 1880s. It was one of the principal pioneers of trade with Japan. By 1890 it ran services from Hamburg, Antwerp and London to Singapore, Hong Kong and Yokohama. The concern suffered a number of setbacks in the early 1900s including substantial losses in the Russo-Japanese War. There were then moves to prop up Shire financially but by 1911 it too was wholly owned by the Royal Mail Shipping Group.

The two lines did not show much greater profitability under Royal Mail ownership which in 1920 took the logical step of completely integrating the sailings of the two concerns under the title of the 'Glen and Shire Lines'. In 1930 the Royal Mail Group collapsed and the constituent companies were placed under various interim administrations. The Ocean Steam Ship Company **(112)** was most interested in purchasing the Glen and Shire Lines. They had provided considerable competition for it over the years and Ocean was anxious they did not fall into the hands of others. Ocean first expressed an interest in purchasing the combined Glen concern in 1930 but it was not until 1935 that it was sold to them for the bargain price of £675,000 (including related property). Ocean maintained Glen as a separate line. Indeed the only major shipping orders which Ocean placed in the late 1930s were for eight fast vessels for the Glen Line. However Ocean did takeover the responsibility for designing and maintaining the Glen ships; for deciding the routes they would run on; and for all matters relating to crewing. C.E. Wurtzberg was brought home from the Straits Steamship Company, Singapore **(617)** in 1937 to be managing director of Glen and he remained in this post until his death in 1952.

The Glen vessels played a distinguished part in the second world war but immediately after the war Ocean decided against renewing the fleet, preferring to rehabilitate the existing vessels. This did not immediately affect profitability as, without German and Japanese competition, there were many windfall gains from post-war reconstruction. However Glen carried only about a quarter of Far Eastern cargoes from British east coast ports and by the 1950s it faced particularly vigorous competition from the faster ships of the Ben Line **(114)**. So in 1960 four new 20-knot ships were ordered with four more of a different class in 1964. These additions took Glen to the close of its separate existence. With containers taking over in the shipping world, Ocean and the Ben Line agreed in 1974 to form a joint service, under the name of 'Ben Ocean', for all their remaining conventional shipping services. This action marked the effective end of the Glen Line. The last ships owned by the line were sold in 1977.

See also Ocean Steam Ship Company **(112)** *for related material on the history of the Glen Line after 1935.*

The Blue Funnel legend: a history of the Ocean Steam Ship Company 1865-1973. By Malcolm Falkus. Basingstoke: Macmillan, 1990. xix, 411p., ill. Bibliog. Index.

Glen and Shire Lines. By Duncan Haws. [?Hereford: ?TCL Publications, ?1991.] (Merchant fleets; 22.) 85p., ill.
[Cambridge University Library.]

Glen Line Limited. London, The Company, 1949. 24p.
[National Maritime Museum Library.]

'Glen Line to the Orient'. By E.P. Harnack. ***Sea breezes*** (Liverpool), New series, Vol. 19, No. 112 (April 1955), pp. 263-92.
[This article was later issued as a publication by the company.]

'McGregor Gow and the Glen Line: the rise and fall of a British shipping firm in the Far East trade, 1870-1911.' By Malcolm Cooper. ***Journal of transport history*** (Manchester), 3rd series, Vol. 10, No. 2 (September 1989), pp. 166-79.

The Shire Line. By W.A. Laxon. London: Glen Line, 1970. 43p., ill. [National Maritime Museum Library.]

106. HONGKONG AND SHANGHAI BANKING CORPORATION

In the summer of 1864 a group of Hong Kong businessmen formed a Provisional Committee for the establishment of a Hong Kong and Shanghae Banking Company. The initiator was Sir Thomas Sutherland, Hong Kong superintendent of the Peninsular and Oriental Steam Navigation Company **(113)**, who was spurred into action because he had learnt that a rival Bank of China had been set-up in Bombay and was to have its head office in Hong Kong. Sutherland's object was to create a local bank which could finance, and profit from, inter-regional trade between the open ports of China, Japan and the Philippines. The bank commenced business in March 1865. The history of this first company, however, ends in December 1866. At that date a new Hongkong and Shanghai Banking Corporation came into existence following its incorporation by a special Hong Kong Ordinance drafted so as to be consistent with British colonial banking regulations.

The new corporation faced some difficult moments in its early years because of the various banking and economic crises of the 1860s and 1870s. Its first big calamity was the failure of the famous China house of Dent and Company in June 1867 and in 1875 two of the old agency houses from Canton days, Heard and Company and Fearon and Company, suspended payments. The bank also suffered because of unwise advances to the Pier and Godown Company. This company had to be sold off at a considerable loss in 1877. Despite these difficulties HSBC expanded and prospered. It opened its own branches or agencies in Calcutta (1867), Hankow (1868), Bombay (1869), Saigon (1870) and Amoy (1873). External agents were appointed in Bangkok and Manila in 1865. HSBC opened a branch in Yokohama in 1866 and an agency in Osaka in 1872. By 1879 it was, for a brief period, the only foreign bank left in Japan and it played a leading part in financing Japanese overseas trade. HSBC also provided internal banking services while the Japanese were setting up their own banks. By the end of the century HSBC was helping to organise large-scale international loans for the Imperial Japanese Government.

There were a number of reasons for HSBC's early success. The bank actually had its head office in Hong Kong and could respond quickly to local needs. It adopted adventurous commercial practices (such as the acceptance of longer-term bills of exchange) which proved profitable. Its accounts in the East were held and transacted in terms of silver values and it did not use Sterling obtained from London. Consequently it did not suffer unduly from the long-term decline in the value of silver.

In the last quarter of the nineteenth century the bank was guided by Sir Thomas Jackson – known as the 'Great Architect' – who was general manager between 1876 and 1902. They were critical years for its continued expansion. Further branches were opened in Penang, Colombo, Rangoon, Singapore, Lyons, Hamburg and New York. In Java the Bank opened branches in Djakarta and Sourabaya partly to provide finance for the export of sugar to Swires' **(309)** Taikoo Sugar Refining Company. When the bank increased its capital to $Hong Kong 7.5 million in 1882, it had become one of the largest financial institutions in the world and was considerably ahead of its nearest rival in China, the Chartered Bank of India, Australia and China **(102)**.

The bank which Jackson brought into the twentieth century had a range of activities well beyond the founders' emphasis on East Asian regional trade. From its beginnings, the bank had the right to issue Hong Kong currency notes and soon became responsible for 80 per cent of the territory's note issue. On the mainland, the bank became more involved with the Chinese economy and this inevitably brought it into politics and international relations. Besides making its own advances to the Chinese authorities, both local and national, HSBC was appointed an agent to the Imperial Government for the floating of loans on the London market. Jointly with Jardine Matheson **(307)** it established the British and Chinese Corporation in 1898 to promote the development of China's railways. HSBC also acted as custodian bank for payments to the U.K. received under the Boxer Riots indemnity.

In the first decades of the twentieth century the bank's involvement in Chinese affairs became more pronounced with two officers playing a key role. Guy Hillier served as manager of the bank's Peking office between 1885 and 1924 while Sir Charles Addis, having worked for the bank for over twenty years in the East, was transferred to London in 1905. He was to serve as Senior London Manager from 1911 until 1922. Addis, in particular, was able to secure very good terms for HSBC in the various international negotiations on China and preserved the dominant influence of the bank over the country's financial affairs. Both men played an important part in the formation of the China Consortium, a grouping of banks from six nations, which in 1913 made a £25 million reorganisation loan to the new Chinese republic. In 1912 HSBC had extended the first international emergency loan of £1.2 million to the new government.

The bank faced extreme difficulties in China in the inter-war years because of the large number of unstable regional regimes throughout the 1920s, the growing incursion of Japan and the weakness of the economy. In some respects the situation helped the bank because it was seen as a safe haven by individuals, Chinese companies and local governments. Careful management enabled the bank to maintain throughout the inter-war years the indexed value of its capital expressed in sterling terms. HSBC played a major role in the silver crises of the 1930s brought about by fluctuations in the value of the metal. Between March 1934 and April 1935 Chinese currency was no longer convertible and the bank helped to prevent a crash by manipulating the exchange with only very slender reserves. When the link with silver was completely abolished, the bank provided an interim loan of £2 million to the Central Bank of China.

During the second world war most of the bank's Asian branches came under Japanese occupation and it survived because the managers had transferred part of the assets to London before the outbreak of war and had built up substantial reserves. On their return to Hong Kong after the Japanese surrender, HSBC's officials found that the bank's records were virtually in tact. This enabled a speedy return to business. Loans were made to public utility companies to put their plants in order while liberal credits were extended to reputable firms to allow them to re-equip. New branches were opened in Malaya and Borneo while in 1947 branches were opened in Japan. Thereafter HSBC's story is of an East Asian bank becoming transformed into a true multinational. Key events are the acquisition of the Mercantile Bank **(110)** in 1959, the British Bank of the Middle East **(404)** in 1960, the United States Marine Midland Banks in 1980 and the British Midland Bank in 1992.

'After the centennial: a history of the Hong Kong Bank Group, 1966-77'. Being pp. 51-68 of ***Asian policy, history and development: collected essays.*** By Frank H.H. King. Hong Kong: Centre of Asian Studies, University of Hong Kong, 1979.

Eastern banking: essays in the history of the Hongkong and Shanghai Banking Corporation. Edited by Frank H.H. King. London: Athlone Press, 1983. xvi,791p., ill. Index.

Finance and empire: Sir Charles Addis, 1861-1945. By Roberta Allbert Dayer. Basingstoke: Macmillan Press, 1988. xxiv, 431p., ill. Bibliog. Index.

The history of the Hongkong and Shanghai Banking Corporation.

Vol. 1: ***The Hongkong Bank in late imperial China 1864-1902: on an even keel.*** By Frank H.H. King with Catherine E. King and David J.S. King. Cambridge: Cambridge University Press, 1987. 701p., ill. Bibliog. Index.

Vol. 2: ***The Hongkong Bank in the period of imperialism and war, 1895-1918: Wayfoong, focus of wealth.*** By Frank H.H. King with David J.S. King and Catherine E. King. Cambridge: Cambridge University Press, 1988. 720p., ill. Bibliog. Index.

Vol. 3: ***The Hongkong Bank between the wars and the Bank interned, 1919-1945: return from grandeur.*** By Frank H.H. King with Catherine E. King and David J.S. King. Cambridge: Cambridge University Press, 1988. 705p., ill. Bibliog. Index.

Vol. 4: ***The Hongkong Bank in the period of development and nationalism, 1941-1984: from regional bank to multinational group.*** By Frank H.H. King. Cambridge: Cambridge University Press, 1991. 991p., ill. Bibliog. Index.

Wayfoong: the Hongkong and Shanghai Banking Corporation. A study of East Asia's transformation, political, financial and economic during the last hundred years. By Maurice Collis. London: Faber & Faber, 1965. xii, 269p., ill. Index.

107. IMPERIAL AIRWAYS

Immediately after the first world war a number of British commercial airlines were set-up but they made little headway against subsidised foreign competition and by early 1921 all had closed down. The British government then provided subsidies to two of the airlines (later extended to four) so that they could resume operations. These subsidies were continued for three years and during this time the government established the Hambling Committee to advise it on civil aviation policy. The committee recommended the formation of a single private company with a large capital and a guaranteed long-term subsidy. Accordingly Imperial Airways was established out of a merger of the existing companies and it began operating on 1 April 1924. The new airline had a capital of £1 million and a subsidy fixed at £1 million over ten years. (The subsidy was later increased and the Empire Air Mail Scheme, begun in 1934, provided a further and major source of revenue.)

Until the end of 1926 Imperial Airways concentrated on European services but these lost money and so it began developing the imperial routes as a means of obtaining additional income. Here it met with difficulties from the governments over whose territories it wished to fly. Nonetheless a weekly service between Cairo and Basra was started in 1927 and, after agreement with the Persian government, this was extended to Karachi in April 1929. (Difficulties with the Persians were to recur and in the autumn of 1932 the service was re-routed over the Trucial Coast.) A

Karachi–Delhi section was also opened in 1929 run by the Indian State Air Service but this was to be temporarily closed at the end of 1931 for financial reasons. Services between London and the Middle East were bedevilled with problems including difficulties with the French and Italian governments. The company tried a variety of expedients to get round these but between late 1931 and early 1937 passengers were taken by train from Paris to Brindisi. They were then flown to Haifa from where they connected with the air service to India.

From the mid-1930s a major expansion in Imperial Airways' operations took place. During 1933 agreement had been reached with the Government of India for the establishment of Indian Trans-Continental Airways. This was 51 per cent owned by Imperial Airways and 49 per cent by the Indian government. The agreement allowed services to begin to Bangkok and Singapore by the end of the year. Early in 1935 Imperial Airways started to duplicate its services to Calcutta. In August that year it registered a new company called 'Imperial Airways (Far East)'. This was set-up to allow routes to be developed to Hong Kong. Regular services were begun to that city in March 1936 placing it within ten days of London. The route went via Penang, Saigon and Touraine although a shorter route via Hanoi was introduced at the end of 1937. The introduction of flying-boats during 1937 brought a revolutionary change. Although land-based flights were not abandoned, the flying-boats allowed non-stop flights to be made from Hythe to Cairo. In October a flying-boat service to Karachi was introduced with night stops at Rome, Alexandria, Habbaniyah and Sharjah.

Imperial Airways was subject to criticism during the 1930s for its poor labour relations, high dividends, continued use of outdated planes and general inefficiencies. In 1937 the British government established a committee (chaired by Lord Cadman) to investigate the organisation of British civil aviation. Amongst other things, this committee recommended that the chairmanship of Imperial Airways should be a full-time appointment. In conformity with the suggestion, Lord Reith (previously director-general of the BBC) took over the chairmanship in June 1938. Within five months of his appointment the government announced its desire to merge Imperial Airways and British Airways (founded in 1935 and mainly serving Europe) into a public undertaking to be known as the British Overseas Airways Corporation (B.O.A.C.). The new corporation was established in November 1939 and formally took over from Imperial Airways in April 1940. Lord Reith was its first chairman.

Britain's imperial air routes 1918 to 1939: the story of Britain's overseas airlines.

By Robin Higham. London, G.T. Foulis and Company, 1960. 407p., ill. Bibliog. Index.
[This monograph is largely devoted to the history of Imperial Airways. Chapters 5, 6, 8 and 11 cover Imperial Airways' operations in Asia.]

'Imperial Airways, 1924-40.' By A.J. Quin-Harkin. ***The Journal of Transport History*** (Leicester), Vol. 1, No. 4 (November 1954), pp. 197-215.

The seven skies: a study of B.O.A.C. and its forerunners since 1919. By John Pudney. London: Putnam, 1959. 320p., ill. Bibliog. Index.

108. INCHCAPE AND COMPANY

Inchcape and Company was not actually floated as a public company until 1958. Until then the Inchcape family controlled a vast empire of businesses of great diversity but with shipping predominating. The core collection of holdings had been acquired by the first Lord Inchcape (James Lyle Mackay, 1852-1932). Lord Inchcape's broad strategy was to leave the various businesses he took over under the control of their existing managements which remained responsible for developing them. He even permitted competition between the various concerns.

The history of the Inchcape Group has been seen by Griffiths as involving four well-marked stages. In the first stage, from the end of the nineteenth century, Lord Inchcape gradually acquired the shares of the Calcutta managing agents, Mackinnon Mackenzie. In the next stage (in India) Mackinnon Mackenzie took over Binny and Company **(505)** in 1906 and purchased in 1915 both Macneill and Company and Barry and Company. In the third stage, the group formed the Macdonald Hamilton partnership in Australia during 1915. Finally the family took control, after the first world war, of the London merchant house, Gray, Dawes and Company, which itself from 1936 onwards took over Smith, Mackenzie and Company and Gray, Mackenzie and Company. These purchases brought East Africa and the Persian Gulf within the range of the group.

Apart from these key businesses, Inchcapes' acquisitions included: Delmege, Forsythe and Company (Sri Lanka); Assam Company **(502)** and Kilburn and Company (India); Anglo Thai Corporation (India and South-East Asia); Borneo Company **(603)** (South-East Asia); Caldbeck, Macgregor and Company, Dodwell and Company **(303)** and Gibb, Livingston and Company (China); Gilman and Company (East and South-East Asia); and Gellatly, Hankey and Company **(104)** (Asia general). Brief details are given below of those Inchcape companies within the scope of this bibliography that are apparently without a significant printed history.

Anglo Thai Corporation

The corporation had a complex history which began in 1825 with the founding of the Liverpool agency of Gillanders and Ogilvie. In 1834 the Liverpool firm decided to establish a partnership in Bombay with which it could trade. By the 1880s one of the interests of the Bombay concern was timber by virtue of the agency it held for the Bombay Saw Mills Company. The firm commissioned C.H. Dennis to search for supplies of teak in South-East Asia. In 1885 he successfully secured the lease of a forest in north-west Thailand and the Siam Forest Company of Bombay was formed to take up the lease. In 1897 a London firm of the same name took over the Forest Company and in 1917 it was re-named the Anglo Siam Corporation.

In 1921 the corporation acquired the entire businesses of the various founding partnerships now located in London, Bombay and Karachi. This meant it had thriving and extensive interests in timber and rice in Thailand and trade in general produce in India. During 1936 it purchased Hendersons' business in Karachi which gave the corporation its first entry into the wines and spirits trade. The corporation merged with Inchcapes in 1975.

Barry and Company

Dr J.B. Barry was a tea garden doctor who bought a tract of land in Chittagong in the early 1860s for tea cultivation. His firm was to produce and buy tea in Calcutta and ship it to London where it would be sold by an associated partnership. The company later diversified into jute, setting-up the Bengal Jute Mill. There were unsuccessful ventures into sugar and gin distilling. In 1949 Barrys was merged with Macneill and Company to form Macneill and Barry.

Caldbeck, Macgregor and Company

This firm was formed by the purchase of George Smith and Company of Shanghai in the middle of the nineteenth century. It specialised exclusively in trading wines and spirits and expanded throughout East and South-East Asia. It was acquired by the Anglo Thai Corporation in 1967.

Delmege, Forsythe and Company

The company's origins go back to 1850 when it was set-up in Galle. It acted as coaling and shipping agents and specialised in the import of flour and sugar into Sri Lanka. It was acquired by Lord Inchcape in 1918.

Gibb, Livingston and Company

The company dates from 1836 when Thomas Augustus Gibb and William Potter Livingston founded a 'factory' in Canton. The firm imported cottons and yarns and exported tea and silk. It acted as agents for a large number of companies and owned its own tea clippers and other vessels. By 1850 the concern had branches in Hong Kong, Shanghai and Foochow. In Hong Kong the partners became much involved in banking and insurance. By the twentieth century Gibb, Livingston had diversified into engineering and manufacturing. It was acquired by Gray, Dawes and Company in 1921.

Gilman and Company

The firm was set-up around 1840 in Canton. After the foundation of Hong Kong it moved there and mainly engaged in the shipment of tea but also became involved in trade with Japan and it imported items from Manchester. The company had a chequered career financially and had to be rescued from near bankruptcy on several occasions. It became involved with the import of sandalwood into South China and later in the twentieth century turned to insurance and the import of motor vehicles, radios and refrigerators. It was acquired by Inchcapes in 1968.

Gray, Mackenzie and Company

The company was founded about 1862 when the British India Steam Navigation Company **(101)** won the contract to carry mail from India to the Persian Gulf. Gray, Mackenzie were to act as agents for B.I.S.N.C. in Basra. The original partners were Archibald Gray, Sir George Mackenzie, Edwin Dawes and John Halliday. A similar partnership was established for Bushire. By the 1880s the concern had diversified greatly and acted as ship repairers, insurance agents and lighterage contractors. It was one of the most important traders in the Gulf. Besides its agency business, it traded in dates, grain, wool and other country produce and imported sugar and general commodities.

In 1905 the firm joined with Lynch Brothers to form the Persian Transport Company which was to operate a concession on the Karun River in Persia as well as a concession from the Shah to build roads and operate transport. Gray, Mackenzie played a major role in helping to organise the Mesopotamia campaign in the first world war. In 1920 it merged with Lynch Brothers to form a concern that became known as the Mesopotamia Persian Corporation (Mespers). The merger was not a success and was ended in 1936 with Gray, Mackenzie holding the management of the Euphrates and Tigris Steam Navigation Company **(403)**. In the second world war the firm again was very involved in providing logistical support for the allies in the Middle East theatre. After 1945 its activities became centred on the new oil economies of the Gulf. The company supplied tankers, barges and tugs. In the 1950s it founded the Bahrein Slipway Company, the Busreh Slipway Company and the Dilmun Navigation Company. (The latter company was the legal owner of Gray, Mackenzies' vessels.)

Kilburn and Company

The firm was started in Calcutta in 1842 by C.E. Schoene who entered into partnership with E.D. Kilburn in 1849. Its first trading activities were the import of cotton goods and yarn and the export of local silk, hides, indigo, jute and shellac. In the 1860s Kilburn and Company acquired the agencies of two important insurance companies together with the Assam Company agency in 1865. In 1873 it obtained the Calcutta agency of the India General Steam Navigation Company **(514)**. The company was acquired for the Inchcapes by Macneill and Barry in 1956.

Mackinnon Mackenzie

The agency house was the result of a partnership between Sir William Mackinnon and Robert Mackenzie in 1847. Mackinnon had been running a sugar refinery near Calcutta while Mackenzie, at Ghazipur, had dealt mainly with the export and import of piece goods and oilman stores. At first the firm acted as general merchants and then combined this with chartering ships to send cargoes from Calcutta to Britain and Australia. In 1856 Mackinnon established the Calcutta and Burmah Steam Navigation Company to carry the mail between Calcutta and Rangoon for which he had won the contract. In 1862 this became the British India Steam Navigation Company **(101)** when the company won further contracts to carry mail from Calcutta to Singapore and to Bombay and the Persian Gulf. Mackinnon Mackenzie held the British India Calcutta agency throughout their existence and it made them into one of the great Eastern agency houses. They were however to be vulnerable because of their almost total commitment to the one activity of shipping. Mackinnon Mackenzie was sold to P. & O. **(113)** in 1958.

Macneill and Company

The company was formed in 1872 by two nephews of Sir William Mackinnon, Duncan Macneill and John Mackinnon. The two men acquired the agencies for the Rivers Steam Navigation Company, the Equitable Coal Company and the Kalline Tea Company. The firm later acquired agencies for jute and rope companies and set-up a number of tea gardens in Assam. In due course they became managing agents for the Assam Railways and Trading Company **(503)**. By the early 1900s the firm had extensive coal interests in India. In 1949 Macneills was merged with Barry and Company to form Macneill and Barry. In 1975 Macneill and Barry merged with Williamson Magor **(526)** to form Macneill and Magor. However Inchcapes sold off its interests in the new concern during 1982.

Conclusion

Inchcapes played a major role in the rationalisation of British business in Asia after the second world war. However even it found it difficult to operate in a climate of state interventionism and the requirement by many countries that companies should be mainly the property of their own nationals. Nonetheless for three and a half decades, from its flotation in 1958 to the mid-1990s, Inchcape and Company was a remarkably profitable and successful business. However in the late 1990s it suffered heavily from the collapse of the Asian economies and other unwise investments. Eventually the decision was taken to restructure the concern into an international motor distributor and sell off all other operations.

An East India tradition within the Kilburn family with some general remarks and information or comment on matter of family interest. London: Printed by the Westminster Press, 1930. 78p.
[A privately printed work which is primarily a family history and does not throw a great deal of light on the development of Kilburn and Company.]

'From regional trade to global shipping: Mackinnon Mackenzie & Co. within the Mackinnon Enterprise Network' by J. Forbes Munro. Being pp. 48-65 of ***The multinational traders.*** Edited by Geoffrey Jones. London: Routledge, 1998.

A history of the Inchcape Group. By Sir Percival Griffiths. London: Inchcape & Co., 1977. ix, 211p. Index.

The Inchcape Group including Inchcape and Co. Limited and subsidiaries and associated companies. London: The Group, 1963. 86p., ill. ['For private circulation. Not for publication.' – Front cover.]

James Lyle Mackay: first Earl of Inchcape. By Hector Bolitho. London: John Murray, 1936. xxiii, 264p., ill. Index.

'The management of British India steamers in the Gulf 1862-1945: Gray Mackenzie and the Mesopotamia Persia Corporation' by Stephanie Jones. Being pp. 25-63 of ***The Gulf in the early 20th century: foreign institutions and local responses.*** Edited by R.I. Lawless. [Durham]: Centre for Middle Eastern and Islamic Studies, University of Durham, 1986. (Occasional papers series; no. 31.)

Trade and shipping: Lord Inchcape 1852-1932. By Stephanie Jones. Manchester: Manchester University Press, 1989. xiii, 222p. Bibliog. Index.

Two centuries of overseas trading: the origins and growth of the Inchcape Group. By Stephanie Jones. London: Macmillan in association with Business History Unit, University of London, 1986. xxii, 328p., ill. Bibliog. Index.

109. KILLICK MARTIN AND COMPANY

James Killick was sent to sea by his father in 1833 when he was 16. By the early 1840s he was already commanding vessels sailing to Canton and continued throughout that decade to be in charge of ships journeying to the East. In 1852 he was put in command of a newly-built fast clipper, the *Challenger*, and he remained with that ship until his retirement from the sea in December 1860. Evidently looking for a land-based career, Killick founded the firm of Killick Martin with James Henry Martin early in 1861. Martin was twenty years younger than Killick and had been trained in a shipping office. In 1863 the two men were joined by J.H. Ritchie.

For the first 25 years of its existence, the partnership engaged in both shipowning and shipbroking. The arrangement was that Killick looked after the ships while Martin and Ritchie found the cargoes. Until 1886 the firm held shares in around 20 different sailing ships but rarely owned a vessel outright. At first the firm's main activity was bringing tea from China in return for mixed cargoes but 1878 was the last year in which tea comprised the largest single item in a Killick Martin ship bound for London. The depression in the shipping business, coupled with the formation of the Far Eastern Shipping Conference in 1879, forced Killick Martin to look for alternatives to the China trade. Instead the firm carried sugar, hemp and tobacco from the Philippines; pepper and rattans from Penang;

and rice from Bangkok and Rangoon. It also began sailing to the west coast ports of the United States.

The course of the firm's history was changed in 1883 when they unexpectedly received the agency for Wm. Thomsons' fleet of six Ben Line steamers **(114)**. (Killick Martin was to hold the agency for over a hundred years.) In 1887 the firm were also chosen as loading brokers for Holts' Ocean Steam Ship Company **(112)**. It was possible to hold the two commissions as Holts' ships loaded at west coast ports in the United Kingdom and at northern European ports while Thomsons loaded on the British eastern coast and more southerly European ports. The work was basically to find cargoes for the two owners but in the case of the Ben Line, Killick Martin were more closely involved with the berthing and loading arrangements of the ships.

These developments brought an end, by the mid-1880s, to Killick Martins' own shipowning activities. James Killick was reluctant to make the transition to working with steamships but his death in 1889 freed the firm from his objections. Around this time Walter Johnston and Henry Godin were admitted to the partnership. The two men were to be the main force in Killick Martin for most of the following four decades. It was a time of steady growth – by 1910 the firm had 4 partners and 25 staff. In the 1920s Killick Martin became involved in chartering, acting for Holts on the Baltic Exchange. They were also appointed agents for the new Far East Line set-up by Holts and Ellerman and Bucknall. During the 1930s the firm acted as shipping agents for the Chinese Government Purchasing Commission. In 1933 they became freight agents for the Elder Dempster Line. This took Killick Martin into the West African trade which was to prove a useful standby in the second world war when Far Eastern traffic was brought to an end.

Killick Martin lost the Holts agency in 1945 but this did not prevent them from expanding vastly in the post-war years into one of the largest independent firms of loaders and brokers. They became greatly involved with containerisation from the 1970s and with tankers and bulk cargoes. They also took on a wider geographical spread. In the 1960s and 1970s they agreed to act as agents for the Geest Line (West Indies), the Lykes Line (New Orleans) and the United Arab Shipping Company. By 1974 their staff had risen to 530 although the number had dropped back to 370 in 1985.

The China Bird. The history of Captain Killick, and the firm he founded: Killick Martin & Company. By David R. MacGregor. 2nd revised edition. London: Conway Maritime Press, 1986. 224p., ill. Index.

110. MERCANTILE BANK OF INDIA

The bank was established in Bombay in 1853 on the initiative of a Parsee, Cowasjee Nanabhoy. The bank functioned initially as a rupee co-partnership and did not have the benefit of limited liability. The original shareholders were drawn from both the Indian and British communities. The bank's first ten years were extremely successful because of its firm local roots in Bombay, conservative lending policies, and high-calibre management and staff. In addition the bank benefited from an economic boom generated by the American Civil War. Offices were established in Colombo, Canton, London, Kandy and Shanghai in 1854; in Calcutta and Madras in 1855; in Singapore in 1856; in Hong Kong in 1857; and in Penang in 1860. The bank received a charter in 1857 and the following year its head office was moved to London which meant that the shareholders became predominantly British. The bank took as its name 'The Chartered Mercantile Bank of India, London and China'.

The 1870s and 1880s were a more difficult period for the bank caused partly by economic downturns but also by the falling value of silver into which much of its sterling capital had been converted. The value of its capital therefore depreciated. The bank also unwisely invested in a substantial holding of rupee government securities in 1881 just before their price fell and in 1892 it was the subject of a large and cleverly concealed fraud by an important customer. In 1893, therefore, the bank was forced to reconstruct. This meant writing off half the value of its capital; obtaining new capital; and exchanging its charter for limited liability. It then took the name 'Mercantile Bank of India'.

The reconstructed bank started life at a difficult moment when confidence was strained as a result of the Barings crisis in London. It survived these years through the caution of its new general manager, James Campbell, who held office until 1913. Campbell closely vetted the bank's expenditure and closed branches in Malacca and Batavia. He judiciously acquired the Bank of Calcutta from the Yule family during 1906. Particularly good results were achieved at this time by the Colombo branch. Just before the first world war further expansion became possible. Extra staff were taken on and new offices were opened mainly in Malaya to take advantage of the rubber boom.

The first world war and its aftermath brought huge profits to the Mercantile Bank. (In 1920 the real profit figure was £666,000 although much of this was concealed in inner reserves.) The bank took over the Bank of Mauritius in 1916 and opened a New York office in 1919. The

1930s depression posed serious problems but in the end the bank weathered the storm better than the other Eastern exchange banks. There was less decline in the Mercantile Bank's asset values and profits. By the late 1930s the bank's business was expanding at a greater rate than that of its competitors. In particular, substantial profits were being made by the Shanghai branch.

During the second world war many of the Mercantile's branches were taken over by the Japanese and the bank invested heavily in government bonds to secure an income. (In 1943 some 51 per cent of its assets were held in this form.) After the war the bank appeared in a strong position because of its secure South Asian base. However it soon became clear that this strength was somewhat illusory and that the real growth area was in the Far East. South Asia suffered from regulatory and other difficulties. In India the bank was only allowed to open very few new branches while in Sri Lanka taxation levels were to reach over 70 per cent.

The Mercantile Bank was taken over by HSBC **(106)** in 1959. For some years it was left to operate much as it always had. The Mercantile Bank took the decision to pull out of Pakistan in 1969 and had completely left Sri Lanka by 1974. (Its interests in Burma had been nationalised in 1963.) In 1966 the bank's head office was moved to Hong Kong and between 1972 and 1976 its central functions were integrated with those of HSBC. By the end of the 1970s HSBC was starting to wind up the Mercantile Bank and merge its operations with its own. In 1984 all that remained were banking licences in Hong Kong and Thailand and a skeleton branch network in Thailand. These were sold that year to Citibank Corporation.

The Mercantile Bank suffered from the fact that it was always a small bank and never reached the size of its competitors. In the post-imperial age size was to become crucial. In addition the bank was heavily centred on South Asia. It did investigate the possibilities of diversifying into Africa and the Americas during the 1950s but decided there was no room for it in these continents. Managements adopted a very cautious lending policy and the decision-making structure was highly centralised on London. The bank was never in a position to take big strategic decisions and depended on turning its money round quickly. Consequently it was not able to become involved in major infrastructural projects. Nonetheless the Mercantile Bank can be credited with helping to develop tea, coffee, tobacco and other plantations; the jute and cotton industries, the timber trade and rice-milling. It is ironical that the bank's last ten years were particularly successful with profits rising from £1.06 million in 1973 to £1.97 million in 1982. India, too, was at the heart of this achievement.

Crisis banking in the East: the history of the Chartered Mercantile Bank of India, London and China, 1853-93. By Stuart Muirhead. Aldershot: Scolar Press, 1996. xiv, 379p., ill. Index.

'The Mercantile Bank in Madras and financial antecedents'. By N.S. Ramaswami. Being pp. 700-8 of ***Eastern banking: essays in the history of the Hongkong and Shanghai Banking Corporation.*** Edited by Frank H.H. King. London: Athlone Press, 1983.

'The Mercantile Bank of India on the east coast of Malaya'. By S.W. Muirhead. Being pp. 655-99 of ***Eastern banking.***

'The Mercantile Bank's Royal Charter'. Being pp. 42-50 of ***Asian policy, history and development: collected essays.*** By Frank H.H. King. Hong Kong: Centre of Asian Studies, University of Hong Kong, 1979.

The paradise bank: the Mercantile Bank of India, 1893-1984. By Edwin Green and Sara Kinsey. Aldershot: Ashgate, 1999. (Studies in banking history.) xii, 242p., ill. Index.

111. NEW ORIENTAL BANK CORPORATION

The Oriental Bank was established in 1842 as the Bank of Western India. In 1845 the bank moved its head office to London and took on its later name. It obtained its Royal Charter in 1850. The Oriental Bank was the first true Eastern exchange bank and it acquired a considerable reputation. The core of the bank's operations were in India but widely scattered branches were opened in such places as Melbourne and Singapore. In addition there was a costly head office building in London. A variety of factors (including the decline in the value of silver) brought about its collapse in 1884.

The New Oriental Bank opened for business in July 1884 in an attempt to retain the goodwill of the Oriental Bank and to restart its business. Some of the factors in the new bank's later collapse were inherent in the business which it took over. It acquired the costly premises and over-extended branch network of the old bank. These were out of all proportion to its very small capital. The shares it issued were fully paid up and there was no provision to make calls for extra capital. The bank made things worse by opening further unprofitable branches in Persia, the Seychelles, Madagascar and elsewhere.

For the first few years the bank paid dividends around the 5-6 per cent mark but it transpired that some of its profits were fictitious. It unwisely lent money to four of its directors amounting to £70,000 and many of its commercial loans were badly judged with dubious security. The bank was caught by the fall of the value of silver and its foreign exchange business was incompetently handled at the branches. In 1891 the bank lost a million pounds in fixed deposits and early in 1892 there was a run on the bank by Parsee depositors in Bombay. The bank was closed down in June 1892. Subsequently its losses through bad lending were found to amount to more than three-quarters of a million pounds.

'The New Oriental Bank Corporation Limited: a lesson in bad banking'. ***Bankers', Insurance Managers' and Agents' Magazine*** (London), Vol. 57, No. 598 (January 1894), pp. 69-80.

112. OCEAN STEAM SHIP COMPANY

The Ocean Steam Ship Company, which ran the Blue Funnel Line, was set-up in Liverpool in January 1865 by two brothers, Alfred and Philip Holt. Alfred was a consultant engineer with a particular interest in the steam engine and he believed it was possible for the new steamers to cover very large distances on a reliable timetable. The Holts decided to concentrate on the China run, mainly carrying dry goods, and they used the Suez Canal from its opening. The company insisted on designing its own ships and employing the best officers in the merchant navy. These key principles remained a part of its philosophy right up to the 1950s. For most of its existence, Ocean was an élite Liverpool business run principally by the Holt family with Asian services as its mainstay. Managers' meetings had the flavour of discussion in an Oxbridge common room and Holt ships, which were given classical names, were always of a standard above A1 at Lloyds.

Ocean began with three steamers and in 1866 the first vessel, the *Agamemnon*, sailed from Liverpool to Mauritius non-stop continuing to Hong Kong via Penang. It was the first time a steamer had sailed so far. Ocean achieved considerable prosperity up to 1875 by which time the company had a fleet of sixteen steamers. From that date Holts' ships did not keep up with the competition and were considered too small and too slow but they did nonetheless return profits. Early in the 1890s the managers took the courageous decision to re-build and expand the fleet. Particularly under the influence of Sir Richard Holt, a nephew of the founders, Ocean grew and diversified. Sir Richard was to serve as senior manager from 1904 until shortly before his death in 1941. He was behind the takeover by Ocean of the China Mutual Steam Navigation Company in 1902; he expanded the routes covered by Blue Funnel Services; and he increased Oceans' property holdings in the Far East. Up to about 1890 Ocean concentrated almost wholly on Liverpool-Far East trade but in the 1890s it diversified within the Far East. Local services were built up between Singapore, Java and Western Australia. Then early in the twentieth century a U.K.-Australia service was begun (with regular passenger services from 1910) as well as services from the Far East to the western United States ports.

In 1914 Ocean with its 73 ships was a major trader between Europe and the Far East. Its tonnage was approaching that of the P. & O. **(113)** and it was the largest cargo line using the Suez Canal. Oceans' fortunes had been helped considerably from the 1880s by the shipping conference arrangements and under the 1911 Far East agreement (which divided U.K. sailings between east and west coast ports). Holts received henceforth a near monopoly of west coast sailings. Like Inchcape at the P. & O., Ocean bought up other lines during the first world war partly to compensate for shipping losses. In 1914 it took control of the Straits Steamship Company **(617)** while in 1915 it acquired the Indra Line (seven steamers) which operated from China to New York. In 1917 Ocean took over the Knight Line (four vessels) which ran services across the Pacific. Ocean lost 16 ships in the war and another 29 were badly damaged.

The first world war proved profitable for Ocean but wisely (and in keeping with usual practice) the Holts ploughed the profits back into reserves rather than into paying inflated dividends. Initially there was a post-war boom and Ocean ordered two large cargo-passenger ships as part of its reconstruction plans. But 1920 was to mark the high point in the history of the Ocean Steam Ship Company. From then on the inter-war years were extremely difficult in the shipping business. The miracle is that Ocean survived and was the least affected of the shipping companies. In 1931 Ocean was in a dire position and the last dividend instalment was passed. But dividends were resumed in a small way in 1932 to be increased in 1936. By 1935 Ocean had fully recovered and was able to benefit from the acquisition of the Glen Line **(105)** that year.

There were a number of reasons for Oceans' relative immunity from the inter-war depression. Firstly the Far Eastern Shipping Conference was quickly re-established after the war. Secondly Ocean had a lower dependence on U.K. trade than most British shipping concerns. During the 1920s it had added many European ports to its routes. Finally Ocean had a good portfolio of trades and areas. Amazingly, the South-East Asian and China trade held up well. Although China suffered much disruption, it was regional and Oceans' trade was not confined to one item (such as oil). A falling-off in one area was generally made up elsewhere.

Ocean suffered very heavily in the second world war both as regards property in the Far East and ships. The very strength of the Holts' vessels meant they were selected for the most arduous and dangerous tasks of the war. (It took two torpedoes to sink a Holts' ship, the company was proud of saying.) Ocean lost 41 ships and in 1945 only 38 remained. (This last figure includes two ships built during the war.) After 1945 there was a massive buying programme and new vessels were ordered. Between 1947 and 1959 some 45 new ships were acquired. Down to the early 1950s the company was very profitable and maintained high dividends and well as having very liquid reserves. The Korean War boom helped and South-East Asia and China were growing areas of world trade. However after 1957 there were declining earnings from shipping and the company suffered particularly from the very fast vessels of the Ben Line **(114)**. In addition, the managers exhibited much vacillation as to the future direction of ship construction.

In 1965 Ocean celebrated its hundredth anniversary but the year was also to prove a fundamental divide in the firm's affairs. Firstly it floated as a public company. Secondly, with P. & O. and others, it established Overseas Containers Limited thus entering the world of shipping containerisation Finally Ocean purchased the West African shipping line of Elder Dempster. These changes were followed in 1972 by the purchase of Wm. Cory. Corys specialised in the related activities of warehousing, transportation, forwarding and distribution (especially food). Henceforth this was the direction which Ocean would take and appropriately in 1973 the concern's name was changed to Ocean Transport and Trading. By the early 1980s, the company's conventional shipping services to Asia had ceased. In 1983 Ocean sold its large shareholding in Straits Shipping while in 1986 the Group left Overseas Containers severing its last link with the Far East. Ocean was out of deep-sea shipping altogether by 1990.

Blue funnel: a history of Alfred Holt and Company of Liverpool from 1865 to 1914. By Francis E. Hyde with the assistance of J.R. Harris. Liverpool: Liverpool University Press, 1956. xvii, 201p., ill. Index.

The Blue Funnel legend: a history of the Ocean Steam Ship Company 1865-1973. By Malcolm Falkus. Basingstoke: Macmillan, 1990. xix, 411p., ill. Bibliog. Index.

Blue Funnel Line. By John Clarkson. Preston: Ships in Focus Publications, 1998. 192p., ill.
[National Maritime Museum Library.]

Blue Funnel Line. By Duncan Haws. Crowborough: TCL, 1984. (Merchant fleets; 6.) 149p., ill.
[National Maritime Museum Library.]

The Blue Funnel Line. Liverpool: Alfred Holt and Company, 1938. 30p.
[National Maritime Museum Library.]

A merchant fleet in war: Alfred Holt & Co. 1939-1945. By S.W. Roskill. London: Collins, 1962. 352p., ill. Index.
[A history of the Blue Funnel and Glen Lines during the second world war.]

113. PENINSULAR AND ORIENTAL STEAM NAVIGATION COMPANY

Brodie McGhie Willcox started business as a shipbroker in 1815. He took into his employment Arthur Anderson, a Scot of humble origins, and in due course made him a partner in the concern. In 1825 Willcox and Anderson entered the perilous world of shipowning and by 1835 they were running irregular services to Spain, Portugal and Gibraltar under the name of the 'Peninsular Steam Navigation Company'. Two years later they were advertising a fleet of seven steamships and by that time Richard Bourne had joined the concern. He was to provide most of the ships for its operations. On 22 August 1837 the Peninsular company signed the contract to ship mail to and from Spain and Portugal and this date is generally taken as the true beginning of P. & O. Mail subsidies were crucial for the operations of P. & O. throughout the nineteenth century and allowed it to run the fast, luxurious liner services which became synonymous with its name.

In 1840 the concern was granted a Royal Charter and an extension of its mail contract as far as Alexandria. Hence the new name of 'Peninsular and Oriental Steam Navigation Company'. The Charter laid an obligation on the company to extend its services to India within two years. There were difficulties here as the East India Company held a monopoly of routes east of Suez. However it was eventually agreed that P. & O. vessels might run from Suez to Calcutta via Aden, Ceylon and Madras. Passengers were taken by land across the Suez peninsular. Regular services began in 1843 but it was not until 1854 that P. & O. vessels called at Bombay. In 1845 the company started its Far Eastern service to Hong Kong via Ceylon or Calcutta then Penang and Singapore. Feeder services with smaller steamers operated from Hong Kong to Macao, Canton and Shanghai. The transport of opium between India and China was important for the mid-Victorian company's revenues.

Willcox, Anderson and Bourne provided dynamic leadership in the early days of the concern which possessed 23 ships in 1850 and 51 by 1867.

However Bourne died in 1851 and Willcox resigned in 1854 leaving Anderson to soldier on as chairman until his death in 1868. By this time his abilities had declined and he had turned his attention to other matters. The result was a rather moribund concern, existing on mail subsidies, which was unprepared for the opening of the Suez Canal and had bought the wrong type of vessels. A downturn in trade following the end of the American Civil War was calamitous for P. & O. and in 1867 it announced a huge loss and the passing of the dividend.

The company was saved by the appointment of Sir Thomas Sutherland as managing director in 1872. Sutherland had served the company for 12 years previously in Hong Kong and was to remain at the helm until 1914. Early on he took the crucial decision to opt for a new fleet of high quality mail steamers rather than cheap freighters but he did also purchase a number of tramp steamers to link in with the liners' schedules and give P. & O. freight business. Sutherland made severe economies, centralised the running of the concern on London and mounted a determined effort, through the offering of loyalty discounts, to capture freight business, particularly tea traffic. He was also active in the various shipping conferences of the late nineteenth century which restricted competition. Sutherland used them to maintain P. & O's right to charge premium fares for its superior level of service. In 1910 the company took over the Blue Anchor Line which specialised in emigration traffic to Australia. When P. & O. merged with British India **(101)** in 1913 it possessed 70 steamers totalling 548,000 tons.

The first Lord Inchcape took over as chairman on Sutherland's retirement and almost immediately had to face the effects of the first world war. P. & O's mail services were not restricted until 1917 but the concern suffered heavy shipping losses through enemy action. The combined group entered the war with 1.1 million tons of shipping; lost over half a million tons but had 1.5 million tons by the armistice. This was partly because Inchcape decided that he must acquire other shipping companies to help make up his deficit. In 1917 he acquired the Union Steamship Company of New Zealand; Hain Steamship Company and James Nourse. In 1918 he bought the Orient Line while in 1919 he acquired the Khedivial Line. In 1920 he purchased General Steam Navigation and in 1923 the Strick Line. In addition the P. & O. group bought 98 ex-enemy ships.

The first ten years after the first world war were a relatively prosperous time for P. & O. It benefited from the post-war boom; there was a renewal of passenger traffic and a great rise in emigration. Between 1919 and

1924 dividends of 12 per cent were paid. In 1929 the *Viceroy of India* entered into service offering new standards of opulence. Five new 'Straths' to similar high standards were also being built. However shortly before he died in 1932 Inchcape had to note that he had not seen such a depressing period for shipping in his lifetime. P. & O. vessels were leaving port with much of their cargo accommodation empty. Dividends were suspended from 1932 and it was not until 1936 that a deferred 4 per cent dividend could be paid. It took all of Inchcape's successors' time to keep the company going. P. & O. then had to face a second world war which brought about even larger shipping losses than the first. The group had 371 vessels in 1939 of which 182 were lost because of the hostilities. Even with replacements the fleet was reduced by 111 ships.

Post-war shortages and high raw materials costs made the building of new ships extremely expensive in the late 1940s. However by this time new developments were occurring which were to fundamentally alter the nature of P. & O's activities. The coming of independence in Asia (to British, French and Dutch colonies) greatly reduced the amount of passenger traffic the company received. The growth of air travel also took its toll. P. & O. began to diversify into a small number of cruise liners, large cargo vessels and tankers. In 1965, through North Sea Ferries, it bought its first Roll-on-Roll-off ferry. The same year P. & O. took a share in Overseas Containers Limited – the start of containerisation. (P. & O. was to takeover the whole of O.C.L. in 1985.) In 1969 P. & O. withdrew its regular passenger services to the Far East and in 1970 it made its last passenger sailing to India. The company had already sold its major Indian interests in 1960 – the Bombay and Calcutta ship repair yards and the pilgrim carrying Mogul Line.

It was clear by the early 1970s that shipping would only form a minority part of the future P. & O. group's activities. This trend was evident when the company finally acquired the building and property concern, Bovis, in 1974. The arrival of Lord Sterling as chairman in 1983 accelerated matters further. In 1985 he organised the takeover of the giant Sterling Guarantee Trust and also Stock Conversion, a major property company.

'Allies or subsidiaries? inter-company relations in the P. & O. Group, 1914-39.' By Christopher J. Napier. ***Business history*** (London), Vol. 39, No. 2 (April 1997), pp. 69-93.

Arthur Anderson: a founder of the P. & O. Co[mpan]y. By John Nicolson. Paisley: Alexander Gardner, 1914. 117p., ill.
(New and revised edition: Lerwick: T.& J. Manson, 1932. 110p., ill.)

Beneath the house flag of the P. & O. By Peter Padfield. London: Hutchinson, 1981. 148p., ill. Index.

Business in great waters: the war history of the P. & O. 1939-1945. By George F. Kerr. London: Faber and Faber, 1951. 196p., ill. Index.

A hundred year history of the P. & O.: Peninsular and Oriental Steam Navigation Company 1837-1937. By Boyd Cable [i.e. Ernest Andrew Ewart]. London: Ivor Nicholson and Watson, 1937. x, 289p., ill. Index.

Merchant adventurers 1914-1918. By F.A. Hook. London: A.& C. Black, 1920. viii, 319p., ill. Index.
[A history of the P. & O., British India and Associated Lines during the first world war.]

'The P. and O. Company.' By Demetrius Boulger. ***Asiatic quarterly review*** (London), Vol. VII, No. 14 (April 1889), pp. 241-58.

'The P. & O. Company: flagships of imperialism.' By Freda Harcourt. Being pp. 6-28 of ***Charted and uncharted waters: proceedings of a conference on the study of British maritime history.*** Edited by Sarah Palmer and Glyndwr Williams. London: National Maritime Museum in association with Department of History, Queen Mary College, University of London, [1982].

The P. & O. Line and Princess Cruises: a celebration in pictures of the Peninsular and Oriental Steam Navigation Company. By Carola Ingall. Cottishall, Norfolk: Ship Pictorial Publications, 1997. xii, 172p., ill.

The Peninsular and Oriental. By G.E. Mitton. London: Adam and Charles Black, 1913. (Peeps at great steamship lines.) 88p., ill.

A statement of the position and operations of the company, from its incorporation to the present time. By the Peninsular and Oriental Steam Navigation Company. London: The company, 1866. 73, vp.

The story of P. & O.: the Peninsular and Oriental Steam Navigation Company. By David Howarth and Stephen Howarth. London: Weidenfeld and Nicolson, 1986. 224p., ill. Index.
(Revised edition with additional text by Stephen Rabson. London: Weidenfeld and Nicholson, 1994. 240p., ill. Index.)

These splendid ships: the story of the Peninsular and Oriental Line. By David Divine. London: Frederick Muller, 1960. 255p., ill. Index.

114. WM. THOMSON AND COMPANY (BEN LINE)

James Thomson was an Edinburgh builder with an interest in Italian marble from Leghorn then much used in his trade. His sons Alexander and William set-up in business as shipbrokers in 1825 while retaining their connection with the family building business. In fact they continued to describe themselves as 'merchants and marble-cutters'. Their interest in sea-trading was however undoubtedly encouraged by their sister's husband, Thomas

Henderson, who was established in Leghorn in the shipping and export business. (Thomas was the brother of Patrick Henderson who founded P. Henderson and Company **(609)** so there were close family ties behind the setting-up of these two major shipping companies.)

In 1839 the Thomsons acquired their first ship the *Carrara* specifically to carry marble from Leghorn to Leith and then in the 1840s the brothers started a regular trade between Leith and Canada. Coal was shipped out and exchanged for timber. As the 1840s progressed the marble-cutting side of the business was separated from the shipping operations and in 1847 Alexander withdrew from the shipping side leaving William in control and the firm took on William's name. Throughout the 1840s new ships were acquired and by mid-century the Thomson fleet was considerable.

In 1851 the latest Thomson ship, the *Araby Maid*, set-out on a new venture to obtain sugar from Mauritius and during that decade Thomson ships started calling at Indian and Mauritian ports. The tenth voyage of the *Araby Maid* in 1859 took her to China and Japan (via Singapore) and lasted for two years. It was the start of a very considerable interest in the Far Eastern trade for the Thomson firm. During the 1860s, William took his two sons into the partnership and in 1871 he built his first steamship the *Benledi*. On William's death in 1889 the fleet was composed of two sailing ships and ten steamships. By that time the Canadian trade had declined and had been replaced by a subsidiary trade to the Baltic though this too was largely ended with the coming of the first world war.

By 1914 a regular berth service for the carriage of general cargoes to the Far East was in operation while many of the region's primary products were being brought back on the return journeys. Ben steamers came to load more and more at London and other east coast ports. The company entered the first world war with a fleet of nineteen vessels and were to lose two of their Baltic ships and three of their Far Eastern ships in the conflict. After the war a new company 'Ben Line Steamers Limited' was set-up to takeover the running of the ships.

In the inter-war period the Ben Line altered the composition of its fleet. Large vessels of around 6,000 tons were built specifically for the Far East trade and other ships of a similar size were purchased. By 1939 Ben owned twenty ships of some 145,000 tons in total. However the depression years were extremely difficult for the concern and it was fortunate to survive. Its ships were not able to compete with the much faster vessels which P. & O. **(113)** and Ocean **(112)** introduced. Bens' directors showed much ingenuity and tenacity in handling this difficult situation. Ships were diverted from the Far East to wherever cargoes could be found. The Ben

Line ended up carrying strange cargoes to unfamiliar parts of the world. There was much tramping. However no Ben vessel was ever laid up for lack of work.

The company lost fifteen vessels in the second world war but it recovered very rapidly. Under the leadership of Sir Douglas Thomson (director 1941-72 and chairman 1966-70), Ben exploited a new-found strength with early effect on the main routes and in subsidiary areas neglected by the established operators. Ben acquired four heavy-lift ships and began a policy of 'doing awkward things well'. It specialised in carrying heavy and awkward cargoes and explosives. During the 1950s the Ben Line introduced very fast passenger ships. In 1966 the journey from London to Singapore was reduced to sixteen and a half days. During the 1950s the company expanded throughout East and South-East Asia and offices were set-up in Port Swettenham, Kuala Lumpur, Hong Kong and Bangkok.

By 1970 the Ben Line operated 33 conventional liners but, with the profound changes then occurring in shipping, the company adopted a deliberate policy of diversification which was so successful that by 1980 it owned no more than three conventional liners. Instead Ben moved into (1) chemical tankers; (2) ship management; (3) container ships and bulk carriers; (4) managed oil tankers and (5) (for a limited time) air ventures. In 1973 Ben went into offshore oil-drilling in alliance with Odeco of New Orleans and in 1976 it acquired the Sheaf Shipping Company of Newcastle upon Tyne which brought it bulk carriers and semi-submersible drilling rigs. In 1974 the Ben Line and Ocean Transport and Trading agreed to form a joint service, under the name of 'Ben Ocean', for all their remaining conventional shipping services. The joint service was organised from Edinburgh. The Ben Ocean service was disbanded in 1982.

Ben Line: fleet list and short history. By Graeme Somner. Kendal: World Ship Society, 1967. 60p., ill.

The Ben Line: the history of Wm. Thomson & Co. of Leith and Edinburgh, and of the ships owned and managed by them 1825-1955. By George Blake. London: Thomas Nelson and Sons, 1956. ix, 222p., ill. Index.

The Ben Line: the story of a merchant fleet at war 1939-1945. London: Thomas Nelson and Sons, 1946. xi, 107p., ill.

The Ben Line 1825-1982: an anecdotal history. By Michael Strachan. Norwich: Michael Russell, 1992. viii, 248p., ill. Index.

'British shipping in the nineteenth century: a study of the Ben Line Papers.' By T.E. Milne. Being pp. 345-66 of ***Studies in Scottish business history.*** Edited by Peter L. Payne. London: Frank Cass and Company, 1967.

CHAPTER 2

History relating to Central Asia

201. CENTRAL ASIAN TRADING COMPANY

The independent state of Eastern Turkistan, or Kashgaria, had only a brief existence. During the 1860s the Amir Yakoob Beg, commander of the Khan of Kokand's army, succeeded in capturing the area. In 1864 he gained control of Kashgar, the main town, and he subdued Yarkand in 1865. However by 1878 Yakoob Beg was dead and the Chinese were back in control of the area. Following the conclusion of a treaty between Yakoob Beg and Russia in 1872, the British, at the second attempt, signed a trade treaty with the Amir in February 1874.

At this time a young British merchant, Thomas Russell, had settled in the Kangra hills of the Punjab. Russell was interested in the possibilities of trade with Central Asia and established the Central Asian Trading Company for this purpose. Following the conclusion of the 1874 treaty, Russell received permission from the British authorities to proceed to Eastern Turkistan. A caravan was despatched to Yarkand in mid-1874 with goods to the value of 300,000 rupees. The consignment mainly consisted of arms, ammunition, English piece goods and tea.

It is clear that Russell had little experience of trading in the East. He set his prices at exorbitant levels (profits of around 75 per cent seem to have been allowed for on the piece goods) and he expected trade to take place on a retail basis without bartering. When sales did not go well Russell was not above adopting a threatening posture and declaring he was being obstructed. At the same time he sought to involve the local British authorities in his trading activities. The Amir made constant attempts to improve the situation. He remitted the customs duties payable on Russell's goods and even offered to buy the arms.

Russell left Yarkand in April 1875 entrusting what remained of the consignment to his assistant Andrew Dalgleish. The assistant adopted an open and more flexible approach offering sales on three months' credit. Consequently there was something of a rush to buy and Dalgleish claimed that he could have sold more tea and prints had he had them. By the autumn of 1875 everything appears to have been sold and matters were wound up.

However the authorities in Calcutta felt that many more Russells would be disastrous for British relations with the Amir. Trade with Eastern Turkistan was best left in native hands. Dalgleish returned to trade profitably in Chinese Turkistan in the 1880s before he was murdered on the Karakoram in 1888. However little more is heard of the Central Asian Trading Company.

'The venture of the Central Asian Trading Company in Eastern Turkistan, 1874-5.' By Bir Good Gill. ***Asian Affairs*** (London), Vol. 31, Part 2 (June 2000), pp. 181-8.

CHAPTER 3

Histories relating to East Asia

301. CHINA LIGHT AND POWER COMPANY

In April 1900 the China Light and Power Syndicate was registered in Hong Kong by Shewan, Tomes and Company – one of the island's foremost agency houses. The senior partner of the agency was R.G. Shewan, a formidable but unhappy man, who was to lead China Light through its most difficult years until his firm was ousted as China Lights' managing agents in 1932.

During 1900 the syndicate took over the Canton Electric Fire and Extinguishing Company (which was to supply electricity to Canton) and also acquired land in Kowloon on which to build a power station for the area. However by 1901 the syndicate was clearly in need of further capital so a new public China Light and Power Company was incorporated. From then until 1918 the company faced great difficulties and only paid a dividend once in 1906. Operations in Canton did start to become profitable as the 1900s progressed but by 1909 the company was the subject of anti-foreigner sentiment in the port and it was forced to sell out on the best terms possible. Unlike Hongkong Electric **(305)** on Hong Kong Island, China Light did not make sufficient profits to pay for the maintenance and upgrading of equipment. So there were continual demands for fresh capital from the shareholders and new issues. The situation reflected the relatively undeveloped state of Kowloon at this time. In 1918 the original company was wound up and a new one set-up.

From 1919 until 1941 China Light paid regular dividends. It faced difficult periods in the 1920s because of nationalist agitation on the mainland – in the third quarter of 1925, for example, its revenues fell off by a half. However by 1929 the company's fortunes were clearly improving. In that year it obtained the government's agreement to supply the New Territories (achieved by 1932) and it signed a major contract with the Green Island Cement Company. From 1937 onwards the exodus of manufacturers and individuals from the mainland had an extremely beneficial effect on China Light. In 1938 there was an overall annual increase in sales of more than 30 per cent.

It was after 1945 that China Light really took off under the leadership of Albert Raymond and then Lawrence Kadoorie. The company profited from the surge in manufacturing activity in its area and further encouraged this by guaranteeing adequate and uninterrupted power supplies. New power stations were built and output rose more than 37 times between 1947 and 1964. In 1941 China Light had 33,000 consumers; in 1964 there were 289,000.

The year 1964 in fact marked a watershed in the company's history. It was faced with the prospect of nationalisation (which never in fact came about) and was blocked from raising further capital for future development. At this juncture it entered into an agreement with Esso (Standard Oil) under which Esso would inject 220 million dollars. Additional power requirements were to be supplied to China Light by a joint company (the Peninsular Electric Power Company or PEPCO) in which Esso would have a 60 per cent stake and China Light would own 40 per cent. Another two supply companies were established on a similar basis in the 1970s and 1980s. In 1979 China Light began supplying the Guangdong Power Company on the mainland with a million kilowatt hours of electricity a day.

Power: the story of China Light. By Nigel Cameron. Hong Kong: Oxford University Press, 1982. x, 277p., ill. Bibliog. Index.

302. DEACON AND COMPANY

Albert Deacon was a Londoner who had joined the famous American agency house of Augustine Heard and Company at the age of nineteen and served in Canton and Foochow as a tea inspector. Four years later in 1856 he set-up on his own in Canton as a public tea inspector and commission agent. In 1858 he was joined by his brother James and the firm of Deacon and Company was formed. Other brothers were to enter the partnership but the family had all left Canton with considerable riches by 1890 and the house passed into other hands.

For its first twenty years the firm handled little else than tea. Then in the 1870s Deacons built up an agency business and moved into banking, insurance and shipping. It took over the HSBC agency in Canton in 1885. Tea exports peaked in 1889 and then declined considerably. So the firm moved into silk. The heyday of this trade had passed but Deacons developed a regular business in silk waste which was to be one of its major export items well into the 1920s. The firm remained in Canton throughout even though it declined as a Treaty port. It was however forced to sell its property on the Bund and move to less imposing quarters.

The first half of the twentieth century was to bring the firm a series of major misfortunes and yet almost unbelievably it survived. In 1908 its compradore absconded owing $90,000 to the firm and $62,000 to HSBC. As a result HSBC decided it was better to establish its own office in the port and ended the agency arrangement. Fortunes were restored with much hard work. The staff laboured so often into the night that Deacons became known locally as 'The Lighthouse'. The firm did extremely well in the first world war and between 1915 and 1917 the four shareholders averaged dividends of 50 per cent a year. However there were lean times after the war and in addition the firm faced labour problems and nationalistic agitation culminating in the local boycott of British concerns in 1925 and 1926. Between June and November 1925 Deacons did very little business and just survived with the help of friendly German firms which shipped goods for it.

Although the Deacons' position eased in the early 1930s, it was badly affected by the activities of Harold Staples-Smith, the managing-partner from 1916, who treated the organisation as if it were a medieval fiefdom and caused half of the firm's capital to be removed by the partners as dividends. For much of the period he was absent in Britain. In addition the firm suffered a second case of its compradore absconding in 1934. On this occasion some $27,500 was lost. The two remaining partners were forced to sell investments to restore liquidity. However, with an improvement in international trade, the firm was soon back on its feet and made its best profit for 13 years in 1937 of some $54,000. At this point the Japanese occupation overtook Canton and the firm stayed in business by what amounted to running the Japanese blockade. G.R. Ross, who had recently joined the firm, was to open an Hong Kong office in October 1938 to assist with these operations. However the company was forced to suspend trading in Canton in 1939. At this low point in its fortunes, Harold Staples-Smith and another key partner sold out. Deacons only survived through the return of Harold Smyth, a partner who had walked out in 1925 but now re-invested funds out of a sense of duty.

Deacons made considerable profits in the early years of the second world war but with the Japanese occupation of Hong Kong many staff ended up in prisoner-of-war camps. The post war history of the firm centres around Smyth and more particularly Ross. With the communist takeover of the mainland it was soon clear that it would not be possible to work from Canton and the office was formally closed in 1955. It also became clear that the sort of exports Deacons had been involved with previously would not be suitable in the new world order. There was therefore a search for new roles. At first the firm became involved in the forwarding and packing business helping with the movement of Chinese from the mainland to Hong Kong. It also chartered ships to move surplus war machinery to Asia. The shipping operations had all ended by 1959 and with the development of Hong Kong as a major manufacturing centre, Deacons found its new role. It became a leading export agency for the vast ready-to-wear textile trade destined for Europe and North America. It also exported shoes and toys. By the 1990s, the firm was sourcing material for the West from Taiwan, Korea, Indonesia, Thailand and the Philippines as well as Hong Kong.

The merchants of Shameen: the story of Deacon & Co. By Robin Hutcheon. [Hong Kong:] The Company, 1990. vii, 140p., ill. Bibliog. Index.

303. DODWELL AND COMPANY

The company traced its origins through an earlier firm, W.R. Adamson and Company. Adamson was sent to China by a group of Macclesfield silk weavers in 1852 to explore the possibilities of increasing supplies of raw silk. The firm he founded was registered in London in 1858. During 1867, Adamson took on a new partner, a Mr Bell. Adamson retired from the business in 1886 leaving Bell in control. Bell adopted a risky policy of making large speculative purchases which tied up substantial amounts of capital. This practice worried a number of members of the firm and Bell made an agreement with G.B. Dodwell and A.J.H. Carlill that should Adamson, Bell and Company fail, a new company would takeover its interests. Dodwell prepared carefully for such an eventuality as he was anxious not to loose any of the firm's agencies. When Adamson, Bell and Company's bankruptcy actually occurred in 1891, a new company, Dodwell, Carlill and Company, was quickly established. The head office was moved almost immediately to London. The firm was to become Dodwell and Company when it took on limited liability in 1899.

In the Adamson era the company had three main operational areas – silk, tea and shipping. The firm is claimed to have been the first shipping concern to establish a regular steamship line across the North Pacific. This was the result of an agency received from the Canadian Pacific Railway for the charter and management of ships between Hong Kong and Vancouver. Unfortunately the new firm of Dodwell, Carlill and Company lost the agency in 1892 but by 1895 it was running a similar service for the North Pacific Railroad Company which lasted until 1903. At that point Dodwells became Holts Blue Funnel agents on the United States and Canadian Pacific coasts. During the Alaskan gold rush Dodwells ran a profitable shipping line between Puget Sound and the ports of Alaska.

By the twentieth century Dodwells had become a major merchant house centring on China but with branches in Japan, Ceylon, the United States and Canada. The house had a substantial network throughout the treaty ports of China. This included a permanent presence in Hankow from 1907 where Dodwells was the leading tea buyer. Japan had also become of increasing importance to the firm. It had been in Yokohama and Kobe from the 1870s and, besides silk, was exporting coal to Singapore and Shanghai and braid for straw hats in Europe. During the Russian-Japanese War of 1905, Dodwells were the agents through whom ships were chartered by the Japanese government. Meanwhile the head office in London was exporting steel, chemicals and dyes for the developing industries of Asia. Dodwells also moved into the supply of office equipment holding an agency for the Underwood Typewriter Company.

The first world war greatly stimulated the company's activities. In 1919 it made record profits and was able to double its capital from reserves. However most of the inter-war period was to prove difficult. There was considerable depression, China was in chaos and Japanese firms started to deal directly with overseas suppliers. The company was only able to pay a dividend once in the years 1926-36 and in 1936 it reduced its capital. From 1937 matters considerably improved. Dodwells became involved with the supply of cars, buses, automobile engines and electrical equipment. It held an important agency from the Chrysler Corporation. Substantial profits were made in Japan and even in China the company did reasonably well.

During the Pacific War the company's activities in the Far East were completely wiped out. Dodwells however occupied itself with a range of new activities in Britain including the manufacture of rubber products. After the war Dodwells was soon back in business in the Far East. Until the communist revolution of 1949 the company made satisfactory profits in China despite many difficulties. In Japan and Hong Kong recovery was rapid and the company supplied goods and services needed for re-construction. Throughout the 1950s exports from Hong Kong amounted to a million pounds annually. Dodwells began a policy of diversifying during the 1950s. In 1951 it opened in East Africa selling Marks and

Spencers' products among other activities while in 1952 it commenced business in Australia. From the mid-1950s the firm acted as specialised buying agents in Asia for department and chain stores throughout the world. In order to undertake this work special export buying offices were set-up in a number of Asian countries. Dodwells was acquired by Inchcape and Company **(108)** in 1972.

'George Benjamin Dodwell: a shipping agent in the Far East, 1872-1908.' By Stephanie Jones. ***Journal of transport history*** (Manchester), 3rd Series, Vol. 6, Part 1 (March 1985), pp. 23-40.

The House of Dodwell: a century of achievement 1858-1958. London: Dodwell & Company, 1958. viii, 159p., ill.

304. GLOVER AND COMPANY

Thomas Glover was born in Fraserburgh. In 1859, when he was 21, he arrived in Nagasaki shortly after the port had been opened to western trade. At first Glover acted as a clerk to Kenneth Ross Mackenzie who was a Scottish merchant and agent to Jardine Matheson **(307)**. But when Mackenzie moved to Hankow in 1861, Glover set-up as a general commission agent and took on the agencies of Jardine Mathesons, Dents and Sassoons **(521)**. In February 1862 he founded Glover and Company in partnership with Francis Groom and later that year two further partners joined the firm. The new concern became involved in the re-firing of Japanese tea with financial assistance from Jardine Matheson. In 1863 it was employing a thousand Japanese in this activity but was making no profit. The firm also engaged in the import and export trade.

Between 1864 and 1867 there was a considerable expansion of the business and Glover and Company became the largest western firm in Nagasaki. In addition it opened branches in Shanghai and Yokohama. (The Shanghai branch was to establish the Union Steam Navigation Company which challenged the monopoly of Yangtze shipping held by Russell and Company's 'Shanghai Steam Navigation Company'.) Glover and Company expanded its agency activities and by 1868 was acting in Japan for Lloyds and six insurance companies. It also represented HSBC **(106)** and the Oriental Bank. The firm went into currency arbitrage operations making money out of different rates in Yokohama and Nagasaki but these ended in 1865 when the rates had equalised in the two ports. There was an attempt to enter the bullion trade but this failed because of inferior gold supplied through Jardine Matheson.

The main area of Glovers' success was in the sale of ships, arms and ammunition to the Japanese. At this time the country was in considerable turmoil, involving a number of factions, which was only ended with the establishment of the Meiji government in 1868. Glover appears to have traded with all sides and did so with Jardine Matheson finance. Sometimes Glover took items like rice, raw silk, tea and seaweed as payment from the various factions. It appears that profits on some of the ship sales were split equally with Jardine Matheson.

Glover and Company declined after 1867 and ultimately went bankrupt in August 1870. The coming of political stability seriously affected the firm's speculative activities and there was also the start of a trade depression which particularly hit Nagasaki. The partnership was not renewed in 1868 and Glover formed a new one with Mackenzie (who had returned to Japan). The new partnership did not control any of the Shanghai operations.

Glover responded to the difficult conditions after 1867 in a number of ways. He opened branches at the new ports of Hyogo and Osaka. He planned advanced methods of tea re-firing but these were of no use because of competition from Chinese merchants. Most importantly he tried to change direction by becoming an entrepreneur rather than a merchant. He constructed a patent slip dock in Nagasaki and began mining Takashima coal. A considerable deposit was found in 1869. Had the coal-mining operation reached the intended level of production more quickly than it did, Glover and Company might not have become insolvent. As it was, many of the firm's assets were sold to the Netherland Trading Company in May 1870 in return for a large loan with which it intended to repay its debts. This was not fully achieved and the firm became insolvent with debts of 87,418 Mexican dollars. Glover, however, had paid back all that he owed by 1877.

'Thomas B. Glover: a British merchant in Japan, 1861-70.' By Shinya Sugiyama. ***Business history*** (London), Vol. 26, No. 2 (July 1984), pp. 115-38.

305. HONGKONG ELECTRIC COMPANY

The company was incorporated in 1889 on the initiative of Bendyshe Layton of Gibb, Livingston (*see under* Inchcape and Company **(108)**). Layton formed a Board of Directors comprising some of Hong Kong's most important businessmen. Most famous was Sir Paul Chater who served for 37 years and played an important part securing various land deals for the company. William Henry Wickham, of the British electrical firm of

Johnson and Phillips, was appointed as the first in a long line of distinguished chief engineers. The company built its original power station at Wanchai and began supplying electricity for street lighting in December 1890. Throughout its history Hongkong Electrics' operations have been confined to Hong Kong island.

The initial response to the company's flotation was good but its early years were not easy. The 1890s were years of depression and plague in Hong Kong. There was also some resistance to the idea of electric lighting from the Chinese community. Wickham's enthusiasm undoubtedly helped prevent bankruptcy in the mid-1890s and when the share capital was doubled in 1899, the issue was taken up very quickly. By then dividends were of the order of 6 per cent. They continued to rise as between 1903 and 1908 the number of consumers trebled. Electricity was also starting to be used to power fans and lifts. By 1914 it was decided to open a new power station at North Point. This became operational in 1919 and Wanchai was closed in 1922.

In the early years of the century there had been threats of competition from various quarters, most notably Hongkong Tramways **(306)**, but by the 1920s these had gone away and the company was even supplying power to the Taikoo Dockyard and other industries. In 1924 the company was producing the cheapest electricity in the world but it did not have a large enough market to maintain this record. There were various attempts in the 1920s to takeover or amalgamate with China Light and Power **(301)** in Kowloon but these came to nothing. The company also suffered from a number of strikes one of which was a response to the situation on the Chinese mainland. Supply of electricity roughly trebled during this decade. It was a trend which continued. On the eve of the Japanese War, Hongkong Electric had installed a total of 51,000 meters and was valued on the Hong Kong Stock Exchange at 36 million Hong Kong dollars. In the 51 years it had been running (apart from two small incidents), the company had only shutdown its electricity supply for two hours and fifty minutes.

The Japanese took apart most of the generating sets in the North Point station during their occupation but they left Set No.7 which had acquired a reputation of having a spirit of its own. It was this set which was used to supply electricity in the early months after the end of hostilities. In the post-war period the company faced further labour difficulties and there was a big increase in demand because of refugees from the communist mainland. There were also the requirements of the new manufacturing industries to be met. Output increased from highest loads of 30,000 kilowatts in 1949 to 300,000 kilowatts in 1970. By this time the company had diversified into property development, retail electrical sales and consultancy. It had also opened a further power station at Aplichau.

A mountain of light: the story of the Hongkong Electric Company. By Austin Coates. London: Heinemann, 1977. viii, 209p., ill. Bibliog. Index.

306. HONGKONG TRAMWAYS

The construction of various tramway lines in Hong Kong was first authorised by an ordinance of the Hong Kong Legislature in 1883. However the Hongkong and China Tramways Company Limited which was promoted under the ordinance was not a success as it did not attract sufficient funds from the public. In 1901 a further ordinance was passed and in 1902 the Hong Kong Tramway Electric Company Limited was incorporated in London and took up the powers in the new ordinance. Before the end of the year the company had passed under the control of the Electric Traction Company of Hong Kong Limited. In 1910 this concern was re-named the Hongkong Tramway Company Limited. By 1913 the company was able to pay a dividend of 7.5 per cent. However the directors all remained United Kingdom residents. In December 1914 they resigned and were replaced by six Hong Kong residents and board meetings moved there. In 1922 a new company was formed called Hongkong Tramways Limited. This company took over the assets and liabilities of the 1910 company.

The route of the tramway, partly opened in 1904, was from Kennedy Town to Shaukiwan on Hong Kong Island with a branch to Happy Valley. This was to remain the extent of the system throughout the history of these tramway concerns although considerable technical improvements were made over the years. By 1931 a three minute service had been introduced and all but a mile of the tracks had been doubled. In the 1930s Hong Kong had the cheapest tram fares in the world. During the occupation the Japanese took over the system while letting it run down and using its maintenance workshop to manufacture grenades. Between November 1944 and April 1945 services were suspended for lack of coal and by the end of the war only 15 cars were in use although the full fleet of 109 was still in existence. The track was in very poor condition. With the help of the Royal Navy it was possible to get a service restarted in the centre of the city in October 1945 with a nominal fleet of 40 cars and by the end of the year all routes had a service. Following an expert report in 1946 recommending the retention of the tramways, a complete rehabilitation of the system had been achieved by 1948. In the 1950s there was further upgrading of the track and the Russell Street works was rebuilt. In 1964 the company started attaching trailers to its cars so as to increase capacity. At the end of the decade the trams remained Hong Kong's largest public service carrier.

Hongkong tramways: a history of Hongkong Tramways Limited and predecessor companies. By R.L.P. Atkinson and A.K. Williams. London: The Light Railway Transport League, 1970. 96p., ill.

307. JARDINE MATHESON AND COMPANY

The company can trace its origins as far back as the late eighteenth century and records from that time remain in existence. It was around 1780 that the East India Company granted permission to John Henry Cox to proceed to Canton to collect his late father's debts. Necessarily he had to take payment in goods and before long he had set-up on his own running two ships between Canton and Calcutta and becoming an active trader. Cox died in 1791 but by then he was in partnership and there followed changes to the partnership, a merger with another firm and at least one partner being declared bankrupt. By 1823 the concern was entirely in the hands of three brothers of French Huguenot ancestry and traded under the name of Charles Magniac and Company. Six years earlier to this, Dr William Jardine had left the service of the East India Company's Marine, where he had been a ship's surgeon, and took up residence in London. Jardine went out to Bombay in due course and it was there in 1820 that he first met a fellow Scot, James Matheson, who had become involved with the Canton opium trade after leaving his uncle's Calcutta firm. Matheson was to go into a partnership with a Spaniard in 1821 while from 1822 Jardine decided to base himself in Canton where he was eventually to join Magniacs. By 1827 Jardine was running Magniacs as the other partners had died, retired or withdrawn. Early in 1828 Matheson joined the business bringing with him, it is said, a capital of $60,000.

There then began three and a half critical years in which Jardine and Matheson increased their investments in the house and eased out the Magniac interests. From the shell of Magniacs was established Jardine Matheson and Company on 1 July 1832. It was easily the largest of the handful of British firms then operating in China and it is the only British-Chinese company to survive from the years before the Treaty of Nanking of 1842 (which opened up China to foreign trade). The two men's greatest success was in the opium trade but they also dealt with less profit in silks, piece-goods and teas. (In 1831 they appointed an agent in Manchester to supply the piece-goods.) The secret of their success was initiative, optimism and close attention to the needs of clients. Jardine and Matheson had an unerring ability to come out of financial crises in tact while learning from the experiences. Between 1832 and 1837 their profits increased by about 50 per cent each year. It would appear that these profits mainly came from private investments as commission work brought only moderate returns. Early in 1839 Jardine retired to England and shortly afterwards the Chinese Commissioner Lin seized and destroyed the stocks of opium held in Canton and confined the Europeans to their factory. Matheson and the other Europeans eventually were allowed to go to Macao while Jardine in London was an important advisor to Lord Palmerston in the months before he took the decision to start the Opium War.

Early in 1841 Matheson settled in the new trading post of Hong Kong and began establishing Jardine Matheson on the island before himself retiring to London. Matheson moved quickly because there were substantial stocks of opium which needed selling but in so doing he was to inaugurate a new era of expansion and consolidation in the company's history. Wharves, warehouses and offices were built and in 1844 Jardines started a branch in Shanghai which was to take Lot no.1 on the Land List there. Following the opening of foreign trade by Japan in 1859, Jardine Matheson were at the forefront of European traders establishing themselves in the country. William Keswick (a great nephew of Dr Jardine) opened a branch in Yokohama the same year. (Keswick was later to become managing director of Jardines for eleven years and, after leaving China in 1885, effectively ran the London end of the business until 1912. The Keswick family were to take control of Jardines.) Trading was difficult in Japan because the authorities at first were hostile and wanted it confined within relatively small limits. But Jardines prospered because of a flexibility and responsiveness to change which marked the firm's approach throughout its history. It was in a position to advance large sums of money in Japan for the purchase of tea and silk, earn freights with its sizeable shipping fleet, sell insurance and engage in larger enterprises such as a tea firing plant built in Yokohama in 1861. When forced out of the silk trade because of high prices, Jardines moved into banking. When HSBC and the other banks arrived, it moved into the export of Japanese raw cotton and the sale of its out-of-date trading vessels.

The second half of the nineteenth century (particularly the 1860s and 1870s) in fact marked a fundamental change in the focus of Jardine Matheson. While it continued even into the twentieth century to buy and sell commodities in the East on its own account, Jardines was changing into a multi-faceted modern business house becoming involved in high finance, creating insurance companies (e.g. Hong Kong Fire Insurance Company, 1868), cotton mills (e.g. EWO Cotton and Spinning Company, Shanghai, 1895), a sugar refinery (China Sugar Refinery Company, 1878), banks (e.g. EWO Bank, Peking 1870), wharves and warehouses (e.g. the Hongkong and Whampoa Dock Company, 1865), a real estate company (Hongkong Land Investment and Agency, 1889) and a large shipping company which ran services on China's rivers and on the region's seas (The Indo-China Steam Navigation Company, 1881). Jardines were to open offices in all the major trading cities of China as well as Japan and Taiwan. The company found in China that it was best to engage in trade by encouraging co-operation and joint investment with the local Chinese merchant community. Outside trading, Jardines learnt that infrastructural investment was only possible with the approval of officials who were unwilling during the Ch'ing empire to allow foreigners to manage government enterprises. Many of Jardines' operations, therefore, were channelled through agency services, expert technical advice and the location of the cheapest capital sources for government. This was particularly the case with railway development which is probably Jardines' most celebrated activity in China. After 1898 this was largely accomplished through the British and Chinese Corporation, a joint enterprise with HSBC **(106)**.

The inter-war years were a particularly difficult time for Jardine Matheson. In the 1920s there was general instability because of the many warlord regimes in China while in the later 1930s the company had to face the consequences of a Japanese takeover of much of the country. China's economy was weak, its problems being accentuated by a fall in the price of silver. The company was beset with labour problems and at one point there was a strike in its dockyards. However some expansion continued. Further cotton mills were acquired in 1921 and in the 1930s the firm moved into brewing and into the manufacturing of agricultural and other machinery.

Jardine Matheson lost almost all its assets during the Japanese occupation of East Asia in the second world war but soon re-established itself after the war. It was, however, forced to leave mainland China again in 1951 following the communist revolution. This led to diversification into South-East Asia in the first place by acquiring a share in the capital of the Singapore merchants, Henry Waugh and Company. In later years Jardines moved into Australia, South Africa and the Middle East. The company was listed on the Hong Kong Stock Exchange in 1961 and in 1984 it moved its registered office to Bermuda. This was in preparation for the ending of British rule in Hong Kong in 1997.

Aux origines de Hong Kong: aspects de la civilisation commerciale à Canton: le fonds de commerce de Jardine, Matheson & Co., 1827-1839. Par Alain Le Pichon. Paris: L'Harmattan, 1998. (Collection Recherches asiatiques.) 602p., ill. Bibliog. Index.
[British Library of Political and Economic Science.]

British trade and the opening of China 1800-42. By Michael Greenberg. Cambridge: Cambridge University Press, 1951. xii, 238p. Bibliog. Index. [From Chapter 3 onwards, this volume is substantially based on the Jardine Matheson archive and provides much historical detail of the early company and the predecessor concerns.]

Eastern traders: some men and ships of Jardine, Matheson and Company and their contemporaries in the East India Company's Maritime Service. A collection of articles by Captain A.R. Williamson. [Hong Kong: Privately published by the company, 1975.] 212p., ill.

History of the Mathesons with genealogies of the various branches. By Alexander Mackenzie. Inverness: A. & W. Mackenzie, 1882. viii, 72p.

Hongkong and Whampoa Dock Company, Ltd.: a record of thirty-six years. Hongkong: Printed at the 'China Mail' Office, [1902]. 23p.

Jardine Matheson: traders of the Far East. By Robert Blake. London: Weidenfeld & Nicolson, 1999. viii, 280p., ill. Bibliog. Index.

Jardine, Matheson & Co., afterwards Jardine, Matheson & Co., Limited: an outline of the history of a China house for a hundred years 1832-1932. [Edited by James Steuart.] London, Hong Kong: Privately printed for the company, 1934. 88p., ill.
[East Asian Research Center, Harvard University.]

Jardine, Matheson & Company: an historical sketch. Being an account to show the circumstances in which the Company came into being and how it was consolidated over the last century. Hong Kong: The company, [1960]. 64p., ill.

Jardine's centenary in Japan, 1859-1959. Tokyo: Jardine Matheson and Co. (Japan) Limited, 1959. 47p., ill.

Jardines in Japan 1859-1867. By John McMaster. Groningen: V.R.B. Offsetdrukkerij, 1966. 162p. Bibliog. Index.

Mandarins and merchants: Jardine Matheson & Co., a China agency of the early nineteenth century. By W.E. Cheong. London: Curzon Press, 1979. (Monograph series, Scandinavian Institute of Asian Studies; no. 26.) xii, 298p. Bibliog. Index.

The thistle and the jade: a celebration of 150 years of Jardine, Matheson & Co.

Edited by Maggie Keswick. London: Octopus Books, 1982. 272p., ill. Bibliog. Index.
[Faculty of Oriental Studies, University of Cambridge.]

Western enterprise in late Ch'ing China: a selective survey of Jardine, Matheson and Company's operations, 1842-1895. By Edward Le Fervour. Cambridge, Massachusetts: Harvard University Press, 1968. (Harvard East Asian monographs; no. 26.) vii, 215p. Bibliog. Index.
[Faculty of Oriental Studies, University of Cambridge.]

308. RATHBONE, WORTHINGTON AND COMPANY

The famous Liverpool house of Rathbones was established in 1746. It traded in a wide variety of products throughout the American colonies, the West Indies and Europe. However by 1800 American cotton had become the firm's main interest. This continued to be the case until the 1830s when Rathbones started to diversify into the China trade. In the early 1840s the house of Rathbone, Worthington and Company opened in Canton. The founding partners were: James Worthington, Thomas Moncreiff, William Rathbone junior and Samuel G. Rathbone. The purpose of the business was to sell British manufactured goods sent to it by Rathbones and to buy tea and silk for export to Britain. Later in the 1840s a branch was set-up in Shanghai.

The Canton operation was not regarded as a success and was closed down in September 1850, the company's trading in the port being transferred to a friend of the partners. Shanghai seemed a more attractive prospect as better prices could be obtained there for manufactures. It was also closer to the tea production areas and consequently tea was less expensive. However Rathbone, Worthington and Company only survived for two more years in Shanghai, the business being wound up at the end of 1852.

There were a number of reasons for Rathbones' failure to maintain its own agency house in China. The accounts of the China operation were produced locally and for some years it was not possible to determine the financial state of the business. Indeed Samuel Rathbone was sent out to China in 1850 expressly to put the 1845-50 accounts in order. The firm's capital was widely dispersed and there was an inadequate marketing organisation in Britain for the Chinese imports. In addition Rathbones was over-influenced by the way it conducted its American trade. The partners in China were constantly having to refer matters back to Liverpool. Most significantly, Rathbones was uncomfortable running an agency house in a country where opium sales were so central to commercial activity.

The business was handicapped by its small size but it did gain prestige with the Chinese brokers for its honesty and by paying its bills on time.

'China houses' being chapter 8 (pp. 85-98) of ***Rathbones of Liverpool, 1845-73.*** By Sheila Marriner. Liverpool: Liverpool University Press, 1961. [This chapter centres on the history of Rathbone, Worthington and Company.]

309. JOHN SWIRE AND SONS

The first John Swire probably launched into business on his own in Liverpool in 1816. Soon he was engaged in trades such as the import of rum, sugar and cotton from Jamaica; indigo from Calcutta; oil from Nova Scotia; and cotton from the U.S.A. When he died in 1847 it would appear that he left his two sons a solvent but not particularly thriving business. Of these sons, John Samuel Swire was the more important. (William Swire suffered from ill health and retired during 1876.) John Samuel was clear-minded as to his objects; showed great entrepreneurial skills; and was not averse to taking calculated gambles. By the time of his death in 1898 the firm had been moulded into the shape it was to assume in the first half of the twentieth century.

It seems reasonable to conclude that the Swires' attention was drawn to the Far East in the 1860s as a consequence of the American Civil War which affected the cotton trade and forced the firm to look for alternative business opportunities. The Swires had been one of the initial subscribers to the Ocean Steam Ship Company **(112)** and it was suggested that they should look after the agency interests of the company in the Far East. In addition the two brothers were concerned about the financial stability of the American house of Augustine Heard which represented their firm in the region. So with the Yorkshireman, R.S. Butterfield, the Swires set-up in the autumn of 1866 the managing agency of Butterfield and Swire. The partnership with Butterfield was to last only until August 1868 but the Swires then carried the agency on by themselves and made Butterfield and Swire into one of the most famous names in the East.

Butterfields opened its first office in Shanghai in January 1867 and branches followed in Yokohama later that year and in Hong Kong in 1870. Further branches were to be opened in Foochow, Swatow, Tientsin, Hangkow, Kobe, Amoy and Chefoo. The work for the Ocean Steam Ship Company was always at the forefront of the agency's concerns. In addition there were Swires' own interests and Butterfields also acted for the Scottish,

Oriental and Pacific Steam Ship Company, for a number of insurance companies including Royal Exchange **(720)**; and for Standard Oil in some ports.

The main firm of John Swire and Sons was very active in the 1870s in the produce trades with the Far East but had abandoned this for other activities by the early 1880s. In 1872 the Swires established the China Navigation Company which was to operate shipping services on the lower Yangtze and other Chinese rivers and in 1874 they formed the Coast Boats Ownery mainly to ship beans and beancake from Manchuria to Swatow and Amoy. (The Ownery was absorbed by the China Navigation Company in 1883.) John Samuel Swire was one of the main founders of the Far Eastern Shipping Conferences which he hoped would protect his shipping interests. In 1881 he began construction of the Taikoo Sugar Refinery designed to supply finished sugar to China and the surrounding region. All told, John Samuel created a series of interlocking businesses of considerable complexity. The key to his success was what might be termed cross-subsidisation. Although one particular activity might not appear to be profitable at any given time, Swire would keep it going as it would be providing revenues for other parts of the group and hence was helping to keep the whole concern profitable.

After John Samuel's death, Swires established the Tientsin Lighter Company in 1904 and opened the large Taikoo Dockyard in Hong Kong in 1907. (Construction had begun in 1900 and the dockyard in due course was to be one of the island's largest employers.) In 1914 Swires became a limited company. The inter-war years in China were difficult for the firm but in the 1920s there was a considerable expansion of the China Navigation Company's fleet to more than 80 vessels. Inland routes in China were much extended and the vessels also carried emigrant labour to the Straits Settlements returning with timber from Bangkok. In 1934 Swires established the Orient Paint, Colour and Varnish Company in Shanghai.

The second world war was devastating for the company. Its property in China was looted and ruined; the London office was gutted in the blitz; the CNC's fleet was scattered and more than 30 vessels were lost; and in Hong Kong the dockyard and sugar refinery were reduced to rubble by American bombing. However the work of reconstruction began immediately after the war and by 1950 the sugar refinery was back in production and the dockyard had made its first 6,000 tons' ship. In 1948 the paint factory was transferred to Hong Kong. The company used the opportunities of renewal to begin altering its direction. It took a stake in Cathay Pacific Airways and by 1948 had acquired a controlling interest in that concern. Swires also became very involved from the early 1950s in Australia, New Zealand and the Pacific Rim providing a wide range of services throughout the region. Eventually the firm was to be in the forefront of the changes connected with containerisation. In 1972 the dockyard was closed down and merged with the Hongkong and Whampoa yard (*see under* Jardine Matheson **(307)**). The same year the sugar refinery was closed and that business thereafter concentrated on specialised sugar products and packaging. In Hong Kong, Swires were to add property development to their other activities and Butterfield and Swire on the island was re-named John Swire and Sons (HK) Ltd. from the beginning of 1974. At the same time Swire Pacific was formed from six Swire Group divisions.

Beyond Lion Rock: the story of Cathay Pacific Airways. By Gavin Young. London: Hutchinson, 1988. x, 245p., ill. Index.

'A British trading firm in the Far East: John Swire & Sons, 1867-1914.' By Shinya Sugiyama. Being pp. 171-202 of ***Business history of general trading companies.*** Edited by Shin'ichi Yonekawa and Hideki Yoshihara. Tokyo: University of Tokyo Press, 1987.

The China Navigation Company Limited: a pictorial history 1872-1992. London: John Swire and Sons, 1993. 118p., ill.
[National Maritime Museum Library.]

A guide to the papers of John Swire and Sons Ltd. By Elizabeth Hook. London: The Library, School of Oriental and African Studies, 1977. 176p. Index.
[Contains a brief history of Swires.]

In China seas: a history of the China Navigation Company. [By B.L. Butcher.] [s.l.: Swire Group, 1978.] 45p., ill.
[A slightly amended reprint of an article in ***Sea Breezes*** (Liverpool) for February and March 1964.]

The senior: John Samuel Swire 1825-98. Management in Far Eastern shipping trades. By Sheila Marriner and Francis E. Hyde. Liverpool: Liverpool University Press, 1967. xv, 224p., ill. Index.

A short history of the firm of John Swire and Sons. Letchworth: Arden Press [for the company], 1914. 56p.
[University of London Library.]

The Swire Group in old China. By Zhang Zhongli, Chen Zengnian, Yao Xinrong. Shanghai: Shanghai People's Publishing House, [?1992]. 344p. Bibliog.
[Translation of a Chinese work published in 1991.]
[Seen by courtesy of the Swire Group.]

Taikoo. By Charles Drage. London: Constable, 1970. 320p., ill. Bibliog. Index.
[Covers the years 1894-1925.]

CHAPTER 4

Histories relating to the Middle East

401. ANGLO-PALESTINE COMPANY

Theodor Herzl, founder of the World Zionist Organization, had the idea in the last years of the nineteenth century of a Jewish Colonial Trust which would provide finance to support Jewish emigration to Palestine. The trust was set-up in 1899 but failed to attract sufficient funds to begin operations. So in February 1902 a small subsidiary company, the Anglo-Palestine Company, was registered in London with no more than £16,000 in fresh capital. The company's first managing director (until 1924) was Zalman David Levontin, an able entrepreneur who had a deep knowledge of the social, economic and political conditions of Palestine.

The company soon took on the character of a bank. A branch (to become head office) was opened in 1903 in Jaffa and by the first world war there were further branches in Hafia, Hebron, Jerusalem, Tiberias and Safed. There was constant harassment from the local Arab and national Turkish authorities and the company had to invoke the powers of the British consuls under the capitulations. Nonetheless the concern prospered and established itself. Although it faced a run on its reserves in 1907 and there were difficulties during the monetary crisis of 1911, the Anglo-Palestine Company came through these years easily and its 'emergency cheques' were widely accepted when gold was in short supply. Between the end of 1904 and 1913 its total assets increased six times and reached more than half a million pounds. However, it did not live up to Herzl's original political expectations. In the early years it did not loan money on any significant scale for the purchase of real estate. At no stage before 1914 did long-term loans amount to more than 10 per cent of the company's portfolio. The remainder of the company's lending was against bills of exchange and other short-term securities.

After the first world war the Anglo-Palestine Company attempted to obtain the role of government bank and bank of issue but not until the state of Israel was established did it approach the status of a central bank. The name of the concern was changed to the Anglo-Palestine Bank in 1930. During 1950 the company was incorporated in Israel under the name of the Bank Leumi le-Israel.

'The Anglo-Palestine Company: the formative years, 1903-1914.' By Nachum T. Gross. Being chapter 7 (pp. 219-53) of ***Ottoman Palestine, 1800-1914: studies in economic and social history.*** Edited by Gad G. Gilbar. Leiden: E.J. Brill, 1990.

402. ANGLO-PERSIAN OIL COMPANY (BRITISH PETROLEUM)

The Anglo-Persian Oil Company was established in April 1909 but the story goes back to May 1901 when William Knox D'Arcy, a Devon man and socialite, secured a 60-year concession from the Shah of Persia to prospect for minerals over half a million square miles. D'Arcy had made his money from the Australian gold rush and had a hunch that another fortune was to be made from oil. However this was not to come about immediately. D'Arcy's first two wells were unsuccessful. Oil was struck in the second in 1904 but it was not found in any quantity. In 1905, with his money running out, D'Arcy formed a Concessions Syndicate jointly with Burmah Oil **(606)** who also repaid part of the expenditure already incurred. Drilling was moved to another part of Persia but again proved unproductive. In 1907 operations were transferred to a spot which became known as Masjid-i-Sulaiman after the nearby ruined Mosque of Solomon. Had these operations been unsuccessful, the venture would almost certainly have been wound up but on 26 May 1908 oil was struck at a depth of 1,180 feet and in very large quantities.

The company was accordingly established to work the oilfields with Burmah Oil. The Concessions Syndicate held almost all its capital. D'Arcy then sold out for just over £200,000 and 170,000 fully paid Burmah shares. The company began constructing an oil refinery on Abadan Island at the head of the Gulf (completed in 1912 but not in full working order until early 1913) and laid a pipeline 138 miles long linking the field with the refinery (pipeline completed in July 1911). At the outset of the first world war, the British Government was very anxious to obtain adequate supplies of oil for its navy. It therefore agreed to invest some two million pounds in Anglo-Persian and in return obtained a voting interest in the company of just over 50 per cent. Thereafter it appointed two ex-officio directors and had a restricted power of veto over the company's affairs to be used only with respect to 'broad strategic issues'.

By 1915 the company had balanced its accounts and soon after declared a modest dividend. At this time it decided to build its own tanker fleet and formed the British Tanker Company for the purpose. Production of crude oil was 274,000 tons in 1914 rising to 1,385,000 tons in 1920 and 4,333,000 tons in 1925. Although production continued to rise there was some levelling off to 5,750,000 tons in 1931 because of the depression. The following year Reza Shah, who was exasperated at the fall in royalties accruing to Persia, declared the concession annulled. A new concession was negotiated in April 1933 which reduced the concession area by more than a half. In the longer term no more than 100,000 square miles were to be included. However the lease was extended from 1961 until 1993 and the Persian government received £0.20 on every ton of oil exported or sold in Persia. In 1935 the company changed its name to the Anglo-Iranian Oil Company.

By 1939 the company appeared to have excellent prospects before it. Some 13 rigs were drilling oil and a production plant at Gach Saran was under construction. 9,584,000 tons of crude oil were produced in Iran that year. After the outbreak of war the British Government decided to source its oil supply from North and South America as shorter distances were involved. This meant a cutback in Iranian production which was more than restored when Japan entered the war. As a result of enemy action the company lost 44 vessels out of a tanker fleet of 93.

After the war, new fields were opened in Haft Kel, Agha Jari and Gach Saran but by 1947 the nature of Anglo-Iranian's concession was arousing considerable opposition from nationalist circles in Iran. A law of October that year committed the government to re-examine the concession. Negotiations took place in 1948-9 and in July 1949 a Supplemental Agreement was signed by the company and the Iranian government considerably improving the revenues payable to Iran. However the agreement was never ratified and in May 1951 the nationalisation of the Iranian oil industry took place under the leadership of a new Prime Minister, Dr Musaddiq. In September the remaining British staff were asked to leave the country. This marked a turning point in the company's fortunes. Although it was to return to Iran in 1954 it only did so as part of an international consortium in which it had no more than a 40 per cent share. Profit was divided 50-50 between the consortium and the Iranian government. The company, over time and from various sources, was to receive about £200 million in compensation for the 1951 takeover. In the future Iran was only to play a minor role in the company's affairs – a fact which was reflected in its change of name to the British Petroleum Company in 1954.

The company survived the 1951 crisis because of its financial strength (it had not raised capital from the public since 1923) and because of early diversification which was now increased. Since the mid-1920s it had had a 23.75 per cent stake in the profitable Iraq Petroleum Company (see **409**) which also operated in Qatar, the Trucial Coast and South East Arabia. In 1934, jointly with Gulf Oil, it had formed the Kuwait Oil Company. So in 1951 the company was in a position to purchase crude and refined oil to satisfy its customers. Thus while in 1950 its total sales of all products amounted to 42 million tons, these had dropped to 24 million tons in 1952 but had already been restored to 37 million tons in 1954. The future for British Petroleum lay in developing new oilfields, particularly at sea. Important offshore concessions were begun in the waters around Abu Dhabi in the 1950s and in the North Sea during the 1960s. B.P. was also to become very involved in the so called 'downstream' activities of distributing and selling oil throughout the world.

Adventure in oil: the story of British Petroleum. By Henry Longhurst. London: Sidgwick and Jackson, 1959. 286p., ill.

Ambassador for oil: the life of John, first Baron Cadman. By John Rowland and Basil, second Baron Cadman. London: Herbert Jenkins, 1960. 191p., ill. Index.

[The first Baron Cadman joined the Anglo-Persian Oil Company in 1921 and was its Chairman between 1927 and 1941.]

'The early management organisation of British Petroleum and Sir John Cadman.' By R.W. Ferrier. Being pp. 130-47 of ***Management strategy and business development: an historical and comparative study.*** Edited by Leslie Hannah. London: Macmillan, 1976.

East of Suez: a study of Britain's greatest trading enterprise. By J.R.L. Anderson. London: Hodder and Stoughton, 1969. 288p., ill. Bibliog. Index.

Fifty years in pictures: a story in pictures of the development of the British Petroleum Group 1909-1959. London: Contact Publications for the Group, [1959]. 160p., ill.

The history of the British Petroleum Company

Vol. 1: ***The developing years 1901-1932.*** By R.W. Ferrier. Cambridge: Cambridge University Press, 1982. xxx, 801p., ill. Index.

Vol. 2: ***The Anglo-Iranian years 1928-1954.*** By J.H. Bamberg. Cambridge: Cambridge University Press, 1994. xxvii, 639p., ill. Bibliog. Index.

Vol. 3: ***British Petroleum and global oil, 1950-1975: the challenge of nationalism.*** By James Bamberg. Cambridge: Cambridge University Press, 2000. xxviii, 637p., ill. Bibliog. Index.

403. EUPHRATES AND TIGRIS STEAM NAVIGATION COMPANY

The firm of Lynch Brothers began trading in Baghdad in 1841 and during 1860 and 1861, with British government help, it obtained navigation rights on the Tigris and Euphrates rivers from the Porte. A Euphrates and Tigris Steam Navigation Company was incorporated in April 1861 with a capital of £15,000. The company's principal operation was a river service on the Tigris between Baghdad and Basra which carried mail. For the next sixty-five years the Lynch family were to be closely connected with the running of the concern. During its history the Euphrates Company suffered from considerable hostility and obstructionism by the Turkish or other local authorities. There were various attempts to set-up rival government concerns which for the most part were unsuccessful.

Little is known of the company's early history but business must have gone well since a second steamer was put into commission in 1865. Close relations were established with the British India Steam Navigation Company **(101)** and around 1879 Sir William Mackinnon obtained a controlling interest in the Euphrates Company but left its management in the hands of Lynch Brothers. By this time through bookings were being made between Britain, India and Baghdad. A third steamer was added in 1880 and throughout the 1890s – indeed up to the first world war – traffic continued to expand. Before 1900, however, it was frequently necessary to suspend through bookings to allow accumulations of cargo to be worked off. It was not until 1899 that the Turkish authorities finally allowed the steamers to tow barges which enabled extra traffic to be carried. By 1914 the company had a fleet of fourteen vessels.

In 1903, at the suggestion of the British government, the company floated the Persian Transport Company which was to become involved in the construction of a road from Teheran to Ahwaz in Persia. Unfortunately the road was not completed and the section which was constructed never became a paying proposition. In 1912 the Euphrates Company set-up a further company, jointly with the Deutsche Bank, designed to carry materials for the construction of the eastern section of the Berlin-Baghdad railway. The company was given the name of the Société de Transports Fluviaux en Orient. This company's work was brought to a close with the onset of the first world war.

The Euphrates Company's fleet was commandeered during the war for the use of the British India Expeditionary Force in the Mesopotamia campaign. There were heavy losses and the remnant was returned to the company in 1917. The company prospered in the commodities boom which followed the war. Some £200,000 was invested in new vessels. However the company faced intense competition in the changed circumstances of the post-war world. A railway was built connecting Baghdad and Basra while two or three local shipping firms remained in existence. (The company was to take over one of these firms – the Khedery Line – in 1924.) By 1926-7 it had become necessary for the Euphrates Company's capital to be written down by some 40 per cent.

'The story of the Euphrates Company.' ***The Near East and India*** (London), 24 November 1932, pp. 948-54.

404. IMPERIAL BANK OF PERSIA (BRITISH BANK OF THE MIDDLE EAST)

The bank was established in 1889 by virtue of a sixty year concession granted by Naser od-Din Shah. It was to act as the state bank and had an exclusive right of note issue in Persia as well as tax free status. The Imperial Bank was floated in London with David Sassoon and Company **(521)** purchasing about a third of the share issue. The bank, which began operations in December 1889, took over the Persian branches of the New Oriental Banking Corporation **(111)** the following April. The board of the Imperial Bank sat in London and day-to-day operations were the responsibility of a chief manager in Tehran.

The first few years of the bank were not markedly successful. The bank was the object of anti-foreigner feelings with rumours that it had cornered fuel supplies. There were periodical runs on the bank, sometimes organised by local moneylenders. Early ventures into mining and transportation (allowed under the concession) were a disaster. Agencies which the bank opened in Iraq were unsuccessful and had to be disposed of to the Imperial Ottoman Bank **(405)**. Similar agencies were opened in India from 1891 and were profitable at first but had to be abandoned by 1900. The fact that the bank survived at all owed a great deal to the first general manager, Joseph Rabino, who held office until 1908. He successfully floated the first of Persia's foreign loans in London in 1892 which gave the bank status. (Another loan was floated by the bank in 1911.) He saw that the future of the bank lay in the construction of a viable banking business within Persia. From the beginning he lent money to Persians realising that expatriate firms would generate little business. By 1908 Rabino had opened twelve offices in Persia yet when he resigned he was largely discredited. In part this was because he would not follow standard British banking practice which called for short-term loans with collateral. Notwithstanding Rabino's unconventional approach, the bank suffered few losses in Persia through bad debts.

The bank faced a good many difficulties during the first world war as the Persian central government lost control of large parts of the country. Branches had to be evacuated and in some cases bank treasuries were looted. The bank opened branches in Basra and Baghdad during the war and these were to survive until 1964 but a branch opened in Bombay in 1919 lasted only until 1934. The immediate post-war years up to 1923 were successful ones for the Imperial Bank. It made several substantial loans and net profits were around the £80,000 level annually. Branches continued to increase and in 1928 there were 24 in various Persian cities.

By the end of the 1920s, however, the Imperial Bank's fortunes were changing fundamentally. The new Pahlavi dynasty, which had come to power in Persia in the mid-1920s, was anxious to construct an indigenous banking system. It set-up the Bank Melli – or State Bank – in 1928. During 1933 the Imperial Bank lost its right to issue notes to the Bank Melli. Although the Imperial Bank played an important part in the foundation of textile mills in Isfahan, Shiraz and Yazd during the 1930s, it suffered badly from government exchange controls and barter agreements which destroyed its business in financing foreign trade. The bank itself was now being run by ageing board members and some of its staff were not of the highest calibre. The branch network was reduced to 12 offices in Iran by 1939. Published net profits throughout the 1930s, however, were not markedly different from the levels of the early 1920s.

During the second world war the bank enjoyed something of a renaissance as Iran was occupied by British and Russian troops. However by the late 1940s the bank had become subject to a number of irksome regulations imposed by the Iranian government. The last straw was the government's refusal to issue the Imperial Bank with foreign exchange during the dispute over the nationalisation of the Anglo-Iranian Oil Company **(402)**. The bank thereupon decided to leave the country. Its chief office in Tehran was the last branch to close in July 1952.

Until the second world war, the Imperial Bank did not open offices outside Persia (with the exception of Iraq and India). However, beginning in 1942, the bank extended its operations and embarked on a transformation which, between 1950 and 1952, was to create virtually a new bank. In 1952 its name was changed to the British Bank of the Middle East. This transformation, one of the most rapid in the history of British banking, was to ensure the bank's survival when operations in Iran were no longer viable. The chief people behind this change in strategy were: (1) Lord Kennet, an innovative chairman who held office during the years 1942-52 and 1953-5; (2) F.H. Johnson, branch manager at Khorramshahr; and (3) Sir Geoffrey Prior, British Political Resident in the Gulf, 1939-41 and

1942-6 who gave the bank much support. Prior, even by the early stages of the war, considered that the bank had no future in Iran.

The bank's diversification began in Kuwait in late 1941 where it was granted a fifteen year monopoly of banking. Three years later a branch was opened in Bahrain. The bank was to hold a duopoly of banking there with the existing Eastern Bank for the following ten years. In 1946 the ruler of Dubai granted the bank a monopoly of banking in his state for twenty years. Between 1946 and 1960 the bank opened or acquired branches in Lebanon, Syria, Oman, Jordan, Saudi Arabia, Tunisia, Morocco, Bombay and Calcutta. It thus acquired a very considerable geographical spread. Bank deposits increased by 107 per cent between 1945 and 1951 – significantly only 12 per cent of the total was held in Iran by 1952. There were a few years of decline but by 1961 deposits had increased by a further 124 per cent. It was the Gulf, and Kuwait in particular, which generated the profits that carried the bank through the 1950s and 1960s.

In 1960 the bank was acquired by HSBC but for two decades more it retained a great deal of autonomy. These twenty years were difficult for the bank as the Middle East was subjected to wars and general instability. Many countries nationalised foreign banks – Syria in 1961, Iraq in 1964, Aden in 1969 and Libya in 1970. The bank effectively left Tunisia in 1973 and Morocco in 1975. On the other hand it re-started operations in Iran in 1959 with a 49 per cent stake in a joint venture. The British Bank was required to cease business in Kuwait in 1970 and the branches were taken over by a locally-formed bank. However this did not affect the profitability of the British Bank as additional income was being generated in Oman and other Gulf states. By the end of the 1970s, the bank's operations in Saudi Arabia and Iran had been taken over.

At the close of 1979, HSBC decided to end the British Bank's autonomy and move its head office from London to Hong Kong. General management functions were integrated within the structure of HSBC. The bank's network was reduced to 38 branches by 1986. The bank, however, remained very profitable. In 1984 its balance sheet stood at its highest ever at over £2,250 million.

Banking and empire in Iran. By Geoffrey Jones. Research by Frances Bostock, Grigori Gerenstein, Judith Nichol. Cambridge: Cambridge University Press, 1986. (The history of the British Bank of the Middle East; Vol.1.) xxiv, 418p., ill. Bibliog. Index.

Banking and oil. By Geoffrey Jones. Research by Frances Bostock, Grigori Gerenstein, Judith Nichol. Cambridge: Cambridge University Press, 1987.

(The history of the British Bank of the Middle East; Vol. 2.) xxi, 359p., ill. Bibliog. Index.

'A brief history of the British Bank of the Middle East in Iran (formerly the Imperial Bank of Persia, Iran).' By V.L. Walter. ***Journal of the Iran Society*** (London), Vol. 1, No. 5 (1954), pp. 176-90.

The foundation of the Imperial Bank of Persia. By G.A. Calver. [Hong Kong:] The Hongkong and Shanghai Banking Corporation, 1980. 29p.

'The Imperial Bank of Iran and Iranian economic development, 1890-1952.' By Geoffrey Jones. ***Business and economic history*** (Williamsburg, Virginia), Vol.16 (1987), pp. 439-50. (Reprinted in: ***Multinational and international banking.*** Edited by Geoffrey Jones. Aldershot: Edward Elgar, 1992.)

'International banking and its political implications: the Hongkong and Shanghai Banking Corporation and the Imperial Bank of Persia, 1889-1914.' By David McLean. Being chapter 1 (pp. 1-13) of ***Eastern banking: essays in the history of the Hongkong and Shanghai Banking Corporation.*** Edited by Frank H.H. King. London: Athlone Press, 1983.

405. IMPERIAL OTTOMAN BANK

The Imperial Ottoman Bank opened for business in Constantinople in June 1863. It was an Anglo-French combination and later on there was to be a sizeable number of Turkish shareholders. The management structure of the bank matched the position on ownership. An English committee in London and a French committee in Paris laid down major policy guidelines while the day-to-day activities of the bank and its branches were managed by the board in Constantinople. At times (particularly from the start of the twentieth century) the French group predominated. However the bank at various stages of its existence came under British influence and was often described as a British concern. For that reason it is included in this bibliography.

During the 1860s the Imperial Ottoman Bank was simply a continuation of the pre-existing Ottoman Bank (a traditional British joint-stock type bank). By 1867 the new bank had branches in Alexandria, Beirut, Constantinople, Larnaca, Salonica and Smyrna. It was granted a monopoly of bank note issue in the central Ottoman lands. In 1875 the bank received a new convention from the Porte by which it took on the role of revenue collector and was able to provide greater finances for government. For most of the 1880s over half the bank's assets were in the form of loans to government or advances against the Turkish national debt. By this time the bank was making fairly good returns but its management had become unadventurous. Throughout the 1870s and 1880s there was no extension of the geographical area which the bank covered.

Between 1872 and 1889 the Bank's director-general was Morgan Foster, a former British civil servant. He was succeeded by Sir Edgar Vincent (later Lord D'Abernon). Vincent, only 32, was to serve until 1897. He was responsible for the Bank opening branches in Bulgaria and helping to finance the Serbian debt. Through his friendship with Cecil Rhodes, he involved the bank in a large South African speculation. Unfortunately in 1895 there was a dramatic fall in the value of kaffirs and this caused a run on the Imperial Ottoman Bank which was rumoured to have made heavy losses. Vincent was followed as director-general by another Englishman, Sir Hamilton Lang, who remained until 1902. Lang was financially much more conservative and oversaw the closing of the Bulgarian branches. In the years up to 1914 the bank tried to extend beyond its primary role as a government banker but remained very much confined operationally to the Ottoman lands. As far back as 1893 it had made an agreement with the Imperial Bank of Persia **(404)** promising not to open offices in Persia. In return the Imperial Bank of Persia withdrew from the Ottoman lands and sold its branches in Baghdad and Basra to the Imperial Ottoman Bank.

The Imperial Ottoman Bank continued in existence after both the first and second world wars but it dropped the word 'Imperial' from its name in 1925. The agreement with the Imperial Bank of Persia broke down during the first world war and in retaliation the Imperial Ottoman Bank opened a branch in Hamadan in 1919. The same year it sold its eight branches in Syria and Lebanon to the French Banque de Syrie et du Grand Liban. The bank always conducted considerable business in Iraq and was one of the most significant foreign banks in the country until the early 1960s. The position was similar in Jordan and when the Jordan Currency Board was set-up in 1949, it appointed the Ottoman Bank as its agent. In the late 1940s the bank also functioned as Jordan's foreign exchange controller. In 1957 the Ottoman Bank assisted in the creation of the National Bank of Bahrain while in the early 1960s it began banking operations in Abu Dhabi. The interests of the Ottoman Bank outside western Europe and Turkey were taken over by National and Grindlays Bank **(516)** in 1969.

La Banque impériale ottomane. By André Autheman. Paris: Comité pour l'histoire économique et financière de la France, 1996. xii, 294p. Bibliog. Indexes. [British Library of Political and Economic Science.]

La Banque impériale ottomane: thèse pour le doctorat. Par Adrien Biliotti. Paris: Imprimerie Henri Jouve [for Faculté de Droit de l'Université de Paris], 1909. 340p. Bibliog.

Gold for the Sultan: western bankers and Ottoman finance 1856-1881. By

Christopher Clay. London: I.B. Taurus, 2000. (International library of historical studies; Vol. 20.) x, 698p. Bibliog. Index.
[The early history of the Imperial Ottoman Bank forms a major part of this study.]

A history of the Ottoman Bank. By Edhem Eldem. Istanbul: Ottoman Bank Historical Research Center, 1999. xxiii, 608p., ill. Bibliog. Index.
[Cambridge University Library.]

'The Imperial Ottoman Bank in the later nineteenth century: a multinational "national" bank.' By Christopher Clay. Being chapter 8 (pp. 142-59) of ***Banks as multinationals.*** Edited by Geoffrey Jones. London: Routledge, 1990.

406. IONIAN BANK

The bank was established in London in 1839. This was at a time when the Ionian Islands were under British suzerainty and the bank was set-up at the instigation of two British high commissioners so that the islands would receive efficient banking services. Until 1920 the Ionian Bank had the right to issue local banknotes.

In 1907 the bank established a branch at Alexandria where Greeks were a large element in the foreign population. Despite commencing operations at a time of economic crisis, the new branch proved successful. It undertook the buying and selling of Egypt's main crop – cotton – acting solely as an agent. By the end of 1909, the Alexandria branch was supplemented by seven further offices throughout the country. In the 1920s the Ionian Bank repeatedly headed the list of institutions handling arrivals of cotton in Alexandria.

During the second world war the bank was unable to function in Greece but its Egyptian operations benefited greatly from the inflationary boom created by Allied expenditure in the area. By the end of 1943, the bank's deposits were as large as those it had held in 1939 when it was still operating in Greece. The bank faced considerable problems after 1947 when Egypt left the Sterling Area as funds had henceforth to be found in the local currency. The Ionian Bank, however, made special arrangements with the National Bank of Egypt **(407)** in order to surmount this problem. In 1951 a new branch of the Ionian Bank was opened in Cairo. The bank's Egyptian branches were nationalised during the Suez crisis of 1956 and in 1957 its branches in Cyprus were acquired by the Chartered Bank **(102)**.

Ionian Bank Limited: a history. London: The Bank, 1953. 47p., ill.
[Guildhall Library]

407. NATIONAL BANK OF EGYPT

Despite its name, and despite the fact that the bank operated from Cairo, the National Bank of Egypt was effectively a British-operated or British-influenced bank for its first forty years. The intention of its founders was that the National Bank of Egypt should become the country's central bank. However although the bank exercised some of the functions of a central bank, it was not until 1940 that it began to resemble one.

The National Bank of Egypt was established by Khedivial decree in 1898. One of the principal founders was the financier Sir Ernest Cassel who organised a London consortium which provided half the initial capital of a million pounds. The remainder of the capital was subscribed by leading houses in Cairo and Alexandria. The bank was granted and retained the exclusive right of note issue in Egypt. British investors were allowed special rights in the running of the bank. Three members of its board were to be resident in London and were to constitute a special committee sitting there. In general the duties of this committee were consultative. However it was granted special voting powers in respect of: (1) transactions over £100,000; (2) increases in the bank's capital; (3) the agenda for general meetings; (4) amendments to the statutes; and (5) approval of the final balance sheet each year.

In 1899 the bank opened a department for agricultural loans to small farmers. This became the separate Agricultural Bank of Egypt in 1902 with which the National Bank was closely connected. The Agricultural Bank was wound up in 1936. The National Bank was also involved with the formation of the Bank of Abyssinia in 1905 and helped to run it. By 1911 the National Bank of Egypt was a successful commercial operation. It had come through the 1906-7 banking crises in Egypt and had 10,000 clients served by 16 offices in Egypt and the Sudan. However the bank was disliked by other banks in the region who resented its attempts to control them. In addition it was not popular with Egyptians because its staff were mainly foreign.

The bank did well in the first world war years. It was helped because the Egyptian Government allowed it to suspend gold payments for its notes in 1914. In 1916 it was also permitted to use sterling Treasury Bills as backing for notes in place of gold. The bank played a key part in financing the Cotton Control Commission Scheme of 1918. Similar schemes continued throughout the 1920s with the bank's participation.

By 1920 the bank's heyday had passed. It was to find the inter-war years difficult because of the repatriation of funds to Europe and declining cotton prices. Its total accounts which were valued at about 27 million Egyptian pounds in 1918 declined to 21 million Egyptian pounds in 1938. Nonetheless the bank was making significant advances to cotton growers and helped float a key government loan. It was able to pay dividends around the 15 per cent mark throughout the 1920s and 1930s.

The bank played an important part in the second world war effort. When exchange control was introduced in Egypt at the start of the war, the bank was delegated as the controlling authority. It took over the running of the national debt and helped convert the debt into new loans during 1943. The bank raised a cotton loan for the Egyptian Government and acted as paymaster for the British government departments (other than the military authorities who banked with Barclays DCO **(701)**).

In 1940 the bank's charter was renewed for a further forty years with the intention of turning it into a true central bank. Under the new arrangements the London Committee was abolished; recruitment to the staff was henceforth restricted to Egyptians (except in special cases); and a majority of the board was required to be Egyptian by 1945. Future presidents were also required to be Egyptian. These requirements were complied with and the bank could no longer be viewed as a British-controlled concern by the end of the war. During the Suez crisis of 1956 the remaining British share of the bank was sequestrated.

National Bank of Egypt 1898-1948. [Cairo:] The Bank, [1949]. 155p., ill. Index.
National Bank of Egypt: seventy-fifth anniversary, 1898-1973. [Cairo:] The Bank, 1974. 77p.
[British Library of Political and Economic Science.]

408. NATIONAL BANK OF TURKEY

The bank was established in 1909 on the model of the National Bank of Egypt **(407)**. The idea appears to have originated with the Young Turk government which had taken power in 1908 and which had pro-British sympathies. Once again Sir Ernest Casel was behind the scheme and he persuaded Sir Arthur Henderson and Lord Revelstoke (of Barings) to join him in finding capital. Sir Henry Babington Smith, who was Secretary to the British Post Office, was persuaded to become the first president of the bank.

Unfortunately the National Bank of Turkey did not achieve the success of its Egyptian counterpart. The bank carried relatively little weight in Constantinople and suffered at the hands of the well-established Imperial

Ottoman Bank **(405)** which at this time was strongly under French influence. The British government did not have a dominating position in Turkey, as it had in Egypt, and the bank's interests were often sacrificed to the need to keep good relations with the government's Triple Entente partners of France and Russia. The bank did not help matters by pursuing schemes which were in French or Russian areas of interest. Again its wish to be involved in the development of oil in Mesopotamia threatened the position of the Anglo-Iranian Oil Company **(402)** which the British Government was supporting because of the need for oil for its warships. The overall attitude of the British government caused the founders of the bank to consider liquidating it on several occasions.

The National Bank negotiated a number of public sector loans in the years before the first world war which enabled it to stay profitable. In 1909 there was a 5 per cent Constantinople municipal loan. This was followed in 1911 by finance for the first stage of the Mesopotamian irrigation scheme. The bank also provided funds for the purchase of warships in England. In 1912 the bank acquired a Baghdad municipal loan at 6 per cent while in 1913 it supplied a loan at 5.5 per cent for the construction of docks and arsenals. By the end of 1913 the bank had decided to withdraw from operations in Turkey but went back on the decision early in 1914. Instead it agreed to sell out to the Salonica Bank. The enlarged bank was to trade under the National Bank's name and the old bank's backers were to have a 25 per cent stake in the new concern. These arrangements were overtaken by the war during which the National Bank lost considerably more than its paid-up capital. In 1919 the bank was bought by the British Trade Corporation. It was profitable after the war but was having to set large sums aside for depreciation of assets. The National Bank was finally liquidated in 1931. In that year the Turkish authorities had set-up a state bank and required foreign banks to subscribe to the capital.

'Agent of empire? The National Bank of Turkey and British foreign policy.' By Marion Kent. ***Historical journal*** (London), Vol. 18, Part 2 (1975), pp. 367-89.

409. TURKISH PETROLEUM COMPANY

The Turkish Petroleum Company was registered in London in September 1912 having been originally set-up in 1911 as African and Eastern Concessions Limited. The company was yet another venture of Sir Ernest

Cassel. The financier wished to acquire all prospecting rights to the Mesopotamian oilfields and also wanted to be allowed to look for oil elsewhere in the Turkish Empire. At the time three concerns had vague claims to prospecting rights in Mesopotamia. They were the Deutsche Bank, Royal Dutch Shell and Anglo-Persian Oil **(402)**. Cassel received the support of the first two but not Anglo-Persian. However under British government influence an agreement was signed by all interested parties in March 1914 which gave control of the Turkish Petroleum Company to Anglo-Persian. In June 1914 the Turkish Grand Vizier informed the British and German Ambassadors in Constantinople that the Ottoman government would lease to the company all petroleum deposits in Mosul and Baghdad subject to an agreement on the Turkish share in the enterprise and other matters.

The agreement was not reached before the outset of the first world war and matters remained in abeyance for its duration. By 1919 Britain was in control of Mosul and Baghdad but under the San Remo Oil Agreement of 1920 a 25 per cent share of the company was given to the French in addition to Royal Dutch Shells' 25 per cent stake. (Anglo-Persian was therefore left with a 50 per cent holding.) In 1922 a provisional agreement gave U.S. companies a 25 per cent share in the company. Eventually, under agreements between 1925 and 1928, Anglo-Persians' share in the Turkish Petroleum Company was reduced to 23.75 per cent.

Turkish Petroleum could not therefore be considered a British concern after 1922. Oil was not struck in Iraq until 1923 and commercial production did not begin until 1927. During its British years the concern must be viewed as a shell company making no profits. In 1929 the company was re-named the Iraq Petroleum Company.

'The Turkish Petroleum Company – a study in oleaginous diplomacy.' By Edward Mead Earle. ***Political science quarterly*** (New York), Vol. 39, Part 2 (June 1924), pp. 265-79.

CHAPTER 5

Histories relating to South Asia

501. ASIATIC STEAM NAVIGATION COMPANY

The company was founded in 1878 under the auspices of the Liverpool merchant house of Turner and Company and their Calcutta associates, Turner, Morrison and Company. The aim was to develop steam communication in the Bay of Bengal. Laxon claims that there was no intention of competing with the fast mail steamers of the British India Company **(101)**. Asiatics' vessels were designed primarily for the carriage of cargo and Indian emigrant labour. The original Asiatic fleet of four ships worked on the Calcutta to Bombay run (calling at various intermediate ports) and later augmented this by a service from Calcutta to Chittagong, Rangoon and Moulmein.

By 1892 Asiatic had built up a fleet of ten vessels and this allowed it to begin sailings from Calcutta to Java via Malayan ports. The company also won the mail contract between Calcutta and the Andamans. Just before the beginning of the first world war, Asiatic had 17 vessels and was operating an impressive network of services criss-crossing the Bay of Bengal including regular sailings to Sri Lanka. The principal cargoes carried were teak, rice, coal and sugar.

Asiatic lost four ships in the first world war. In 1935 British India acquired a controlling interest in Asiatic but Turners remained the managing agents. Asiatic suffered considerably in the 1930s from subsidised foreign competitors but in 1939 it was able to start a large re-building programme. Eight ships were lost in the second world war but, because of the re-building programme, the company finished the war with fourteen ships rather than the thirteen it had had in 1939.

Like the British India Company, Asiatic was excluded from the Indian coastal trade after independence. It also lost its Burma-India rice trade and the Java-India sugar trade. As a consequence the company's activities changed greatly and many of its vessels spent time on charter to other members of the P. & O. group **(113)**.

In 1960 the company ceased to use Turners as its managing agents and the following year P. & O. acquired the remainder of Asiatics' equity. Its fleet thereafter became much more closely integrated within P. & O.

Asiatic Steam Navigation Co. Ltd., 1878-1963. By W.A. Laxon. Kendal: World Ship Society, 1963. 9p., ill.

502. ASSAM COMPANY

During his time as Governor-General, Lord Bentinck was attracted by the idea that tea should be grown locally in India. In 1834, at his suggestion, the East India Company set-up a committee to look into the possibilities. A short while after C.A. Bruce was appointed as Superintendent of Tea Culture. He took over government trials with tea plants and seed from China although it was his brother Robert who had been one of the first to point out in 1823 that the tea bush was indigenous to Upper Assam. Following increasing British involvement in the administration of Assam, the Assam Company was established in London in 1839 to try to make a commercial success of tea-growing on the basis of what had been learnt in the government trials. The promoter of the company was the merchant and businessman, Sir George de Hochepied Larpent, who brought together a group of traders which included Richard Twining. One of the company's first acts was to amalgamate with the Bengal Tea Association which had been set-up previously in Calcutta with similar objects. This meant that in the early years, the Assam Company had a London and a Calcutta board which gave rise to many differences of judgement. From the beginning the company only grew the native Assam bushes.

It is hardly surprising, since this was a pioneering operation, that the first thirty years of the Assam Company were difficult and included two very bad phases when the whole operation might have been closed down. J.W. Masters was appointed first gardens superintendent of the company and he did much to get the organisation running and hire the considerable volume of labour which was needed. He pressed for government to release C.A. Bruce and Bruce joined him as northern gardens superintendent in 1840. Up to 1843 the company appears not to been profitable and by the end of 1844 it was clearly in a very bad state. Both Masters and Bruce had resigned. The situation had been partly brought about through gross extravagance in setting-up the estates and by the purchase of an unsuitable steamer to take the finished tea down the Brahmaputra to Calcutta. The company was rescued through the efforts of a number of people including Henry Burkinyoung who lent the company money and regularly inspected the estates. In 1848 Burkinyoung was appointed managing director in Calcutta. Around the same time Stephen Mornay was made gardens superintendent, and he was to exhibit great efficiency (and ruthlessness) in the running of the estates. The dividends of the company thereafter improved and when Mornay left in 1852 he was succeeded by George Williamson, junior – one of the great figures in the history of the Assam tea industry – who adopted better and higher yielding methods of plucking tea.

There followed a period of vast expansion, even over-expansion, of cultivation such that by 1860 the company owned 4,725 acres. There were also great difficulties in the hiring of suitable labour. Unfortunately senior employees and managers were allowed to purchase their own tea estates. The tendency was to leave the company's bushes in poor condition while the private estates were cared for. Tea seed and other items were stolen from the company. These circumstances led to sizeable annual losses in the years 1865-7 when no dividends were paid. This time the situation was turned round by a new superintendent, Albert B. Fisher, and by the appointment in 1865 of the Calcutta firm of Schoene Kilburn as managing agents.

By 1870 the Assam Company's pioneering days were over. From then on it followed fairly closely the fortunes of the Indian tea industry as a whole. In the decades up to the first world war the average dividend was above 7 per cent and in individual years dividends could reach 25 per cent or more. The beginning of the twentieth century was marked by very low tea prices but the company cut its production costs by making big improvements in yields. It was also helped by the extension of the Assam-Bengal Railway which gave it a direct connection with the port of Chittagong. The years 1920-30 were very profitable for the company but in 1931 and 1932 it sustained losses despite making considerable economies in working practices. Profits were restored by the International Tea Agreement of April 1933 and during the second world war and up to 1951 the tea price was effectively fixed by the British government through its bulk purchase contracts. The company in Assam was not greatly affected by the partition of India but its communications with the outside world were disrupted. It was forced to revert to river transportation because of railway delays and its direct link with Chittagong was ended because of high Pakistani excise duties.

The company's operations were always confined to Assam and were centred on tea production. (In 1951 its plantations covered about 11,500 acres.) There was some diversification into general farming and from 1890 there were serious attempts at coal mining but the mines were sold off in 1913. The sterling holding company which owned the Assam Company came completely under the control of Inchcape and Company **(108)** in 1980. Inchcapes used the Assam Company a vehicle for all their sterling tea interests and it was to be the last major concern which they owned in India.

A history of the Assam Company 1839-1953. By H.A. Antrobus. Edinburgh: Privately printed by T. and A. Constable, 1957. xv, 501p., ill. Bibliog. Index.

503. ASSAM RAILWAYS AND TRADING COMPANY

In the third quarter of the nineteenth century tea-planters in Upper Assam were suffering badly from the lack of good communications with Dibrugarh on the Brahmaputra from where their tea could be taken by river to Calcutta. They were forced to use an unmetalled cart-track some sixty miles in length which at times was virtually impassable. Under the leadership of a local benefactor, John Berry White, and with the approval of the Chief Commissioner for Assam, a prospectus was issued in December 1879 for a company which would construct a light railway linking Upper Assam with Dibrugarh. Unfortunately the prospectus met with inadequate public support. At this point the London engineer, Benjamin Piercy, agreed to underwrite the scheme on condition that the new company opened up the Makum coalfield and exploited known timber and petroleum rights. The new Assam Railways and Trading Company was incorporated in July 1881 and the share issue was oversubscribed.

The railway was completed and the Makum colliery was opened in 1883-4. Another colliery was opened in Ledo in 1882. Between 1896 and 1940 a further seven coalfields were opened up. In 1909 the railway was extended up the Brahmaputra to Saikhoa. The Government of India assumed responsibility for the railway in 1942 and in 1945 purchased it outright. Oil was struck at Digboi in 1889 and in 1893 a concession was granted by government. The Assam Railways and Trading Company promoted a fresh company – the Assam Oil Company – to takeover the concession. (In 1921 the Burmah Oil Company **(606)** were appointed commercial and technical managers of the Assam Oil Company.) For a short while the Assam Railways and Trading Company owned a flotilla which brought materials to Assam for the construction of the railway and collieries and undoubtedly speeded up this work. It also helped develop markets for the coal output. In 1887 the flotilla was sold to the Rivers

Steam Navigation Company (*see under* Joint Steamer Companies).

The company began tea-planting in 1890 and two years later it floated a separate Makum (Assam) Tea Company which by 1894 had about 1,000 acres under cultivation. The Assam Railways and Trading Company then cleared forest in the Namdang area from 1908 onwards and formed a Namdang Tea Company in 1916. By 1950 the Makum and Namdang companies were cultivating an area of some 5,000 acres. The Assam Railways and Trading Company built four factories between 1917 and 1924 for the manufacture of plywood used to make tea chests.

The story of the Assam Railways and Trading Company Limited 1881-1951. [Compiled by W.R. Gawthrop.] London: Harley Publishing Co. for the Company, 1951. 63p., ill.

504. BALMER LAWRIE AND COMPANY

In 1866 the Scot, Alexander Lawrie, set-up in business in Calcutta. He was joined in 1867 by S. Balmer and the firm's name became Balmer Lawrie and Company. However Balmer died soon after the establishment of the business and it was under Lawrie (senior partner until his death in 1908) that the firm developed into one of the major managing agencies in Calcutta. It became a private limited company in 1924.

In many ways Balmer Lawrie engaged in the typical mix of activities undertaken by the Calcutta houses. Soon after its foundation the firm went into the development and management of tea gardens in Northeast India. Eventually it was to manage some fourteen estates including the Jokai (Assam) Tea Company, the Lebong Tea Company; and the Darjeeling Consolidated Tea Company. In 1873 the firm set-up the New Beerbhoom Coal Company and in 1886 it established the Bengal Paper Mills Company. Balmer Lawrie was much involved in flour-milling with managing agencies for the Bengal Flour Mills Company and the Empire Flour Mills Company. The firm represented the Calcutta Ice Association and was an early pioneer in customs clearance and forwarding work through its Anglo-Indian Carrying Company. Balmer Lawrie was local agent for about seven major insurance companies including the Sun Fire Office **(723)** and Phoenix Assurance **(716)**.

Where Balmer Lawrie had acknowledged strengths of its own were in the fields of general engineering and electrical engineering – very much developments of the twentieth century. The firm's machinery department specialised in meeting the mechanical needs of factories, mills and railways.

Through the Bridge and Roof Company it supplied and erected all sorts of structural steel, plate girders and bridges. As agents for the Indian Galvanising Company, founded in 1926, Balmer Lawries were able to deliver buckets, drums and tanks. On the electrical side the firm was managing agents for the British India Electric Construction Company which manufactured specialised switchgear and engaged in transformer re-winding. Balmer Lawrie was sole agent in India for Ediswan lamps and Johnson and Phillips wires and cables.

Balmer Lawrie was badly hit by the 1930s depression, particularly in its tea plantations. It also sustained heavy losses through the non-sale of engineering spares. However the engineering and electrical operations came into their own during the second world war when there was a huge military and civilian demand for these services. After independence Balmer Lawrie and its London arm, Alex Lawrie, ceased to be managing agents for four key companies and instead took them over directly. The companies were: Bengal Flour, Bridge and Roof, Indian Galvanising and British India Electric Construction. While the tea estates remained the hard core of Balmer Lawries' business, it lost control of the Bengal Paper Mills. During the 1950s Alex Lawrie sold a 25 per cent stake in Balmer Lawrie to Steel Brothers **(616)** who had first option for the remainder of the equity. Steel Brothers made the purchase through their subsidiary Indo-Burma Petroleum. Shortly after, the Government of India nationalised the Indian petroleum industry and with it Indo-Burma Petroleum. So when in 1968 Indo-Burma exercised its option for the remainder of the shares, Balmer Lawrie became a Government of India enterprise.

Balmer Lawrie & Co., Ltd.: merchants, bankers, general agents, engineers. London: Sir Joseph Causton and Sons [for the Company], [?1927]. 49p., ill.
[Centre of South Asian Studies, University of Cambridge.]

505. BINNY AND COMPANY

In 1796 John Binny set out from London for Madras where a number of his relatives were already working. At first he found employment as the Nawab of the Carnatic's surgeon but in 1799 he decided to set-up an agency house for the purposes of banking and selling goods on commission. In 1813 the East India Company lost its monopoly of the Indian trade and the firm was thereafter able to export to Britain, chiefly on consignment. Binnys also took on a wide range of agency functions in areas like insurance. From the 1840s onwards the firm became more heavily involved in trade and agriculture. There were experiments with sugar-refining and indigo-planting but neither activity was successful. Much more profitable were ventures into coffee-growing and textile-manufacturing. Binnys wholly or partly acquired coffee estates in Mysore and Coorg and assisted in the flotation of the Manjunhalla Coffee Company, contributing substantially towards its capital. As far as textile production was concerned, the company in 1876 established the Buckingham Mill Company in Madras again taking a substantial share of the equity. In 1881 they set-up the Carnatic Mill on an adjacent site and somewhat later they took on the managing agency for the Bangalore Woollen, Cotton and Silk Mill.

Around 1900 the partners of Binnys made serious errors in the companies they chose to promote and also failed to provide these new companies with adequate managerial control. In particular there were heavy losses with the Godavari Coal Company and the Deccan Sugar and Akhbari Company – the later having to be bought out by Binnys competitor Parrys **(517)**. The failure of the bankers Arbuthnot and Company in 1906 led to a run on Binnys which the house was not able to withstand. After its failure, Binnys was reconstructed by Mackinnon Mackenzie for Lord Inchcape and thereafter the firm held the British India **(101)** agency in Madras gaining also the P. & O. **(113)** agency in 1924. In the twentieth century Binnys were most famous in the areas of textiles and engineering also entering the structural steel business from the 1920s. Inchcapes **(108)** sold off 52 per cent of Binnys to Indian interests in the mid-1960s. Over the next fifteen years the company suffered from serious labour problems and low textile prices which brought it close to bankruptcy. In 1983 Inchcapes sold its remaining holding of 28 per cent of the company.

The house of Binny. By F. de Souza. Madras: Printed at the Associated Printers (Madras) Private Limited, [?1970]. 281p., ill.

506. BIRD AND COMPANY

Bird and Company traced its origins back to 1864 when Captain Sam Bird organised local labour to carry grain across the Jumna River at Allahabad. Bird was already Allahabad agent of the India General Steam Navigation Company (*see* Joint Steamer Companies **(514)**) and that year he had secured the first of a number of labour 'handling contracts' from the East Indian Railway (**903**, Appendix 2). By 1873 Bird and Company were 'labour contractors' to the East Indian Railway over the whole of the railway's now completed line from Howrah to Delhi.

In 1870 Bird started business in Calcutta where he secured further handling contracts from the steamer companies as well as from the Eastern Bengal Railway. These contracts were followed by a rice-handling contract from the Government of India as part of the measures taken to alleviate the Bengal and Bihar famine. By the time of Sam Bird's retirement in 1885 the firm had moved into two areas which were to be crucial for its future – jute (through the Union Jute Mill floated in 1880) and coal (through an agency for the Burrakur Coal Company obtained in 1878).

In 1881 Ernest Cable (later Lord Cable) joined the firm and it was under his leadership that Birds was transformed into one of the most important agency houses in Calcutta. Large numbers of coal and jute concerns were set-up or agencies obtained. In the early 1900s Birds developed a shipping business and in 1917 they acquired F.W. Heilgers with its important paper-making interests. In the 1920s Birds opened a branch in Delhi while Heilgers began trading in Rangoon. Birds were now becoming very involved with timber, iron and steel and concrete.

Lord Cable died in 1927 and ownership of the firm passed to Sir Edward Benthall, his son-in-law. Benthall (with his brother Sir Paul) further developed Birds and also became involved in politics. For at least the last decade before independence Sir Edward was one of the main leaders and spokesmen of the European business community in India. By 1939 jute accounted for about a fifth of Birds' business. The firm at that point managed some twelve mining companies which raised 10 per cent of the coal used in India. It was the largest paper-manufacturing business in the subcontinent and produced a substantial proportion of the raw materials used in iron and steel-making. During the war Birds became much involved in labour-contracting, particularly in the Calcutta docks.

Partition and independence had very serious effects on Birds largely because of the type of activities with which the firm was involved. At least two-thirds of its raw jute supplies came from East Pakistan whose government imposed a ban on exports to India. In India the government fixed selling prices for paper and coal at levels which were not very profitable. During the 1950s Birds' labour-contracting activities became illegal.

Sir Edward Benthall died in 1962 and soon after that the firm came under Indian control. In 1965-6 Birds was split up because it was beyond the size permitted under the Indian Monopolies and Restrictive Trade Practices Act. Both the paper and the coal concerns were taken into government ownership. Eventually Birds got into financial difficulties and was itself nationalised.

Bird and Company of Calcutta: a history produced to mark the firm's centenary 1864-1964. By Godfrey Harrison. Calcutta: Printed by Anna Art Press, [?1964]. x, 340p., ill.

A history of Bird & Co. 1864-1929. [By M.S. Jacomb-Hood.] Calcutta: Caledonian Printing Company, 1929. 2 vols. (xviii, 399p. with continuous pagination through the vols.), ill.
[Centre of South Asian Studies, University of Cambridge.]

507. DUNCAN BROTHERS

Walter Duncan took up an appointment with Playfair, Bryce and Company around 1855 when he was in his early twenties. The Glasgow firm traded mainly with Canada. After a short while Patrick Playfair (who was related to the senior partner of the firm) asked Duncan to go out to Demerara to wind up a business of his which was in difficulties. While Duncan was doing this, Playfair offered him a partnership if he was able to re-establish the concern but Duncan declined as he felt the opportunities in Demerara were too restricted. On his return to Britain he did, however, enter into a different partnership with Playfair. Under its terms he was to go out to Calcutta and start-up a house with the name of 'Playfair, Duncan and Company'. Duncan spent part of 1858 in Manchester learning all he could about the various classes of goods which were sent to India. He then sailed for Calcutta and arrived early in 1859.

The first years were difficult. However the shortages caused by the American Civil War resulted in a brisk trade in Lancashire piece goods and by 1865 the firm had become comfortably profitable. In Calcutta, Duncan shared a building with Charles Stewart Leckie. When Leckie had to return to Britain through ill health in 1860-1, Duncan acted as a forwarding agent for him. This brought an early introduction to jute and tea garden agencies. Walter's brother, William, was admitted to the partnership in 1866 and various other people, mainly connected with Playfair, also joined the business. Besides the activities mentioned, the firm took on agencies for sailing ships.

Matters continued fairly evenly until the partnership came up for renewal in 1874 when Playfair and Walter Duncan were unable to agree on shares. So it was dissolved and a new business was set-up by the Duncan brothers with the other partners in Calcutta joining the new partnership somewhat reluctantly. Unfortunately the loyalty of these junior partners seems to have been questionable and in 1876-7 they left to join Shaw, Finlayson and Company taking almost all the tea garden agencies with them. This was the lowest point in the fortunes of Duncans but the brothers worked steadily at re-establishing their presence in tea. By 1890 the firm held 12 agencies covering 5,795 acres and producing over two million pounds of tea annually. In 1895 the firm decided to go into jute in a serious way and set-up the Anglo-Indian Jute Mills Company.

The story thereafter was one of steady expansion with the 1920s bringing particular prosperity to the firm. In those years Duncans became one of the leading tea agency houses in Northern India. In jute too, with the opening of Jagatdal Mill in 1922, Anglo-Indian Mills became the largest single jute mill company operating on the Hooghly. There followed a difficult period in the 1930s but Duncan Brothers survived to play an important part in the second world war. Jute in particular was used for items as diverse as parachutes, aircraft landing strips and makeshift tea boxes.

The firm was particularly hard hit by independence and partition in 1947. The raw jute used by the Anglo-Indian Mills was grown in East Pakistan and some of the Duncans' tea gardens were also located there. Access to other tea gardens in Assam had at first to be through East Pakistan which imposed many restrictions. The firm reacted to these difficulties by establishing separate public companies in India and Pakistan during 1948-9. On its establishment, the Indian company had the managing agency for 4 jute mills (with 2,500 looms); managed 82 tea estates covering 71,000 planted acres; and produced 55 million pounds of tea annually.

During the 1950s Duncan Brothers began to diversify. It started a new gunny export department in 1951 and in 1953 set-up a tea-buying department. Agencies were taken on for a number of British engineering firms and Duncans became much involved in the marine and fire insurance business. In 1951 the company admitted its first two Indian partners. One of these was K.P. Goenka, a leading Calcutta businessman. During the 1950s the Goenka family acquired a considerable stake and family presence in the business. In 1960 Mr Goenka became chairman of Duncan Brothers and by 1963 had a majority shareholding in the concern. Duncan Brothers was one of the first Calcutta agency houses to come under Indian ownership and was to extend its interests into the holding of investments.

The Duncan Group: being a short history of Duncan Brothers & Co. Ltd., Calcutta and Walter Duncan & Goodricke Ltd., London 1859-1959. London: B.T. Batsford [for the Group], 1959. 184p., ill. Index.
[This centenary history was written by a retired partner of the Group. The preface is signed 'W.W.' which suggests that the author was William Wallace. The first ten chapters are a revised version of a short history (not

by Wallace) compiled and printed for private circulation in 1931.]

508. JAMES FINLAY AND COMPANY

James Finlay set-up as a merchant in Glasgow in 1750. His specialism was the export of cotton goods. However it was his son, Kirkman Finlay, who really expanded the business. Kirkman took over on his father's death in 1790 and between 1798 and 1806 he bought three cotton mills in Scotland beginning manufacture of Finlays' celebrated sheets and towels. Kirkman also developed Finlays' trade with Europe courageously breaking the Napoleonic blockade. In 1816 he sent a ship and representatives to Bombay and out of this came the house of Ritchie, Steuart and Company. Ritchie Steuart were to be Finlays' agents in Western India until the end of the 1850s.

After Kirkman's death in 1842, Finlays lacked direction and it was intended to liquidate the business. The firm was saved through the work of James Clark who was admitted to the partnership in 1847. Clark renewed the machinery in the mills and joined up with another group of merchants. He developed fresh foreign connections; set-up a house in Bombay during 1862 under the name of Finlay, Clark and Company; and established a branch in Liverpool. When he retired in 1867, Finlays had grown into a substantial business.

At this point Finlays' fortunes came to be directed by (Sir) John Muir. Muir had entered the partnership in a small way in 1861 through his marriage to the eldest daughter of another partner. Thereafter Muir has been viewed as ruthless operator and a 'cuckoo in the nest' who managed to expel his colleagues, becoming sole partner in 1883. (The Muir family was to be closely connected with the Finlay house for the rest of its independent existence.) It was John Muir who greatly developed the Indian side of the business. In 1870 he opened the Calcutta house of Finlay, Muir and Company and this was to be his first love. Branches were also established in Karachi (1890), Colombo (1893) and Chittagong (1901).

Muir took the Calcutta house into the produce trade; had an unsuccessful involvement with indigo; and became associated with the Clan Line of steamers (Appendix 1). In 1870 the Champdany Jute Company was founded with two mills and 5,000 workers. In 1872 Finlay, Muir started what was to become the Golabarry Press Company. Finlays entered the tea business in the 1870s by taking on managing agencies of relatively small estates but it was the cotton slump of the 1880s which persuaded the firm to diversify into tea in a big way and invest in the plantations. Muir soon realised that only large groupings would survive and in the last years of the century he set-up four major tea companies. The most famous of these were the Consolidated Tea and Lands Company and the Amalgamated Tea Estates. Thereafter tea-planting and blending was to be one of Finlays' core activities. When Muir died in 1903 the company (as managing agents) had 74,000 acres under cultivation and employed 70,000 people.

The firm faced difficult trading conditions in the early years of the twentieth century but nonetheless in 1908 it floated the Swan Cotton Mill in Bombay. During the inter-war period Finlays was badly hit by the depression in primary products and the company played a major part in the Tea Regulation Scheme. Significantly in 1926 it had set-up the African Highlands Produce Company which was to introduce tea-growing to Kenya and provide opportunities for the firm outside India. In the 1930s Bombay cotton-manufacturing was badly hit by Japanese competition and Finlays responded by re-equipping its works and by manufacturing finer quality goods. In 1932 a branch was opened in Vizagapatam to handle the manganese ore trade.

Finlays were quick to come to terms with the situation in the sub-continent after independence and duplicated main offices in West and East Pakistan. It was realised that there was no future in jute and the firm left the trade. Tea operations became centred in East Pakistan (Bangladesh), Finlays selling their Darjeeling and Cachar interests in the late 1950s. There was an attempt to trade in engineering products and an office was established in Delhi.

By the mid-1960s Finlays were effectively turning their attention from their traditional operations to new activities in developed countries such as confectionery-making, finance, oil-related activities and general trading. In Scotland the cotton mills were wound up while in India tea interests were left under-capitalised. In 1963 Finlays formed a joint company with Tatas and the Tata-Finlay Company was used in 1976 as the vehicle for converting Finlays Indian interests into Indian ownership. In 1983 Finlays sold off its minority holding in the Tata-Finlay company. During the 1990s it was found that Finlays wide range of activities was no longer viable and the company came to concentrate on its tea plantations in Africa, Sri Lanka and Bangladesh and on the making of beverages. In 2000 the firm was taken over by its largest shareholder – Swire Pacific (**309**).

James Finlay and Company Limited: manufacturers and East India merchants.
Glasgow: Privately published by Jackson Son and Company for James Finlay, 1951. xix, 276p., ill. Index.

[A collaborative history. First draft compiled by Colm Brogan. Limited edition of 2000 copies.]

Unacceptable faces of tea: James Finlay of Glasgow. [Compiled from research by Farouk Faisal and Roger Jeffery with the editorial assistance of Joyce McMillan.] Edinburgh: Edinburgh WDM Publications, [1980]. 16p.
[This pamphlet gives a short account of Finlays' history and then discusses the treatment and conditions of workers in Finlays' Bangladesh tea-gardens after 1970.]
[British Library of Political and Economic Science.]

509. GILLANDERS, ARBUTHNOT AND COMPANY

The firm was established in Calcutta in 1819 by a Scotsman, F.M. Gillanders, who was a supercargo to Sir John Gladstone, proprietor of the famous Liverpool merchant house of Gladstone and Company. (A supercargo was the officer of a ship responsible for its commercial operations; the Gladstone family were always to be closely involved with Gillanders.) In 1832 the firm was joined by G.C. Arbuthnot. By this time the proposal for an associated Canton house was under consideration. Arbuthnot had been a captain in the East India Company's Marine and had run his own vessel after he had retired. It was felt he would be very suitable to take charge of operations in Canton. A partnership agreement was drawn up between Gillanders, Arbuthnot and three others which laid down conditions for the future conduct of the Calcutta business. This started using the name 'Gillanders, Arbuthnot and Company' during 1833. However the Canton house never came into existence.

For its first fifty years Gillanders concentrated on importing general merchandise and piece-goods. It also became very attracted by indigo as a way of providing return cargoes to Britain. The firm took on indigo agencies very freely even though a number of these involved it in heavy losses. Sometimes it became necessary to takeover shares in indigo factories as a way of recovering debt. Nonetheless Gillanders prospered and did not finally leave the indigo business until 1906.

From about 1870, under the leadership of H.N. Gladstone, Gillanders began diversifying and expanding. It was to open branches in the principal north Indian cities as well as Bombay and Rangoon. Sub-branches were established in Coimbatore and Hyderabad. Like other Calcutta houses, Gillanders moved into tea and jute from about 1865 and between 1890 and 1910 it became involved in mining, particularly coal, diamonds, tin and copper. It was also to move into chemicals and forestry.

Shortly after Indian independence, Gillanders became a public company and during the 1950s it expanded its operations. It was particularly successful with its copper operations and began trading in a range of Indian produced goods including electrical products, cement and paint. Gillanders also started manufacturing ironmongery and pharmaceuticals.

In 1969 the Gladstone family sold their 60 per cent holding in Gillanders and a substantial part of this was taken up by Indian businessmen. Over the next two decades Indian holdings in the firm increased and by 1990 they formed a controlling majority of the equity. By that date Gillanders had taken control of many of the companies it had previously managed but the Government of India had nationalised some of the firm's copper interests.

History of Gillanders, Arbuthnot & Co. By J.S. Gladstone. London: Printed by Waterlow & Sons [for the Company], 1910. 105p., ill.
[Flintshire County Record Office, Hawarden.]

510. GREAVES COTTON AND COMPANY

There is some doubt as to the exact date when James Greaves arrived in India. However it seems most likely that he reached Broach in Gujarat towards the end of the 1850s or the beginning of the 1860s. His object was to buy raw cotton and to import textile machinery. He also envisaged starting-up cotton-ginning factories and baling presses along the coast. At some point he came to know Sir George Cotton who had come out in 1863 to manage the East Indian Cotton Agency of Bombay. In 1870 the two men set-up a business of their own in Bombay with the name of 'Greaves Cotton and Company'. By that time it appears that both men had gained considerable experience by working as technicians and managers of Indian-owned cotton mills.

Greaves and Cotton arranged for agents to start-up mills on their behalf and in due course other mill-owners placed their concerns under the firm's management. In 1874 James' son, John R. Greaves, joined the firm. He had spent several years with the famous Oldham machinery firm of Platt Brothers and Company and played a major part in the expansion of Greaves Cotton. He later became its head. In 1904 Greaves Cotton controlled a chain of eight mills with a total of 290,000 spindles. The mills had such names as Empress, Connaught, Howard, Bullough, Imperial and James Greaves. Part of the reason for Greaves Cottons' success was that it introduced a technologically superior form of ring spindle in its mills.

The company was also among the first managing agencies to switch over to a system of remuneration which was calculated on the operating mill's profits rather than on sales or output.

Greaves Cottons' growth continued in the early years of the twentieth century and at the outbreak of the first world war the firm is said to have controlled twelve of the fifteen European cotton mills in Bombay. It then had a capital of half a million pounds and was the largest private industrial employer in India. However by 1915 the firm was suffering heavy losses from its cotton mills which ultimately had to be closed down. Most of their output was sent to China in the form of yarn and this trade suffered from wartime depression and disruption as well as from intensive Japanese competition. Greaves Cotton was, therefore, forced to concentrate on other activities. It began manufacturing a wide range of metal products as well as textile and other machinery. In due course the firm entered the heavy electrical machinery business and became much involved in the production of agricultural equipment and irrigation pumps. By 1940 Greaves Cotton had seven offices located in the key cities of India. It held some 40 agencies for British firms in the fields of textile machinery, engines, boilers, lubricants and paints.

A century of progress. [By J.H. Langdon.] Bombay: Greaves Cotton & Co. Ltd., 1959. 105p., ill.
[Centre of South Asian Studies, University of Cambridge.]

511. GRINDLAY AND COMPANY

Robert Melville Grindlay entered the East India Company's Army as a cadet in 1803, reaching the rank of captain in 1817. He was a talented artist and served at one stage as ADC to the Governor of Bombay. He retired on half pay in 1820 but maintained contact with friends and former colleagues in India helping them with their business requirements. In 1828, with a partner, he established an agency in the City of London under the name of 'Leslie and Grindlay'. Grindlay's partner left after two years and by 1843 the firm had become Grindlay and Company. Grindlay, himself, finally retired to Nice in 1842.

Grindlays specialised in making travel arrangements and in clearing and forwarding the personal effects of Indian Army officers. It took care of all the details of life abroad. Between 1847 and 1898 Grindlays even published a regular newsletter on 'Home News' for the benefit of its clients in India. In 1854 the company opened its first Indian branch in Calcutta under G.J. Groom and another was opened in Bombay in 1865 with the name 'Grindlay Groom and Company'. The Indian branches were financially autonomous until 1908 when Groom was bought out by the London head office and their name reverted to Grindlay and Company. Over the next 20 years, branches were opened in, Delhi, Lahore, Karachi, Madras, Peshawar, Quetta and Simla – all places with significant military establishments.

Grindlays engaged in banking from a fairly early stage – its first cheques can be traced back to 1838. However until 1920 the firm restricted itself to running personal accounts. At that date commercial business was introduced and in 1924 the National Provincial Bank took over Grindlays while leaving the business very much as an independent concern. In 1948 Grindlays was acquired by the National Bank of India. (See **516** below for subsequent history.)

100 years of banking in Asia and Africa: a history of the National and Grindlays Bank Limited. By Geoffrey Tyson. London: The Bank, 1963. xii, 246p., ill. Index.

Grindlays, 1828-1978. [By Lord Aldington and others.] London: The Bank, 1978. [16p.], ill.
[Includes reproductions of water-colours of western India by R.M. Grindlay.]

512. HINDUSTAN ENGINEERING COMPANY

The firm was incorporated in December 1936 as the Hindustan Loom Company. It was owned by George Hattersley (an established Yorkshire textile machinery manufacturing company) and its Indian agents, Duncan, Stratton and Company. Hattersleys had already had Indian experience as they had tried to set-up a cotton-weaving business in Bombay between 1920 and 1925 but this had not been a success. They had a 55 per cent stake in the new concern and Duncan, Stratton and Company effectively controlled the remaining 45 per cent. The object of the Loom Company was to produce weaving machinery for the Indian market more cheaply than could be done in Britain. It was initially located in Satara but when its hopes of capturing the South Indian machinery market were not fulfilled, it moved and began production in Bombay in 1939. At that point its capital was increased, its name was changed to the Hindustan Engineering Company and it undertook a wider range of activities including making machine parts, other engineering accessories and more general items like vices. By the early stages of the second world war operations had become profitable but in 1943 the firm's premises were requisitioned by the army (probably unnecessarily). The Hindustan Engineering Company never seriously restarted after the war and was wound up in 1954. There were complex reasons why the firm never resumed operations but Hattersley's in 1945 was preoccupied with its own production difficulties in Britain while Duncan, Stratton and Company had turned its attention to new areas of business.

In its six effective years of existence the Hindustan Engineering Company manufactured some 7,300 looms to a value of more than 2,500,000 rupees. Overall it made a loss of nearly 50,000 rupees although, as indicated above, it was profitable by the end of its existence. It retains the honour of having been the first company to set-up plant to manufacture textile machinery in the Indian subcontinent.

'Machinery manufacture in a colonial economy: the pioneering role of George Hattersley and Sons in India, 1919-43.' By Colin Simmons, Helen Clay and Robert Kirk. ***Indian Economic and Social History Review*** (New Delhi), Vol. 20, Part 3 (July-September 1983), pp. 277-315.

513. IMPERIAL TOBACCO COMPANY OF INDIA

The British American Tobacco Company was established in 1902 as part of a settlement between the warring American Tobacco Company and the U.K. Imperial Tobacco Company. BAT was to handle the tobacco interests of the two concerns in overseas markets. As far as India was concerned there were already distribution networks in existence which BAT was able to takeover and in 1905 it incorporated a firm with the name of the Peninsular Tobacco Company for the purpose of building a cigarette manufacturing plant. A site at Monghyr in Bihar was eventually chosen because Bihar was at the centre of the Indian tobacco-growing region. (It was not appreciated that the tobacco grown there was of the Balkans variety and not the Virginia leaf which the company sought.) In 1910 the Imperial Tobacco Company of India was established and bought up all the BAT interests in India, Burma and Aden. The following year the American Tobacco Company was broken up as a result of the anti-trust legislation in the United States. It was required to sell its holdings in BAT and by 1914 about 70 per cent of the company's shares were owned by investors with British addresses.

The new Imperial Tobacco Company of India quickly felt the need for a further factory which began operating in Bangalore in 1913. A third factory was established in Saharanpur in 1926 and in 1940 the company acquired a factory in Parel from A. & G. Green. In 1912 Imperial set-up the Indian Leaf Development Company at Calcutta to help with the development and procurement of tobacco. It bought 150 acres of land in Guntur District, Madras and began working through brokers to obtain tobacco from farmers. By 1921 the company had gone in for direct purchasing and bonded selected local farmers to whom it issued free seedlings and gave advice on horticulture. A network of buying depots was set-up as was a drying and stripping factory at Chirala. Imperial established Printers (India) in 1928 to manufacture cigarette boxes. This concern started a second factory for the purpose in 1950. In 1944 a joint company, called Eastern Tissues, was set-up with the Bengal Paper Mills to manufacture cigarette paper. This enterprise only lasted until 1951. A wholly-owned company (under the BAT umbrella) with the name of Tribeni Tissues was operating by 1950. On the distribution side Imperial divided India into depot territories and in 1925 replaced its agents with distributors in every large town.

ITC suffered badly in the early 1930s from the nationalist boycott of British goods and sales of its cigarettes declined dramatically. The company was forced to close three depots in Bihar. Eventually it adopted a ploy of manufacturing cigarettes in boxes with Chinese names and giving the impression they had been manufactured in Hong Kong. ITC's position was helped by its acquisition in 1930 of the Indian firm of Vazir Sultan and Sons which operated from Hyderabad. In 1935 (as part of a world-wide arrangement) ITC took over the running of Carreras' Indian factory in Calcutta. (ITC was to acquire all Carreras' Indian interests in 1943.) The effect of these developments was to give ITC about 75 per cent of the total cigarette manufacturing capacity in India and by the end of the 1930s its sales had recovered to the levels of the late 1920s. During the second world war ITC manufactured special non-branded 'V' label cigarettes for the Indian Army. Two types were produced in red and green packs for European and Indian personnel.

ITC found the operating environment in South Asia difficult after Indian independence in 1947. As a response, Indianisation of the management took place and in 1968 the first Indian chairman, Ajit Haksar, was appointed. In 1970 the company changed its name to Indian Tobacco. (The Pakistan Tobacco Company had been created in November 1947.) However these measures could not counteract the effect which the imposition of excise duties and sales taxes had on the market. Perhaps of greater significance was the emergence of the Indian-owned firm of Golden Tobacco. By 1961 Imperials' market share was down to 40 per cent from the 70 per cent it had in the mid-1950s. At the end of the 1960s Golden Tobacco began a campaign against Imperial claiming it was a foreign concern which was draining foreign exchange and had wiped out 200 small local manufacturers. Imperial believed it had an effective answer to these charges and in any event pointed out that Golden Tobacco was open to criticism itself because of its close family structure. However some of the claims stuck – there was no avoiding the fact that 75 per cent of Imperials' shareholders lived overseas and a million pounds was paid annually in dividends to them. In 1973 the Foreign Exchange Regulations Act (FERA) was passed which required the foreign equity in Indian companies to be no more than 40 per cent. Indian Tobacco reached this target in 1976 largely by the sale of equity stock exclusively to Indian nationals. For the company the future lay in diversification. It was to move into the hotel trade, general exports and marine foods.

Challenge and change: the ITC story 1910-1985. By Champaka Basu. Hyderabad: Orient Longman, London: Sangam Books, 1988. xv, 367p., ill.

The global cigarette: origins and evolution of British American Tobacco 1880-1945. By Howard Cox. Oxford: Oxford University Press, 2000. xxii, 401p., ill. Bibliog. Index.

'International business, the state and industrialisation in India: early growth in the Indian cigarette industry, 1900-19.' By Howard Cox. ***Indian economic and social history review*** (New Delhi), Vol. 27, No. 3 (July-September 1990), pp. 289-312.
[Centres on the early history of British American Tobacco in India, particularly the company's opposition to increases in Indian customs duties on imported tobaccos.]

See also the entry for British American Tobacco Company **(702)** *which gives details of the firm's activities elsewhere in Asia.*

514. JOINT STEAMER COMPANIES

The Joint Steamer Companies were the India General Steam Navigation Company and the Rivers Steam Navigation Company. They provided river transportation in northern and eastern India. The two companies' joint working dated from an agreement made in 1889. The agreement set-up a joint management structure for the two companies under which the operational control for services in a particular area was the responsibility of one of the companies.

The **India General Steam Navigation Company** was set-up on the initiative of the Calcutta agency house of Carr, Tagore and Company. It put a draft prospectus to a meeting of the Steam Tug Association held in the city in February 1844 and the new company can be said to date from June of that year. Its first services went up-river from Calcutta into Northern India. In some cases they travelled as far as Garmukhteswar on the Ganges (1,760 miles by river) and Agra on the Jumna (1,640 miles by river). From 1860 the company began an Inland Water Service to the tea-gardens of Assam.

The early years of the India General were not very successful partly because unsuitable vessels were acquired. As a consequence the shareholders removed the first managing director and board in 1847. After this the company entered into three decades of considerable profitability. It did face competition from rival concerns but it absorbed one and some of the others went out of business. The company had to contend with increasing competition from the newly constructed railways and it realised its future lay in Assam and eastern India rather than on the rivers of the north. In the 1880s it entered into a rates war with the RSN company but the losses both companies sustained ultimately led to the joint agreement.

Little is known of the early days of the **Rivers Steam Navigation Company**. It was founded in 1862 with the name of the New Rivers Company by Captain J.H. Williamson who had commanded two IG vessels. Williamson left in 1865 to help found Williamson Magor and Company **(526)** and the steamer concern was entrusted to the Calcutta agency house of Begg, Dunlop and Company. At about this time the steamer company was re-named. It was to became particularly well known for the fast steamer service it ran from Dhubri to Dibrugarh in Assam. Rivers had accepted a subsidy in 1880 from the Government of Assam to run this service for ten years.

The **Joint Companies** arrangement proved extremely successful and enduring. From the beginning the companies established joint agencies at certain steamer stations. Through to the first world war and up to about 1930 they enjoyed steady profitability; there was an expansion of services; and a considerable ship-building programme was undertaken. A new joint workshop was set-up at Sonachora near Dacca. However the companies suffered considerably in the depression of the early 1930s. Jute and tea traffic was curtailed because of overproduction. By 1934 prosperity began to return and the years up to 1939 were some of the most satisfactory in the companies' histories. During the war they were much involved in the movement of stores up the Brahmaputra for onward transmission to China. They also transported refugees from Burma but did not have sufficient capacity for all demands made on them.

Viewed in retrospect the years after partition were bound to be unhappy ones for the Joint Companies as inevitably they would become involved in political tangles despite forming separate companies in India and Pakistan. At first there was a good deal of traffic from political refugees moving from one of the partitioned countries to the other but this had ceased by 1950. Then the companies suffered from loss of skilled labour, strikes and unfair competition. The India General in India was the first company to go; it was effectively taken over by the RSN Company in 1963. However by 1965 the Government of India bought out RSN for one pound. In Pakistan a new company called Pakistan River Steamers Limited was effective from the beginning of 1961. It included a government element and the Joint Companies accounted for about two-thirds of the concern. However in 1972 the new Government of Bangladesh transferred this concern to a nationalised corporation.

A history of the Joint Steamer Companies. By Sir Percival Griffiths. London: Inchcape & Co., 1979. xvi, 156p., ill.

The India General Steam Navigation Company Limited. By Alfred Brame. London: Leadenhall Press, 1900. iv, 249p., ill.

515. JOREHAUT TEA COMPANY

The Jorehaut Tea Company was established in 1859 as the second limited liability tea company in Assam at a time when there was controversy within the Assam Company **(502)** as to how it should be run. Consequently many of the new company's chief officers came over from the Assam Company. For example, the first managing director, William Roberts, had been managing director of the Assam Company between 1853 and 1858. (The Roberts' family were to play an important part in the affairs of the Jorehaut Tea Company. Between 1859 and the 1940s the managing directorship was to pass from father to son and then to grandson in an unbroken succession.) The company began with four estates in Assam of some 831 acres and, despite opposition from his gardens superintendent, Roberts was determined to increase the total to 10,000 acres which he had done by 1862. The company was financially successful from the start – in 1863 a dividend of 36 per cent was paid and only in three years in the period up to 1946 were dividends passed. High dividends were the norm.

Throughout its history the company had a policy of only producing the finest quality teas of which its gardens were capable. The company did not substantially diversify out of tea and it remained based in Assam. In 1869 mechanisation was introduced in the form of a tea-leaf rolling machine. Until 1900 the story was one of steady expansion with ample provision of labour. However the first years of the twentieth century were marked by overproduction of tea in the industry as a whole. The company was forced to reconsider its position faced as it was with a substantial proportion of tea bushes over thirty years old. Areas were taken out of cultivation and different pruning methods were adopted. Thereafter (until 1919) there were continuous rises in the company's prosperity. It absorbed the Borsapori, Desang and Langharjan Tea Companies. The period 1919-29 was probably the most remarkable in the Jorehaut Company's history. There was a large expansion in tea acreages after the first world war which brought in some of the highest profits ever. However the company suffered somewhat in the early years of the 1930s because of the worldwide depression in primary products. Tea production then became the subject of an international tea regulation scheme which lasted throughout the second world war. This brought the company reasonable if not record profits. In 1945 it cultivated 10,175 acres of which 9,904 were bearing tea.

A history of the Jorehaut Tea Company Ltd. 1859-1946. By H.A. Antrobus. London: Tea and Rubber Mail, [?1946]. 368p., ill. Index.

516. NATIONAL BANK OF INDIA

The National Bank of India began life in September 1863 as the Calcutta City Banking Corporation but its name was changed to the National Bank of India the following year. The bank was a rupee company and its first board of directors consisted of four Indian members and three Europeans emphasising the local character of the enterprise. However the need for a wider presence soon exerted itself. A branch was opened in London in October 1864 and during 1865 the bank took over the Indo-Egyptian and London Bank whose business was mainly in Bombay. By this time a debate had grown up between those in the bank who wanted its activities to be centred on Calcutta and those who favoured expansion. The expansionist party won and during 1866 and 1867 the bank's registration and head office were moved to London. Nonetheless rumblings of discontent with the decision continued throughout the early 1870s fuelled by disgruntled ex-employees.

The bank had begun operations at a fortunate moment when the Indian economy was buoyant but it did well to survive the banking crises of the late 1860s. In part this was due to the fact that it was at the time primarily a Calcutta enterprise while the main area of failure was in Bombay. Early losses in Bombay had taught the directors to operate in that city with circumspection. The National Bank of India also began life with an outstanding general manager in the person of Robert Orr Sawers – a Scot who was only 26 when he took on the post. Sawers remained general manager until he died at the early age of 43 in 1880 and during his tenure he showed great qualities of prudence, tact and firmness which established the bank on a sound footing. Sawers was followed by Robert Campbell who was to serve either as general manager or chairman of the board until 1924. Campbell (one of the great figures in Eastern exchange banking) brought the bank to maturity and gave it authority, particularly in India. The decision in 1893 (almost certainly his) to bring the bank's silver back to Britain saved the concern from substantial losses. Henceforward the National Bank was to hold the whole of its capital in sterling and branch managers were required to use local sources of finance for loans.

The last three decades of the nineteenth century were a period of considerable expansion for the bank. By the 1870s it was operating in Hong Kong and Shanghai but its experience of the Far East was not altogether happy. Its first manager in Hong Kong, although an experienced banker, seems to have made many errors of judgement which caused heavy losses. The bank continued in the region for a while but left Hong Kong in 1880 and Shanghai in 1884. Thereafter, alone of the major exchange banks, the National Bank of India never operated east of Burma. Instead it built up a considerable branch network in India, Ceylon and Burma and then in 1893 opened in Zanzibar to help finance Indian Ocean trade. This was the beginning of a major presence in East Africa where the bank obtained important business from the remittances of overseas Indians. In 1894 the bank opened a branch in Aden where for many years it was the only western bank. By 1900 the National Bank of India had nineteen offices in all.

Over a period of about eighteen months at the end of the first world war, the National Bank of India was engaged in negotiations with Lloyds Bank whereby the latter bank would buy up all the National Bank's shares. A figure had been agreed but the takeover was vetoed by the British Treasury. The bank therefore remained independent during the inter-war years which for it were difficult given its considerable commitments to Indian industry and plantations, particularly with seasonal finance. However annual profits in the key years of 1928-32 remained stable at about half a million pounds. During the second world war the bank benefited from not having branches in the Far East. After the war, however, it encountered more difficult operating conditions as the newly independent South Asian states set-up powerful central banks. In 1948 the National Bank of India purchased Grindlays Bank **(511)** from the National Provincial Bank and this gave it a greatly enhanced presence in India and Africa even though Grindlays was not formally integrated with the National Bank until 1958. The bank changed its name to National and Grindlays Bank in 1959 and resources were further strengthened by the acquisition of the eastern branches of Lloyds Bank **(712)** during 1960. By 1963 National and Grindlays had 130 branches. In 1975 the bank was re-named Grindlays Bank and in 1984 the concern was acquired by the Australia and New Zealand Banking Group. In 2000 Grindlays was purchased from ANZ by Standard Chartered **(102)** for £850 million. It was then integrated within the Standard Chartered Group.

100 years of banking in Asia and Africa: a history of the National and Grindlays Bank Limited. By Geoffrey Tyson. London: The Bank, 1963. xii, 246p., ill. Index.

517. PARRY AND COMPANY

It was in 1788 that Thomas Parry, a young Welshman, arrived in Madras intending to follow a merchant's career outside the employment of the East India Company although sanctioned by it. At first Parry went into partnership with Thomas Chase but by 1792 he had set-up on his own. Thereafter Parry sometimes operated on his own but more often he worked with a succession of different partners. There were even occasions when Parry left the running of the business to his partners and went into paid employment. For example, between 1813 and 1818 he served as cashier to the government bank.

The company which Parry started was in many respects a model for British merchant houses in India throughout the nineteenth century. Parry provided much needed banking and insurance services for the British in Madras. He operated freight and passenger agencies and supplied naval stores to the East India Company. He chartered space on Company ships to bring in items such as liquor, canvas and rope and exported piece-goods, indigo, coffee and spices. In due course Parry was to run his own ships. As early as 1805 Parry became involved in a form of manufacturing when he set-up a tannery.

By all accounts Parry was a kind and generous man and advantage was sometimes taken of his good nature. Thus two of his ships' captains acted beyond their instructions and left the firm with debts exceeding 350,000 rupees. Nonetheless the company survived the bad times, mostly notably the depression of 1805-7. Soon after Parry's return to the business in 1818 the partnership broke up and he took on John William Dare as his new partner. Dare was to run the concern from Parry's death in 1824 until his own death in 1838. A much harder type than Parry, Dare took the firm into more nautical ventures including a shipping service between Madras and London.

For the rest of the nineteenth century the firm continued to operate largely on the basis of the established staples. There were attempts at coffee and tea-growing, mining and iron and steel-making but none of these activities was particularly successful. In 1842 the concern moved into sugar-refining and this, together with the associated distilling, was to become very important for it. During the American Civil War, Parrys made very large profits from the export of cotton. Throughout the nineteenth century there was a considerable expansion in Parrys' branch network and in 1899 the firm had twenty branches across South India.

By 1900 it was clear that Parrys' operations were expanding and changing. As early as the 1880s the indigo business had collapsed with the development of German aniline dyes. In 1897 a British firm, East India Distilleries and Sugar Factories (EID), took over most of Parrys' sugar interests although Parrys was closely involved with the firm and acted as its managing agents. Around this time Parrys moved into the fertiliser, chemicals and china industries with operations mainly taking place on its Ranipet site. Parrys was greatly affected by the collapse of the Arbuthnot banking house in 1906 and the subsequent failure of Binnys **(505)**. Parrys itself came under sustained pressure but it survived partly with the help of a loan from a British house. However banking operations never really recovered and during 1919-20 this side of the business was closed down. In the years up to 1914 Parrys moved into the confectionery business and into timber. There was also a vigorous revival in the trade in cotton piece-goods.

The first world war took Parrys into a number of new areas including engineering when the firm set-up a railway engineering department. Sales of confectionery also greatly increased. After the war the firm faced the biggest crisis it had so far encountered when the value of silver suddenly halved in 1920-1. Parrys had considerable sterling liabilities (particularly on the purchase of cotton piece goods) and these now had to be met with greatly increased amounts of silver rupees. The firm pulled through these difficulties largely because of the determination of its senior partner, Sir William Wright. For the rest of the inter-war period Wright avoided any project which was not manifestly safe. He worked only with first rate managing agencies; kept to guaranteed sellers like fertilisers and engineering products; and completely rebuilt and re-equipped EID's main sugar refinery. Needless to say Parrys moved out of the cotton piece-trade.

In the second world war Parrys' fertiliser operations were greatly expanded and the firm entered into new operations like dehydrated foods and wood distillation for acetic acid. The firm played a big role in organising shipping in southern Indian ports and in providing coal for the allied navies. It also produced 'Parrys Naval Gin' which gained great fame in the East.

Parrys survived in the post-independence era because in practice, if not at once in ownership, it Indianised very rapidly. Moreover EID, while not yet becoming a rupee company, moved its seat of management and control to India in 1948. By 1954 no senior European manager who was with Parrys in 1939 remained. In addition, Parrys was to be run by a number of very prominent Indians in the early years of independence. The first of these was C.R. Srinivasan who had been editor of the Tamil-language newspaper *Swadesamitran*. Srinivasan became a director of EID in 1948 and its chairman in 1955. The following year he organised the takeover of Parrys by EID although the name of the group was not changed to EID-Parry Limited until 1962. Under Srinivasan, Parrys became involved in a number of prestigious joint projects. The most famous of these was the formation of Coromandel Fertilisers with an American company. This was to make Parrys the biggest handler of fertilisers in the private sector in India. Meanwhile at Pettavaithalai in Tamil Nadu, Parrys established the Cauvery Sugars and Chemicals Limited.

At the end of the 1950s the EID group took a decision to concentrate on industrial projects and to relinquish sales agencies progressively. At that point Parrys' future seemed to depend mainly on sugar, chemicals and pottery. When Srinivasan died in 1962 he was eventually succeeded by H.V.R. Iengar who had been Nehru's principal private secretary. Iengar was to be faced with declining prospects for fertilisers and he diversfied EID-Parrys taking it into the production of seeds, animal feeds and pesticides. It was under Iengar in 1970 that the decision was taken to turn EID-Parrys into a rupee company. This actually took place in June 1976 while the last European executive director had retired from Parrys in 1972.

During 1969 Parrys lost around 65 million rupees in fertiliser stocks as a result of a disastrous cyclone. It was to be the first of a number of serious misfortunes which would dog the firm in the 1970s and lead to its further takeover in 1981.

Parrys 200: a saga of resilience. By N.S. Ramaswami and S. Muthiah. New Delhi: Affiliated East-West Press, 1988. xv, 304p., ill. Biblog. Index.

Parry's of Madras: a story of British enterprise in India. By Hilton Brown. Madras: Parry & Co., 1954. 347p., ill. Index.

Thomas Parry: free merchant, Madras, 1788-1824. By G.H. Hodgson. Madras: Higginbothams, 1938. vi, 357p., ill.

518. PEIRCE LESLIE AND COMPANY

Robert H. Peirce and Patrick Leslie were good friends and it is probable that around 1850 one or both of them were sent out to Sri Lanka to buy coconut oil for Prices' Patent Candle Company or otherwise represent Prices. In 1851 Peirce became manager of Wilson, Richie and Company of Cochin but in 1862 that firm failed and together with Leslie, Peirce took over the business thus founding Peirce, Leslie and Company. In 1863 Peirce moved up the coast to begin trading in Calicut and the firm's head office was moved there. Leslie returned to London in 1873 and continued to represent the company in Britain for a time. Peirce was intending to dissolve the partnership in 1878 but died before he could do this. The firm continued under the sole-partnership of Stuart Gilkinson who had become a partner in 1874. Gilkinson was noted for his caution and ability to drive hard bargains. These qualities stood Peirces in good stead during the failures of 1906.

Initially the firm had two main activities. Firstly, it acted as local agent for a number of important British companies such as Commercial Union Assurance **(705)** and the British India Steam Navigation Company **(101)**. It was the Lloyds' agents for Cochin. Secondly, acting as produce merchants, the firm helped to market the abundant harvests of the Malabar region. Commodities involved included pepper, ginger and other spices, coconut oils, coir and coconut matting, sandalwood and sandalwood oils. In due course Peirces entered the coffee-curing business. It took over the Anupura Coffee Works in 1891 and bought Morgans' Jeppo Curing Works in 1923. Following from this, Peirces established its own network of up-country agents to procure the raw coffee. In 1890 Gilkinson started an import business which took the firm into cement, bar-iron and steel, chemical fertilisers, soap and piece-goods. Inevitably this extension of its activities increased Peirces' involvement with shipping and provided further work for the shipping agency side of the business.

The twentieth century brought considerable changes in the firm's operations. There was a decline on the produce side so that by 1962, with one exception, these activities were mainly confined to coir products and coffee. The exception was Peirce Leslies' increasing association with the Indian cashew industry which had begun around 1900. In 1925 the firm started shipping cashews in carbon dioxide, rather than in shell, and by 1931 it had 17 roasting and shelling establishments in the vicinity of Mangalore. In 1952 it linked up with Metal Box **(715)** to can cashews.

The major development of the twentieth century was the entry of Peirce Leslie into the plantations sector, generally as managing agents. Besides coffee, it was to become much involved with tea and rubber. For example in 1911 the firm floated the Panora Tea and Produce Company and the Eddivanna Rubber Company. In 1926 it took over some of Binnys' **(505)** properties in Mysore and formed, as managing agents, the Kalasa Tea and Produce Company. When T.H. Allan and Company went out of business in 1931 it acquired a number of its agencies including the Gudalur (Nilgiri) Tea and Coffee Estates Limited. A year earlier most of Peirce Leslies' rubber interests were merged into the new Cochin-Malabar Estates Limited.

Another development of the twentieth century was Peirce Leslies' entry into manufacturing. In 1928 it formed the Cambodia Mills Limited in Coimbatore for the spinning of cotton yarn and in the same year it took over Morgans' Tile Works in Jeppo which produced high quality tiles.

Peirce Leslie merged with Steel Brothers **(616)** in 1975.

Century in Malabar: the history of Peirce Leslie & Co., Ltd. 1862-1962. Edited by W.K.M. Langley. Madras: The Madras Advertising Company on behalf of Peirce Leslie & Co., [1962]. xiv, 150p., ill. Index.

519. THE PRESIDENCY BANKS AND IMPERIAL BANK OF INDIA

The Bank of Bengal, first of the Presidency Banks, began operating in 1809 and grew out of the Bank of Calcutta which had opened its doors in 1806. These banks were the result of government initiatives – it was hoped they would assist in raising funds for military operations and also make the buying and selling of government securities easier. The Bank of Bengal was granted a charter by the East India Company in 1809 and this was renewed a number of times in the next 110 years. The company subscribed a fifth of the total capital of Rs. 5 million and appointed three members to the board. Until the Mutiny, the bank's secretary and treasurer was almost always a senior company official. A similar bank was established in Bombay in 1840 with a capital of Rs. 5.2 million of which Rs. 300,000 was contributed by government. This collapsed in 1868, following frenzied share speculation in Bombay, and a new Bank of Bombay was established with a capital of Rs. 10 million. The Bank of Madras was established in 1843 with a capital of Rs. 3 million of which Rs. 300,000 was contributed by government. The Bank of Bengal was the largest of the three banks and for much of the nineteenth century its assets were greater than those of the other two banks combined.

The charters issued to the Presidency Banks laid down precise conditions under which they were to operate. They were to enjoy a monopoly of government banking business and (until 1861) were allowed to issue banknotes up to certain limits, provided the required reserves were maintained. The banks were allowed to lend to both individuals and government (with specified security) but maximum amounts were laid down and, for most of the nineteenth century, the permitted periods of the loans were relatively short. The banks were not allowed to engage in trade and could not discount bills payable outside India (with the exception of the Bank of Madras which was allowed to operate in Ceylon). Overseas branches could not be established.

The position of the Presidency Banks was somewhat changed in 1862 when, in return for giving up their note issue to the government, they were allowed to invest the balances which they held from government and also took on the management of Treasury work. In practice the banks became agents for the note issue and in order to do this they established branches up-country. For example by 1900, the Bank of Bengal had 17 branches which stretched from Rangoon to Nagpur, Lucknow, Cawnpore and Lahore. The branches became of increasing importance in the twentieth century. Under the terms of the Presidency Banks Act of 1876, the governments no longer held all their balances with these banks. However if the balances fell below certain levels, interest was payable by the government to the banks to reimburse them for the work they were carrying out. In addition, government shareholdings in the banks were abolished and the various governments no longer appointed directors to the boards.

The idea of merging the Presidency Banks into a single national bank was suggested as early as 1866 but the idea was frowned upon and no action was taken. However in 1921 such a merger did come about when the Imperial Bank of India Act was passed. The Imperial Bank continued to function very much as the Presidency Banks had. It received government deposits; acted as banker to the central and provincial governments; and maintained part of the reserves of Indian commercial banks and of foreign banks in India. It granted loans and discounted internal bills of exchange. In 1934 the Government of India established a true central bank under the name of 'The Reserve Bank of India'. (Operations began in April 1935.) At this time the Imperial Bank lost its governmental banking functions except that it continued to act for the state in places where the Reserve Bank of India had no branches. The Imperial Bank was henceforth allowed to discount foreign bills, open overseas branches and operate in the foreign exchange market. In 1951 it had deposits of Rs. 2,309 million representing more than a fifth of all bank deposits in India. It also had 391 branches in the country.

The Presidency and Imperial Banks were subject to considerable criticism. It was claimed (by the commercial banks) that their privileged positions gave them unfair advantages while others have felt that they received many of the benefits of a central bank without having corresponding responsibilities. It has been argued that the banks preferred their own profits to national interests and exploited to the full the highly seasonal demand for money. In 1955 the Indian Parliament nationalised the Imperial Bank and re-named it 'The State Bank of India'.

An account of the Presidency Banks. By J.B. Brunyate. Calcutta: Office of the Superintendent of Government Printing, 1900. 117, xxviiip.

The evolution of the State Bank of India. By Amiya Kumar Bagchi.

Vol. 1: *The roots 1806-1876.*

Part I: *The early years, 1806-1860.* Bombay: Oxford University Press [for the Bank], 1987. xxi, 535p., ill. Index.

Part II: *Diversity and regrouping, 1860-1876.* Bombay: Oxford University Press [for the Bank], 1987. xii, 515p., ill. Bibliog. (covering both Parts). Index (covering both Parts).

Vol. 2: *The era of the Presidency Banks 1876-1920.* New Delhi: Sage Publications [for the Bank], 1997. 664p., ill. Bibliog. Index.

[Professor Bagchi is currently writing a third volume of his history to cover the years 1920-55.]

The history of the Bank of Bengal an epitome of a hundred years of banking in India. By G.P. Symes Scutt. Calcutta: Printed at the Bank of Bengal Press, 1904. iii,166,viip. Index.

[Title page has the heading: 'Private. For Directors and Staff only.']

The Presidency Banks and the Indian economy 1876-1914. By Amiya Kumar

Bagchi. Calcutta: Oxford University Press [for the State Bank of India], 1989. xv, 294p. Bibliog. Index.

520. RALLI BROTHERS

The Rallis were already a well-established and successful Greek trading family when two of the sons, John and Eustratio, set-up in business in London during 1818. A branch was established in Manchester in 1827 to handle the trade in cotton piece-goods and during the following ten years, with the help of other brothers, branches were set-up in Constantinople, Marseilles and Odessa. In 1865 the original partnership was wound up and a new one, based on London, was established by John and Stephen Ralli (son and nephew respectively of Eustratio Ralli). The family was careful to employ Greeks in all the most senior positions and many of the records and accounts were in Greek. Nonetheless the family did take on British characteristics and their firm was a British company. Ralli Brothers therefore fall within the scope of this bibliography.

The partners established a branch in Calcutta as early as 1851 and a further branch in Bombay in 1861. Soon the Rallis were operating in Karachi and Pondicherry and had set-up one of the largest trading networks in India with agencies throughout the country. Indeed India was to be the key area of operations for the Rallis. Until the first world war, they were merchants pure and simple. With the exception of some cotton-ginning and jute-pressing, they distrusted industries and they eschewed all speculation. In Calcutta they imported cotton piece-goods and exported silk, hides, rice, indigo, shellac and jute. In Bombay they exported cotton, sesame seed and grain. In Pondicherry the exports were groundnuts while in Karachi they were grain, cotton, hides and bones. The Rallis had two central operating principles. Firstly they only added small profit margins to the cost of their commodities but they worked with high turnovers. Secondly they stood for absolute integrity and honesty.

From the 1930s Ralli Brothers diversified both by activity and by area. The firm moved into shipping, insurance, cotton mills, agriculture and oilseed crushing. It set-up offices or businesses in East and South Africa, Sudan, Turkey, Hong Kong and West Germany. After the partition of India the Ralli businesses were split between India and Pakistan. In 1951 nearly two-thirds of Rallis' merchandising activities were still connected with South Asia and in India merchandising turnover was of the order of £31.5 million. Cotton was the main article in the firm's trade (accounting for 25 per cent of the turnover) while jute was second (with 20 per cent of the turnover).

In 1959 Ralli Brothers was acquired by Sir Isaac Wolfson's General Guarantee Corporation. Two years later the raw cotton department was moved from London to Liverpool and many trading departments in London were closed down. However trading did continue in jute, jute goods, sisal and coffee. All trading was moved to Liverpool in 1966.

In 1969 Sir Isaac Wolfson's interest in Ralli Brothers was sold to Slater Walker Securities: Mr Jim Slater merged Rallis with Oriental Carpet Manufacturers to form Ralli International. The new concern carried on the Ralli trading operations and took over a number of other international merchant houses. By 1972 Ralli International's profits were up 61 per cent on the previous year and at the end of the year it was sold to the Bowater Corporation to form their International Trading Division.

History and activities of the Ralli Trading Group: commodity merchants for 160 years. London: The International Trading Division of the Bowater Organisation, 1979. [87]p., ill.

Ralli Brothers Limited. [By J.H. Vlasto.] London: The Company, 1951. 56p., ill. [Guildhall Library]

521. SASSOON FAMILY BUSINESSES

The Sassoons were Turkish Jews and the father of David Sassoon (1792-1864) had served as Treasurer to the Pasha of Baghdad. In 1858 David Sassoon sent his third son, Sassoon Sassoon, to London to help look after the family business there and in the following decades six of his eight sons moved to Britain, living and dying in the country. The Sassoon family in subsequent generations became very prominent in British life. On these grounds the Sassoon businesses are treated as falling within the scope of this bibliography.

David Sassoon and Company

David Sassoon was already a prominent merchant in Baghdad when he visited Bombay in 1832. He was much taken by the city and the following year he returned to Bombay for good. The business he set-up carried on the trading activities he had been used to in the Middle East. He sold English textiles for Persian products and oriental weaves. These latter were re-exported to the U.K. by other South Asian merchants. Soon Sassoon's firm became the largest in India to be engaged in the Gulf trade.

Gradually, however, Sassoon became more interested in the possibilities for selling Bombay yarn, Lancashire piece-goods and opium in China. From 1844 each of his sons worked for a time in East Asia. Branches of the firm were set-up in Canton, Hong Kong and Shanghai with agencies in Yokohama and Nagasaki. It was this China trade which raised the house of Sassoon to the very first rank in British India.

With the onset of the American Civil War the firm was at the forefront of the profitable trade of supplying Lancashire with Indian cotton yarn. At this point the business became more directed to the U.K. When David died in 1864 his oldest son, Albert-Abdullah, took the firm into cotton-manufacturing and weaving in Bombay. He constructed the Sassoon Dock in Bombay between 1872 and 1875 – the first wet-dock on the western coast of India. In Calcutta he established the Port Canning and Land Improvement Company which employed some 15,000 people in land development schemes.

By 1900 the firm controlled the Sassoon Spinning and Weaving Company as well as the Sassoon and Alliance Silk Manufacturing Company. It had considerable interests in the Oriental Life Assurance Company and the Prince of Wales Fire Insurance Company. The company did not engage in merchant banking until after the second world war but it did play a part with others in the establishment of the Imperial Bank of Persia **(404)** in 1889. David Sassoons became a limited company in 1901 and successive generations of Sassoons in the twentieth century performed something of a holding operation with the business. There were heavy losses in India and the Chinese investment side was highly volatile after the collapse of the Manchu dynasty in 1911. In the 1930s investments in the Bombay cotton mills were much restricted. The company lost its businesses in China following the communist takeover. David Sassoon and Company thereafter diversified into general world trade; agency work; and the financing of various projects in the U.K.

E.D. Sassoon and Company

The firm was set-up in 1867 by Elias Sassoon a little more than two years after his father's death. It seems likely to have been the result of a disagreement between the brothers because the two firms became bitter rivals and Elias established a competing network of branches in China. His son Jacob, the ablest Sassoon of his generation, extended operations to Japan, the Persian Gulf and Arabia. He also set-up branches in Calcutta, Karachi, Rangoon and London. The firm played a greater part in the expansion of the Indian cotton industry than even the parent company. In 1880 it purchased the Alexandra Mill and soon after it built a series of new mills beginning with the E.D. Sassoon Mill. It also started a dye works. In its heyday E.D. Sassoon directly controlled mills which employed more than 15,000 workers. The company became much involved in banking and Jacob was behind the formation of the Eastern Bank which was registered in London in 1909. During 1920 E.D. Sassoon became a rupee limited company.

From about this point the firm decided it would reduce its Indian commitments and expand into banking. In 1930 a new firm called the E.D. Sassoon Banking Company, registered in Hong Kong, took over the banking interests of E.D. Sassoon. Also at this time the ordinary trading interests of E.D. Sassoon were transferred to Arnhold and Company, an old established house which the Sassoon firm had acquired. E.D. Sassoon divested itself of its produce business in China in 1935. All that remained were the mercantile and manufacturing interests in India. Many of these were also removed to China. E.D. Sassoon's United Cotton Mills fared badly in Bombay in the first half of the1930s and made considerable losses. They suffered from labour unrest, the depression, and the boycott of British goods. By 1937 the mills had become profitable again partly because of the imposition of a protective tariff on imported cotton goods. Sir Victor Sassoon (now head of the concern) started to re-equip the mills as he foresaw the coming of the second world war. By 1943 Sir Victor owned a quarter of the textile plants in the Bombay Presidency and was producing over seven per cent of all India's cotton goods. At this point he decided to leave India and his plants were sold over the following few years. In 1948 E.D. Sassoon and Company was placed in voluntary liquidation in India. The banking business was moved from Hong Kong to Nassau in 1952.

The Sassoon dynasty. By Cecil Roth. London: Robert Hale, 1941. 280p., ill. Index.

The Sassoons. By Stanley Jackson. London: Heinemann, 1968. xv, 304p., ill. Bibliog. Index.

522. SHAW WALLACE AND COMPANY

David Shaw was a partner in a number of Indian agency houses from 1868 onwards but the firm he was running in the early 1880s got into difficulties with a flotation on the London market and had to be wound up. In January 1886, having paid off his debts, Shaw went into partnership with Charles Wallace and thereby founded the famous Calcutta agency house. (Wallace had earlier worked for Shaw at the London end of his business.) The new business had three departments: piece-goods; tea-buying; and silk. Progress was slow at first and was not helped by senior assistants in all three departments engaging in fraudulent activities. Nonetheless during the 1890s the firm took off. The tea side of the Shaw Wallace partnership was particularly important and was always to remain so. Companies in Northeast India were formed or acquired. These included the Assam Frontier Tea Company; the Silloah Tea Company; and the Buxa Doaors Tea Company. Later on Shaw Wallace was to become involved with tea in Sri Lanka but it never owned tea estates in Southern India.

In the 1890s Shaw Wallace went into cotton-manufacturing by purchasing from government the Bengal Nagpur Cotton Mills. The firm also expanded by absorbing four related businesses. The most important of these was Mitchell Reid and Company (acquired in 1891). This was because, amongst other things, Mitchell Reid were agents in India for the Burmah Oil Company **(606)**. At first the oil business did not appear significant. However kerosene became widely used in India for cooking and heating and in addition from 1900 ownership of motor vehicles increased. To look after its oil interests, Shaw Wallace opened branches and oil installations in Aden, Bombay, Cochin, Coconada, Karachi, Marmagoa and Tuticorin. A branch was also acquired in Madras from Binnys **(505)**. Once it had opened branches, Shaw Wallace then used them to engage in whatever other activities appeared attractive locally. For example in Madras, Shaw Wallace sold hides and was to become an important supplier of sulphate of ammonia in the inter-war years. In Cochin the firm went into coir yarn and coir products.

In December 1927 Burmah Oil ended its agency with Shaw Wallace and began direct distribution in conjunction with Shell **(721)**. The loss of the oil business was a severe blow to Shaw Wallace as it also transferred the forty senior assistants involved in oil operations. To make matters worse the severe slump of the early 1930s soon followed and the Karachi branch had to be closed. Shaw Wallace reacted to these events by building-up other areas of its business. It had substantial coal interests in Bengal, Bihar, Rewa and the Central Provinces. These were developed to make Shaw Wallace the fourth largest coal producer in India. In addition the firm was active in flour-milling, insurance, produce, tinplates, shipping, jute fabrics and fertilisers. In 1930 it acquired the Ceylon business of British Fertilisers Limited.

During the second world war Shaw Wallace probably did more war work than any other firm in India. Its tea companies were involved in the construction of the Burma Road and the firm also transported cloth from Bombay to Assam. In Calcutta, Shaw Wallace was busy procuring rice for governments in eastern and southern India and a senior member of the firm helped organise supplies for the Middle East and Russia. From the end of 1941, the firm acted as owner's agent for the China Navigation Company fleet of Swires **(309)**.

Shaw Wallace took on limited liability in 1946 and, in due course, separate companies were established in India and Pakistan. Unlike many agency firms, Shaw Wallace was very successful after Indian independence and some of its biggest profits were made in the early 1970s. The company acquired substantial holdings in all concerns where it had acted as agents. In addition, new or joint ventures were entered into in the fields of: superphosphates; distilling; yeasts; and spraying equipment. From the 1960s the Malaysian firm of Sime Darby **(614)** became very involved in the London end of the Shaw Wallace business and early in 1972 took it over. Between 1978 and 1987 the Indian business was handed over to its Indian management and was for all intents and purposes an Indian company. In 1987, after a bitter battle, Shaw Wallace was taken over by the Chhabrias – an important Indian business family.

A history of Shaw Wallace & Co. and Shaw Wallace & Co. Ltd. Compiled by Sir Harry Townend. Calcutta: Designed and produced by S.H. Benson (India) Ltd. for the Company, 1965. viii, 256p., ill. Index.

523. J. THOMAS AND COMPANY

In 1851 a Welshman, Robert Thomas, set-up business as a general produce-broker in Mission Row, Calcutta with Charles Marten. The partnership lasted until 1854 after which Thomas continued trading on his own. The commodities involved included sugar, saltpetre, silk and shellac. Very early on the company acquired a leading place amongst Calcutta's indigo-brokers. Indeed indigo became the mainstay of the business and it is probable that Thomas's was one of only two official brokers to the Bihar and Bengal planters. The firm went bankrupt following the collapse of its bankers, Agra and Masterman's Bank, in 1866. (Itself a consequence of the Overend Gurney collapse in London.) However Thomas's had discharged its debts within a year and were back in business.

By that time the firm had taken the name of 'J. Thomas and Company' by which it was to be known. The founder had died in 1865 and his relative, John Phillips Thomas, had taken control. 'Jack' Thomas was a consolidator anxious to diversify the firm and (under the influence of his cousin) took it into tea-broking, real estate and banking. (Thomas's had already organised the first public tea auction in India in 1861.) The diversification was wise as trade in indigo declined with the development of synthetic dyes at the end of the nineteenth century. Early in the twentieth century the firm moved into the jute trade in a serious way following the immense increase in the cultivation of the crop in Bengal. In 1902 Thomas's took over the business of G.W. Hope and Company, gunny-brokers, and a year later it re-opened its raw jute department which had been closed down in 1876. It was to acquire H.K. Banks and Company, an up-country jute-purchasing agency, which traded with moderate success in the late 1920s and early 1930s until it became a victim of the great depression.

The first world war brought the firm considerable profits as hessian sandbags were needed in the trenches but after the war the firm was faced with the growth of Marwari dealer-brokers or jobbers in jute who acted on their own account in the markets (something which was forbidden to J. Thomas.) This was a very serious blow for the firm's gunny department. After partition in 1947 trade in jute dried up as many growers were now in East Pakistan. By the 1960s the firm retained a strong presence in tea but had moved from gunny, jute and shellac into bulk transportation shipping. In 1973 it formed the Nilhat Shipping Company.

A hundred and twenty-five years: the story of J. Thomas & Co. [?Calcutta:] The Company, [?1976]. 48p., ill.

524. TINPLATE COMPANY OF INDIA

Tinplate was heavily used in India, particularly for petroleum cans, and there were great shortages during the first world war because of insufficient shipping to bring out Welsh tinplate. Burmah Oil **(606)** therefore took up the suggestion of local manufacture which their agents, Shaw Wallace **(522)**, had made to them. As tinplate is 98 per cent steel, Burmah Oil formed the Tinplate Company of India immediately after the war in collaboration with the Tata Iron and Steel Company. The new concern was one-third owned by Tatas and two-thirds owned by Burmah Oil.

Wisely it was decided to adopt American, rather than Welsh, manufacturing technology. The American process took account of high summer operating temperatures and did not need the same number of skilled workers. It was, however, more costly. Consequently Burmah Oil had to write off about six million rupees and also loan the Tinplate Company additional funds in the form of debentures. Six rolling mills were erected at Golmuri at the edge of Tatas' iron and steel town of Jamshedpur. A small township was also built to house the workers. By the second world war the Tinplate Company was paying dividends of 25 per cent each year although it should be said that the capitalisation was artificially low.

The first tinplate was made at the end of 1922 and the company soon came to supply a large proportion of Indian tinplate requirements. In 1927 the plant produced 41,521 tons of plate annually; by 1943 this had reached 62,378 tons; and in 1963 the figure was 82,778 tons. The equipment used remained basically unaltered throughout the first forty years of operation but in the mid-1960s it was decided to replace it with new continuous mills which were able to take the manufacturing process all the way through from hot-rolled coils to the finished product.

The early years: the Tinplate Company of India Ltd., Jamshedpur. By Sir Harry Townend. Calcutta: Shaw Wallace & Co., [?1962]. 29p.
[Centre of South Asian Studies, University of Cambridge.]

'Tinplates.' Being pp. 87-101 of ***A history of Shaw Wallace & Co. and Shaw Wallace & Co. Ltd.*** Compiled by Sir Harry Townend. Calcutta: Designed and produced by S.H. Benson (India) Ltd. for the Company, 1965.

525. WALLACE BROTHERS

The firm was started in London at the end of 1862 when Lewis Alexander and George Wallace broke with their business partners and set-up on their own. The two men were already middle-aged at this time and came from a family of six brothers all of whom were to become involved in some way with the new firm. Furthermore, all six had already had experience of India. For Wallace Brothers were to be the London correspondents of the Bombay firm of Wallace and Company which had existed under this name since 1848 but had a history going back to 1828. Each brother had been sent over to work for the Bombay firm.

In theory the division of functions was along the lines that while the London firm was responsible for providing finance and chartering shipping, the Bombay concern was the centre of actual commercial activity in such areas as wheat, indigo, pepper, spices, diamonds, wool, cotton, as well as teak through the new Bombay Burmah Trading Corporation **(602)**. In practice most of the policy decisions were actually taken in London especially after the arrangement was instituted that one of the senior managers of the Bombay concerns was to be stationed with Wallace

Brothers in London. This was particularly the case from 1886 when Wallace and Company was divided. The old firm was thereafter responsible for the agency of the Bombay Burmah Trading Corporation while a new concern, the Bombay Company, took over responsibility for general trading and other developments.

With the passage of time the Wallaces' interests expanded considerably. In 1885 they set-up the Arracan Company to engage in the Burma rice trade. In the 1890s they became involved in Indonesia starting-up (in 1902) the Tannadine Company to provide tanning materials from woods in Sumatra. The concern invested in rubber estates by promoting through Wallace and Company an 'East India Rubber Corporation'. In the early 1900s Wallaces turned to industry becoming managing agents for the Lakhshmi Cotton Manufacturing Company at Sholapur. In 1910 the Wallaces started a second mill in the town called the Vishnu Cotton Mill and in 1913 they acquired Dymes and Company of Madras which brought them cotton mills in South India and factories for processing oil seeds. On the failure of Arbuthnot and Company in 1906, Wallaces took over many of its assets. In 1912 the firm entered tea-planting in the Nilgiris although it assigned this activity to the Bombay Burmah Corporation.

The first world war brought particular difficulties for Wallaces but some activities, such as the cotton mills, were spectacularly successful. In fact 1918-19 marks the apex in the fortunes of the Bombay Company. In 1919 the company purchased Ripley and Mackay, a cotton and country-produce merchant. Wallaces suffered considerably during the depression of the 1930s, in part because they made unwise investments in securities. Things were particularly bad in the Bombay Company. The Sholapur mills suffered from Japanese competition, labour unrest and political agitation. In the years 1929-39, Wallace Brothers received only two small dividends from the Bombay Company.

There was some revival of fortunes during the second world war. Substantial profits were made by the cotton mills and the tea estates produced record crops. Obviously all was lost in Burma, Java and Thailand. The attainment of independence by the Asian states after the second world war forced Wallaces into a major re-alignment of interests. In 1959 the East India Rubber Corporation went into voluntary liquidation. In 1958 the Bombay Company relinquished its cotton interests and by 1969 it had effectively ceased trading. It too was soon to be wound up. Wallace Brothers then went into commodity-trading throughout the world, into banking and into shipping. The group was taken over by Standard Chartered Merchant Bank **(102)** in 1978.

Wallace Brothers. By A.C. Pointon. Oxford: Printed at the University Press, 1974. x, 120p., ill. Index.

526. WILLIAMSON MAGOR AND COMPANY

The firm was established in Calcutta in April 1869 by Captain J.H. Williamson and R.B. Magor. Williamson was the younger brother of the pioneer tea planter, George Williamson, junior (*see* Assam Company **(502)**), while Magor was an assistant in the Great Eastern Hotel, Calcutta. The firm acquired agencies for managing the tea estates of many publicly-quoted tea companies and also for selling their teas. Williamson retired from Calcutta in 1875 while Magor continued as managing partner in India until 1884. In 1885 the firm merged with its London agents, George Williamson and Company. Under the merger agreement, control was vested in the partners present in the United Kingdom who constituted a committee of management. By 1895 the firm was handling the affairs of 44 tea estates comprising a total area of 35,000 acres and producing 14 million pounds of tea annually. The firm also had interests in rubber and from 1905 it took on agencies in coal although these were not entirely successful.

During the twentieth century the partnership expanded and the Magor family came to predominate. The Calcutta operations were very successful during the first world war and the partners in London showed great caution in the expansionist phase of the 1920s. Nonetheless the firm was very badly hit by the great depression of the 1930s. A number of its gardens were located in particularly unprofitable areas. The firm and some of the associated tea companies appear to have come perilously close to bankruptcy. Two partners played a crucial role at this time. Stephen Anderson, senior partner, kept the organisation together. E.J. Nichols, its experienced visiting-agent, instituted a 'cool earth' method of cultivation. His rigid disciplines saved Williamson Magor.

The firm suffered considerably during the second world war. There was insufficient management in the gardens and the quality of the teas fell. With the coming of independence in 1947 the morale of the planters was adversely affected and there were difficulties with communications. The company faced up to the implications of independence at a remarkably early date. Briju Khaitan, a member of a wealthy Indian family, was taken onto the board in 1961 and played a major role in the affairs of Williamson Magor over the following thirty years. From 1946 the business diversified into tea cultivation in East Africa. In 1954 Williamson Magor became a company incorporated in India while in 1964 Williamson Tea Holdings was incorporated in London. This latter business owned seven Indian tea companies in 1964 as well as a number in Africa. During the 1970s the George Williamson partnership in London was incorporated as a company and in 1975 Williamson Magor merged with Macneill and Barry (*see under* Inchcape and Company **(108)**) to form Macneill and Magor. The merger did not work and in 1982 Williamson Tea Holdings bought out the Inchcape interests. In 1987 the Williamson Group purchased the tea interests of Guthries **(607)**. This turned it into one of the largest private tea-producers in the world.

Williamson Magor stuck to tea. By Peter Pugh. [Cambridge.] Cambridge Business Publishing, 1991. vii, 213p., ill. Index.

527. ANDREW YULE AND COMPANY

Andrew Yule, whose father was a Scottish linen and woollen draper, arrived in Calcutta in 1863 and set-up his business. However the person who was to dominate the firm's early years was Andrew's brother, George. He went out to India in 1875 and stayed until 1891. Then the Yules' nephew, David (who had also arrived in 1875 aged only 17), took over the running of the business and eventually bought his two uncles out. Until he left India in 1917, Sir David Yule was the driving force in the development of the firm which became one of the biggest British businesses in India.

Sir David had no sons and in 1916 he suggested to Morgan Grenfell that their London and New York houses should buy the company. Morgans persuaded Thomas Catto (later Lord Catto) to take charge in Calcutta which he did in 1919. Eventually (in September 1922) the ownership of the business was settled with Catto holding 25 per cent of the equity, J.P. Morgan in New York holding 37.5 per cent and various people connected with Morgan Grenfell in London holding the remaining 37.5 per cent. Catto remained as managing director in India until 1928 and then returned to London from where, as senior partner, he oversaw the running of the business until 1940.

Andrew Yule had the most diverse range of interests of all the Calcutta business houses. Originally it took on agencies in cloth and insurance but it came to act as managing agents in a wide range of Eastern Indian industries such as jute, cotton, sugar, paper-making and chemicals. Andrew Yule was one of the largest tea concerns in India and controlled ship-repair yards and lighterage operations. It ran a river steamer line between Assam and Calcutta. Through its managing agency of the Bengal Coal

Company, Andrew Yule became the leading coal-mining firm in British India. Lord Catto was responsible for adding to the firm's portfolio the control of investment companies and also the *Statesman* newspaper – Calcutta's most important English-language daily.

Andrew Yule found the early independence years relatively congenial. The coal-mining operations were encouraged by the new Government of India and the coal was shipped all over the world. Tea continued to be produced in 26 tea gardens and paper-making also took place although the Assam papermill (Assam Pulp) was not successful. (This was a joint venture with Balmer Lawrie **(504)**). Jute too was giving many headaches. After 1960 this relatively happy picture changed. Andrew Yule was to lose control of its coal and insurance businesses. Although paper-making remained with the firm it did not perform well. Tea was one of the few good businesses left. Early in the 1970s the Government of India bought up the 24 per cent of Andrew Yule's equity owned by the London arm of the business (Yule Catto). In 1979 the Government of India took over the company completely.

Andrew Yule and Co. Ltd., 1863-1963. Edinburgh: Printed for private circulation by T. and A. Constable, 1963. 34p., ill.

'Die Entwicklung der Managing Agency Andrew Yule & Co.' being Chapter 7 (pp. 195-220) of ***Britische Managing Agencies in Indischen Kohlenbergbau.*** By Henner Papendieck. New York: Arno Press, 1981. [Reprint of doctoral thesis – Freie Universität Berlin.]

Thomas Sivewright Catto, Baron Catto of Cairncatto, 1879-1959: a personal memoir and a biographical note [by H.C.B. Mynors]. Edinburgh: Privately printed by T. and A. Constable, 1962. 119p., ill.

CHAPTER 6

Histories relating to South-East Asia

601. BIBBY LINE

The Bibby Line was under the control of the Bibby family for five generations. It was established in Liverpool in 1807 by John Bibby and John Highfield. Bibby was a farmer's son from a village near Ormskirk and had gone to Liverpool to work for an iron merchant. Bibbys' earliest ships tramped round the U.K. coast and operated a service between Parkgate and Dublin. Within a short while longer sailings were arranged to South America and the Mediterranean ports (where they captured a sizeable part of the trade with Liverpool). After the ending of the East India Company's monopoly of trading in 1813, Bibby vessels began sailing to the East Indies on a regular schedule. By 1839 the fleet consisted of 12 ships. In 1865 it had grown to 23 vessels amounting to more than 31,000 tons.

The senior partner in 1873, James J. Bibby, was not yet prepared to entrust the running of the line to his two nephews so its 18 steamers came under the control of another partner, Frederick Leyland. They formed the nucleus of what was to become the Leyland Line. However in 1889 James provided capital for the nephews to establish a new Bibby fleet (under a firm called Bibby Brothers and Company). The steamers were to be named after the English shires and were to trade between Liverpool and Rangoon (to which Colombo was later added). Here they came into competition with the ships of P. Henderson and Company **(609)**.

Most Bibby ships were requisitioned in the first world war and from July 1916 only the *Warwickshire* carried on the service to Burma. She was joined in 1917 by a new ship, the *Lancashire*. (Both ships survived the war.) In 1930 the line obtained the government contract to run the Indian relief trooping service. At the outbreak of the second world war the Bibby Line had in commission four transports, five motor vessels and two steamers. All were requisitioned and participated actively in the war. There were two losses which were replaced. By 1954 the line employed five ships in the Burma trade. In 1969 it discontinued its services to Rangoon.

(*See under* P. Henderson and Company *for related material on the history of shipping services to Burma.*)

Bibby Line 1807 to 1957. Liverpool: The Line, 1957. 64p., ill.

The Bibby Line 1807-1990: a story of wars, booms and slumps. By Nigel Watson. London: James and James, 1990. 73p., ill. Index.
[National Maritime Museum Library.]

The Burma boats: Henderson and Bibby. By Duncan Haws. [Uckfield: The Author] 1995. (Merchant fleets; No. 29.) 203p., ill.
[Cambridge University Library.]

From sail to oil: the progress of the Bibby Line. Liverpool: Ports and Cities Publishing Co., 1927. xlii, 33p., ill.
[Mainly deals with the development of shipping. Only pp. 29-34 relate to the Bibby Line.]

The history of the Bibby Line. By E.W. Paget-Tomlinson. Liverpool: The Line, 1970. 78p., ill.
[Bodleian Library, Oxford.]

602. BOMBAY BURMAH TRADING CORPORATION

By the 1850s the Bombay trading firm of Wallace and Company (*see under* Wallace Brothers **(525)**) had expanded their business to include the import of Burmese teak. In the first half of the decade they advanced sums to a firm in Moulmein to supply teak and evidently, as time passed, Wallaces became concerned as to how the transaction was progressing. So at some point between 1850 and 1857 the Bombay house sent one of the family, William Wallace, to investigate the position. Once in Burma, William realised there was scope for the expansion of the teak business. He obtained permits from the British authorities in Lower Burma to work timber from forests on the Attaran River and he erected a sawmill near Moulmein. In 1862 he accompanied the Chief Commissioner, Sir Arthur Phayre, to Mandalay in Upper Burma where he obtained a concession from King Mindon to extract teak in the Ningyan area. These activities were involving Wallace and Company in heavy expenditure and to meet future capital needs a public company was set-up in Bombay in September 1863 which eventually took the name of the Bombay Burmah Trading Corporation.

The first twenty years of the corporation's existence were fairly uneventful. Until 1881 it employed another firm, Darwood and Goldenberg, to extract the timber. In 1880 two senior officers, after a year's residence in Mandalay and in the face of severe competition, secured leases in forests over a substantial part of Upper Burma. It was a landmark in the corporation's history but in 1885 the Burmese authorities accused the corporation of bribery and of taking timber without paying revenue. The Burmese threatened fines and cancellation of the leases. Unwisely they declined an offer of arbitration and, as a result, the British annexed Upper Burma in 1886 following the Third Burmese War. The corporation's difficulties were a convenient excuse for excluding the French from Burma but thereafter the firm was very much associated with British imperialism at its zenith.

Although business was fully resumed in Burma by the end of the 1880s, the corporation decided to extend its interests to Thailand. Already in 1884 two senior managers had looked into the possibilities in a journey which had taken them from Moulmein to Chiengmai. By the mid-1890s the corporation had secured leases which gave it a firm foothold in Thailand and in due course it was to become the principal company in that country's timber business. Until about 1909 leases in both Burma and Thailand were short-term for only a few years at a time but between 1907 and 1910 the two countries awarded the corporation fifteen year leases which they renewed for a similar period in the 1920s. This gave considerable stability to the corporation's work.

In the years before the first world war the corporation diversified its activities. There were unsuccessful attempts at oil-drilling in Sumatra and Sabah. An attempt at teak-logging in Java did not last long. The corporation purchased rubber estates which were held in the name of the Indo-Java Rubber Planting and Trading Company. This concern itself was to become a fully-owned subsidiary of the East India Rubber Corporation in which the Bombay Burmah Corporation held a majority interest. In 1913 the corporation started-up tea estates in the Anamallai Hills near Cochin in South India. Nearby estates were purchased in 1919 and in 1928 new estates were established in Tinevelly District. In 1939 the corporation established a tea factory at Namhsan in the Shan States of Burma.

The corporation was badly affected by the great depression – in 1933-4 its profits were only about a tenth of those of 1928-9. After the onset of the Japanese War, it was only the corporation's tea operations in India which brought it any income. The coming of independence in South-East Asia in the years following the war led to major changes in the corporation's activities. It ended its timber operations in Burma in 1949 and virtually all its interests in the country had been wound-up by 1963. The leases in Thailand were not renewed when they expired in 1955. Instead the corporation moved into Sabah. In 1949 it formed, with the North Borneo

Trading Company, a new concern called North Borneo Timbers. This was highly successful and within a few years the corporation, together with Wallace Brothers, had bought out the Trading Company's interests in North Borneo Timbers.

The Bombay Burmah Trading Corporation Limited 1863-1963. By A.C. Pointon. Southampton: Millbrook Press for Wallace Brothers & Co. (Holdings) Ltd., 1964. viii, 143p., ill. Index.

History of the Bombay Burmah Trading Corporation, Ltd. 1864-1910. By R.H. Macaulay. London: Privately printed by Spottiswoode, Ballantyne & Co., 1934. viii, 161p.

603. BORNEO COMPANY

The Borneo Company (BCL) was registered in London in June 1856. The exact background to the flotation is not clear but three Glasgow firms seem to have played an important part. They were W.R. Paterson and Company, R. & J. Henderson and MacEwen and Company. MacEwens' trading interests centred on Singapore and its manager in the port, John Harvey, was to become BCL's first managing director in the East. Everyone behind the new venture was impressed with the economic potential of Sarawak under the rule of the first Rajah Brooke. Almost immediately after its formation, the Rajah gave BCL extensive rights to develop Sarawak's natural resources in return for a royalty.

Throughout its history the Borneo Company proved very adept in taking up any opportunities which might prove profitable. Although its administrative headquarters were at Singapore, the company soon extended its operations over a wide area of Asia including, besides Sarawak, Batavia, Calcutta, Hong Kong and Thailand. In Hong Kong it imported rice, cinnabar and quicksilver and exported silks. The branch lasted until 1890. In Calcutta the company set-up the Barnagore Jute Factory and bought a sugar refinery in 1857 which was later converted to paper-milling. BCL had ended all direct connection with these Indian concerns by 1935.

The main centres of BCL's operation before the first world war were, however, Sarawak and Thailand. In Sarawak the company began by looking for antimony, cinnabar, quicksilver and coal and then moved on to gold-prospecting – an activity which was to dominate its operations in the country between 1897 and 1923. By the twentieth century the company was also starting to plant pepper and rubber estates. It made three attempts to extract timber – in the 1860s, in 1904 and in the late 1930s – but only the last was at all successful.

BCL entered Thailand in 1856 and opened up the export trade in rice and started to represent British banking and insurance companies. It also ran a coastal shipping service from Bangkok. However trade in teak soon came to predominate. By the 1880s the company had acquired concessions in the north of the country and had become Thailand's largest teak firm although it was to be overtaken by the Bombay-Burmah Trading Corporation **(602)** at the turn of the century. In the 1920s, with a decline apparent in teak sales, the company diversified.

This diversification took a number of forms. In Malaya BCL established branches in Ipoh, Kuala Lumpur, Melaka and Penang in the late 1920s. This move followed the promotion of a number of tin and rubber ventures in the Federated Malay States. In Singapore BCL had taken up brick making as early as 1899 and in 1928 it established the Alexandra Brickworks Company there Also in the 1920s, BCL began tea-growing in Sumatra through its Haboko Tea Company. BCL was involved in the motor trade from its earliest days and in 1925 it floated off Borneo Motors Limited which held franchises in South-East Asia from the leading manufacturers. The early 1920s were in many respects the company's most prosperous years; it suffered considerably in the 1930s from the depression in primary products.

By 1942 all the company's property abroad was in Japanese hands. It recovered quickly after the war although some activities, such as tea-growing, were to prove no longer viable. Nonetheless, particularly in the motor trade, it made considerable profits in the late 1940s and early 1950s. At this point, with over 150 agencies, BCL was Malaya's largest importer and it was also one of Malaya's leading manufacturers. However the company then had to face up to problems caused by wide fluctuations in commodity prices, loss of market share in the motor business, the emergency in Malaya and the moves towards independence. It decided to lessen its dependence on tin and rubber and on the entrepôt trade with Indonesia and Thailand. It went into specialist trading and manufacturing, for example taking a controlling interest in Duncan, Roberts and Company, office equipment suppliers. It acquired United States and West German agencies. BCL also redeployed a substantial part of its assets in Canada. In the 1960s various timber interests were acquired in Australia. In 1967 the Borneo Company became a wholly owned Inchcape subsidiary. (*See also entries under* Inchcape and Company Limited **(108)**.)

The Borneo story: the history of the first 100 years of trading in the Far East by the Borneo Company Limited. By Henry Longhurst. London: Newman Neame for the Company, 1956. 120p., ill.

'Business strategy and the end of empire: managing the Borneo Co. Ltd. in Malaya, 1945-1957' being chapter 6 (pp. 223-61) of ***Business, government and the end of empire: Malaya, 1942-1957.*** By Nicholas J. White. Kuala Lumpur: Oxford University Press, 1996.

Sixty years trade in Bangkok, 1856-1926: The Borneo Company Limited. Bangkok: The Company, 1926. 9p, ill.
[Guildhall Library.]

604. BOUSTEAD AND COMPANY

Edward Boustead began his trading activities in South-East Asia on his arrival in Singapore in 1828. He was probably of English ancestry from Liverpool. In 1834 Boustead was joined by Gustav Schwabe. By 1843 the firm was operating in China, Liverpool, the Philippines and Singapore. In time it was to open in Malaya and became particularly identified with the development of eastern Malaya where it was the first large merchant house. In 1851 Boustead returned to England and remained in charge of the London office until his death in 1888 at the age of 88.

Bousteads engaged in a wide range of activities. They acted as general export and import merchants and also as agents for various estates and mines. At one time the company itself refined tin in Penang and the special 'Boustead Brand' had a considerable reputation. The firm operated as coal contractors and was appointed Lloyds' agent in Singapore and the east coast ports of Malaya. By the end of the nineteenth century Bousteads had become agents for some ten shipping lines including the Glen Line **(105)** and the British India Steam Navigation Company **(101)**. The firm was to acquire considerable planting interests in sugar, tapioca, coconuts, rubber and palm oil. It was involved with Marcus Samuel in the bulk oil trade and in 1892 handled the first shipment to Penang. After Samuel set-up the Shell Transport and Trading Company **(721)** in 1897, Bousteads continued to operate an agency in Penang until (in 1920) Shell's local subsidiary opened its own branch on the island. Bousteads became associated with the Tanjong Pagar Dock Company **(619)** and Singapore Cold Storage. It acted as local agent for the Chartered Bank **(102)** up to 1859 and for HSBC **(106)** between 1871 and 1876.

Bousteads was formed into a limited company in 1918 and during the next forty years it greatly expanded its merchandising interests acting as agents for British, American and European manufacturing companies. Further diversification resulted in the firm becoming leading travel agents in Malaysia. During the 1950s Bousteads joined with other partners to start-up a major iron-ore enterprise in Kelantan. In 1960 the London office was turned into an independent operation, trading under the name of 'Edward Boustead and Company'. It was to move into merchandising operations in Australasia. As a result of this de-merger Boustead and Company comprised only the firm's Malaysian interests. It was registered as a Malaysian public company in 1960 with Malaysian shareholders and a proportion of Malaysian directors on its board.

Bousteads. London: Edward Boustead & Co., [?1963]. 40p., ill.
[British Library of Political and Economic Science.]

'The second oldest Malayan firm: the story of Boustead and Company, Ltd.' By H.R. Cheeseman. ***Malaya*** (London), Vol. 5, Part 1 (January 1956), pp. 38-40.

605. BRITISH NORTH BORNEO CHARTERED COMPANY

In 1865 the newly appointed United States Consul to Brunei secured from the Sultan the cession of a large tract of territory in what is now Sabah. The Consul soon sold the concession and in 1865 a company was formed to develop the area. By the mid-1870s other speculators were trying to acquire the concession. The most notable of these was Baron von Overbeck, the Austrian Consul-General in Hong Kong. When he ran out of funds, Overbeck came to London where he met Sir Alfred Dent, the young head of the re-organised China house of Dent Brothers. Dent agreed to advance Overbeck £10,000 and Overbeck returned to Brunei to negotiate a fresh concession from the Sultan. This he secured at the end of December 1877. A month later he obtained a second concession from the Sultan of Sulu who also had rights over areas on the north Borneo coast. Overbeck then moved to Singapore leaving William Pryer as his Resident of the East Coast (Sandakan Bay). Pryer was given instructions to treat the local people fairly.

By the end of 1880 Dent had bought-out Overbeck and had also acquired all the interests of the 1865 company. He formed a Provisional Association to run his concessions and sold out to the association for £120,000. A royal charter was granted in November 1881 and the new British North Borneo Chartered Company acquired all the powers of the Provisional Association. Dent was appointed first managing director and W.H. Treacher was seconded from the British Colonial Office to be the company's first governor of the territory. By 1882 it had been decided that the company should leave commercial undertakings to others and should primarily be an administrative organisation. There were rich natural resources in North

Borneo and exports included: edible birds' nests, rattans, gutta-percha, gum and camphor. To these in the twentieth century were added: timber, tobacco, rubber, copra and manila-hemp. The company obtained an income by taxing these exports and also secured revenue by granting rights to land. It was not a formula for vast riches and when the company did pay dividends, they were never high.

The new company began on an over-optimistic note. Treacher offered employment to more than 40 Europeans and entered into levels of expenditure which could not be sustained. The company was forced to retrench and there followed five years which were the most critical in its history. But from 1887, with revenues from the new tobacco industry and the other sources of income, the budget slowly became balanced. From 1894 W.C. Cowie became the dominant influence in the court of the company and was to remain chairman until his death in 1910. Dent was reviled and Cowie, who had meddled in North Borneo affairs since the early days, set about running the concern his own way. This involved rigid administration from London and the employment of cronies. Unsound schemes were adopted, such as the building of railways and a telegraph line which were not viable. The railway from Jesselton to Beaufort was so badly built that it had to be completely reconstructed and the final cost was around £800,000. On the other hand, the government encouraged the growth of the new rubber industry in the proximity of the railway. By the time Cowie died, North Borneo's exports had more than doubled. However he had saddled the company with debenture loans and left a legacy of maladministration.

Cowie was succeeded by Sir West Ridgeway who immediately relaxed control from London and sought independent advice on the administration. He paid dividends annually of about 5 per cent – by the end of his time these were being paid out of capital. He put money into railways and road-building; resuscitated the Cowie Harbour coal mines; established a state bank in 1921; and put substantial sums into the British Borneo Timber Company (established after the first world war in collaboration with Harrisons and Crosfields (**608**)). By 1924, when the court set-up a committee of enquiry, the company was in debt to the sum of £1,649,800. Ridgeway resigned in 1926 when the committee reported.

The new President, Sir Neill Malcolm, instituted a regime of careful husbandry so that when the Japanese overrun Sabah in 1941, £700,000 of debt had been paid off. These were difficult years for the company with the depression in primary products, particularly rubber. Small dividends were only paid in 1928, 1937 and 1938. Attempts were made to institute various administrative reforms but these were largely unsuccessful. In 1946 it was realised that the company did not have sufficient funds to rehabilitate the territory and the Labour government took it over as a British colony.

'The British North Borneo Company' being chapter16 (pp. 246-62) of ***A licence to trade: the history of English Chartered Companies.*** By Sir Percival Griffiths. London: Ernest Benn, 1974.

A gambling style of government: the establishment of the Chartered Company's rule in Sabah, 1878-1915. By Ian Black. Kuala Lumpur: Oxford University Press, 1983. x, 254p., ill. Bibliog. Index.

The North Borneo Chartered Company's administration of the Bajau, 1878-1909: the pacification of a maritime, nomadic people. By James F. Warren. Athens, Ohio: Ohio University, 1971. (Papers in international studies, Southeast Asia series. (Ohio University, Center for International Studies); No. 22.) xiv, 112p. Bibliog.

Under Chartered Company rule: North Borneo 1881-1946. By K.G. Tregonning. Singapore: University of Malaya Press, 1958. v, 250p., ill. Bibliog. Index. (2nd edition published under the title: ***A history of modern Sabah (North Borneo 1881-1963).*** By K.G. Tregonning. [Singapore]: University of Malaya Press, 1965. v, 275p., ill. Bibliog. Index.)

606. BURMAH OIL COMPANY

During the third quarter of the nineteenth century several British companies were established to refine and market oil in Burma from deposits which local Burmese workers raised by hand. The companies were not a success but the last of them – Rangoon Oil – came to the attention of David Sime Cargill, a Scot who had owned a merchant house in Ceylon. Cargill was persuaded to buy Rangoon Oil for £15,000 on its liquidation in 1876 and over the next ten years he spent £6,000 a year on his oil activities (over and above receipts from sales) but was unable to make a profit. His fortunes changed in 1886 following the British annexation of Upper Burma. He then received a number of concessions to prospect for oil. The Burma Oil Company was registered in Edinburgh in July 1886 to takeover Cargill's interests with Cargill becoming chairman. Drilling was started (in addition to hand-digging) and the first drilled oil was struck in March 1889 at Yenangyaung. The major product the company came to market in these early years was kerosene and by 1900 it was providing most of Burma's requirements. It therefore turned to India and in 1901-2 it was supplying 13 per cent of India's kerosene needs. In 1904, when Cargill died, the company produced a throughput of two million barrels of oil and made a net profit of £264,000.

The central problem which Burmah Oil was to face arose from the fact that, in oil industry terms, it was a small concern. (Even in 1939 it produced only 0.5 per cent of world output and was little-known outside Asia.) If it was to survive it needed to associate with its larger competitors. In 1905 Burmah Oil made an important agreement with Asiatic Petroleum, an enterprise established in 1902 by Royal Dutch Petroleum, Shell **(721)** and the Paris Rothschilds. In various forms this agreement was to last until 1928 and provided that only Burmah would supply kerosene to the Burmese and Chittagong markets while Asiatic alone would supply the product to the Straits, China and Ceylon. In India, Burmah was given prior marketing rights and Asiatic would buy some of Burmah's surplus capacity to distribute elsewhere. The same year as the agreement with Asiatic, Burmah Oil became financially involved with prospecting in Persia which led eventually to the formation of the Anglo-Persian Oil Company **(402)** in 1909. Burmah lost control of Anglo-Persian to the British government in 1914 and its holding was reduced to about a third of the capital. But henceforth Anglo-Persian was viewed as a valuable additional source of revenue for Burmah Oil which could become important if reserves in Burma ran out. Finally in 1905, Burmah signed a contract with the Admiralty for the supply of fuel oil to the Navy. This was not a very profitable deal but it did ensure that henceforth the Admiralty had an interest in the continued existence of the company.

When the first world war came in 1914, Burmah did not in fact supply the Admiralty with a vast amount of oil and the company's role in the war was respectable but hardly heroic. The most significant event was the appointment of Robert I. Watson as head of the London office in 1914. Watson was to dominate the company's affairs from that date until his retirement in 1947. (Between 1920 and 1947 he was Burmah's managing director.) Having worked at the Burma end from 1901, Watson brought a breadth of vision, a clear mind and a gift for lucid explanation to the company's affairs. He centralised operations on London; emphasised the need for economy; and arranged in the 1920s for the Yenangyaung field to receive electricity for its operations. In fact Watson turned Burmah from a small agency house into something of a multinational. Between 1915 and 1924 there were various attempts to merge Burmah with Royal Dutch Shell (and also at one point with Anglo-Persian as well). Watson supported these proposals because they would have meant that Royal Dutch Shell would have become a British concern. Ironically these merger attempts were finally defeated as a consequence of the Admiralty's hostility. In 1927 Burmah Oil and Shell Transport and Trading set-up a joint marketing company in India known as Burmah-Shell. In many ways this was Watson's most noteworthy achievement and indicated that Shell was now very much the junior partner in the subcontinent.

Throughout the inter-war years Burmah's oil production continued to increase. This was helped by output from the Assam Oil Company (where the company had taken a controlling interest in 1921). By 1941 Burmah was producing more than eight million barrels of crude annually. This really marked the high point of Burmah's fortunes in Asia. In 1942 the company's oilfields and installations in Burma were destroyed in a systematic attempt to deny them to the advancing Japanese. (An action for which the company was never effectively compensated.) After the war, production did not return to pre-war levels. Indeed Watson had doubts whether it would be feasible to work in Burma again but operations were resumed in March 1946. It then became necessary for Burmah to evacuate most of its employees from the country in mid-1949 because of rebel activity in the area of the oilfields. There then followed remarkable discussions with the Government of Burma about the possibility of a joint venture for oil production. These continued for a number of years and in 1954 were successful. A new Burmese company – the Burmah Oil Company (1954) – took over, valued at £15 million. The Burmese Government owned 33.3 per cent of the concern; Burmah Oil 55 per cent; and other oil companies 11.7 per cent. The concern traded profitably for seven years but following General Ne Win's coup in 1962 it was nationalised with Burmah and the other oil companies receiving only £4.7 million compensation which also was to cover the takeover of Burmah's distributing interests. Meanwhile in India (which was the main source of Burmah's trading profits after the war and into the 1950s), the company constructed a new oil refinery in Bombay jointly with Shell. However Burmah's oil business in India was to suffer considerably from state-owned prospecting and marketing operations introduced by the Nehru governments. In Pakistan, Burmah came to concentrate on natural gas production from the Sui field. Burmah's Pakistan operations were not considered a success by the company. Between 1947 and 1959 new investments totalling £14 million yielded profits of only £3 million.

In the years after the second world war, Burmah Oil increasingly came to depend on income from its investments. In 1955, for example, only 39 per cent of the company's income was made by trading profits. Under the influence of William Eadie (chairman 1957-64) the board agreed reluctantly to diversify. Burmah acquired oil production interests in the United States, Canada, Peru, Ecuador, Australia and the North Sea. During

1966 the company took over Castrol Limited, a lubricants business which traced its origins back to 1899. Unfortunately during the oil crisis of 1974 Burmah Castrol got into financial difficulties and had to be rescued by the Bank of England. It was forced to sell its British Petroleum shares at very low valuations to the British government. Thereafter the firm reshaped itself into a specialist gas, oil and chemical products business. In 2000 it was taken over by BP Amoco – a concern which, in part, Burmah Oil had helped to create.

'Burmah Oil Co. Ltd.: history and archives to 1966.' By Bridget Stockford. ***Business archives*** (London), No.58 (November 1989), pp. 33-9.

Burmah...the early days. ***Swindon: Burmah Oil Trading Limited, [1986].*** [12] leaves, ill.
[Seen by courtesy of Burmah Oil Trading Limited.]

A history of the Burmah Oil Company. By T.A.B. Corley.
Vol. 1: *1886-1924.* London: Heinemann, 1983. xvi, 331p., ill. Index.
Vol. 2: *1924-66.* London: Heinemann, 1988. xvi, 416p., ill. Index.

'Strategic factors in the growth of a multinational enterprise: the Burmah Oil Company 1886-1928.' By T.A.B. Corley. Being pp. 214-35 of ***The growth of international business.*** Edited by Marc Casson. London: George Allen & Unwin, 1983.

607. GUTHRIE AND COMPANY

In 1816 the young Scot, Alexander Guthrie, went out to work for Thomas Talbot Harrington, a merchant in Cape Town. The two men keenly watched developments further East and saw great trading possibilities in Raffles' Singapore. The new island port came under the control of the Indian Governor-General so in 1820 Guthrie secured an indenture from the Marquess of Hastings (then the Governor-General). This allowed him to reside in Singapore and transact business there on behalf of the house of Harrington. On arrival Guthrie was persuaded by the local Chinese that the best way to trade was through Chinese middlemen and that in order to do this he should employ a Chinese compradore on his staff. He thus adopted a method of conducting business which was to be widely used by British companies in East and South-East Asia during the nineteenth and twentieth centuries.

Harrington retired late in 1823 and shortly afterwards Guthrie entered into a new ten-year partnership with James Scott Clark. When this came to an end in 1833 the firm adopted the name 'Guthrie and Company'. Throughout the nineteenth century the business expanded by taking on partners from the Guthrie family and from close friends. It became much involved in the general entrepôt trade of Singapore. Its transactions with the local Chinese merchants meant it had access to products from the entire South China Sea region. Guthries also established direct trading links with Malaya, Cambodia, Siam, Borneo and Sumatra. The firm became an important landowner and acted as agent for banking, insurance and steamship companies. It was one of the companies behind the formation of the Tanjong Pagar Dock Company **(619)**.

Guthries were very involved in the agitation for the transfer of Singapore from the Government of India to the British Crown (which took place in 1867) and for the British to bring some order to the various Malayan states. However the firm was at first wary of becoming involved on the Malayan mainland. Through personal connections the house had been granted large tin-mining concessions for ten years by the Tungku of Selangor in 1873 but Guthries rapidly transferred the rights to a new company, called the 'Selangor Tin Mining Company'. It was not until 1896 that Guthries moved decisively into Malaya by taking on the agencies for a group of coffee and rubber plantations.

From the late nineteenth century until the 1960s the fortunes of the firm were guided by two outstanding entrepreneurs of their generations – Sir John Anderson and Sir John Hay. These men extended Guthries' branch network in Malaya while ending the firm's unprofitable agencies. The company came to concentrate particularly on rubber production but with important interests in general trading, tin and sandalwood. It was during the first quarter of the twentieth century that Guthries effectively took control of rubber estates like the Cheviot and Glendale, the United Sua Betong and Malacca Rubber Plantations Limited – the largest rubber company in Malaya. In 1908 Guthries set-up the Renong Dredging Company in Thailand (the first tin-dredge to work on land in South-East Asia) and in the 1920s Guthries further diversified into oil palm having substantial interests in the company 'Oil Palms of Malaya' which it established in 1930. Sir John Hay was to became the acknowledged leader of the British rubber industry in the 1930s and was the main architect of the International Rubber Regulation Committee of 1934. Following a difficult time during the years of the Malayan Emergency, the company diversified into a wide range of activities throughout the British Commonwealth.

'The oldest Malayan firm: the story of Guthrie & Co., Ltd.' By H.R. Cheeseman. *Malaya* (London), Vol. 4, Part 1 (January 1955), pp. 37-40.

The Traders: a story of Britain's South-East Asian commercial adventure. By Sjovald Cunyngham-Brown. London: Newman Neame for Guthrie & Company (UK) Limited, 1971. 352p., ill. Bibliog. Index.

608. HARRISONS AND CROSFIELD

In January 1844, the three Liverpool Quakers, David Harrison, Smith Harrison and Joseph Crosfield, entered into partnership with a capital of £8,000 to trade in tea and coffee. Thess activities remained the core of the business until the last decade of the nineteenth century. After losses had started to show up in Liverpool the firm moved in 1855 to London where it soon became the third largest trader in tea. By the 1890s however Harrisons had become rather set in its ways and the tea and coffee business no longer offered attractive prospects for the future.

At this point the firm's fortunes were transformed largely through the admission of Arthur Lampard into the partnership in 1894. Lampard travelled to Sri Lanka in a search for better sources of tea and this led him to take Harrisons and Crosfield into the running of tea plantations. Shortly after, a colleague drew his attention to the potentialities of rubber plantations in Malaya. So in the 1900s the firm first became associated with the estates on which its fame was later to rest. The companies involved included: (1) the so-called 'Three Sisters' in Malaya: the Petaling Company, Golden Hope Rubber Estates and London Asiatic Rubber and Produce Company; (2) London Sumatra in Indonesia; (3) the Malayalam Company in South India; and (4) the Lunava Company in Sri Lanka.

Harrisons did not actually have sufficient resources to buy the plantations for themselves. So with great resourcefulness the firm devised various schemes to allow the new companies to raise their own capital. (A notable example in the rubber industry was the Rubber Plantations Development Trust of 1907.) Harrisons supplied financial and technical expertise to the concerns; acted as managing agents; and were represented on the various boards. The firm placed great stress on the institution of the visiting agent. This was an individual appointed from outside the particular plantation company who inspected the estates and ensured that the best techniques and management systems were introduced. This emphasis on pioneering and experimenting led to what was known in the City of London as 'The Harrisons' Competitive Edge'.

The years from 1914 to 1960 were a period of diversification for the firm caused partly by difficult conditions in the tea and rubber industries. Under the leadership of Sir Eric Miller and Sir Eric Macfadyen it became involved in agencies of all descriptions, general trading, as well as with palm oil and timber production. Harrisons rose to prominence in North Borneo during 1917 when it bought out the established firm of W.G. Darby. This gave Harrisons timber mills, ice works, a slipway and shipping interests. In 1920 it acquired a one-third share of the British Borneo Timber Company. Until 1939 Harrisons and Crosfield were to dominate commerce in North Borneo. The connection with timber was also to bring the firm into the timber and building supplies business in Britain in the second half of the century.

What was ultimately the most significant diversification for the company was its entry into the chemical industry. As early as the 1920s it had shown an interest in this area in order to provide for the particular needs of the rubber industry. However it was in 1947 that it joined with Durham Chemicals to supply zinc oxide to Canada. By 1962 Harrisons had acquired a majority shareholding in Durham and in 1971 they bought out Haagen Chemicals in the Netherlands. This was followed by the purchase of British Chrome and Chemicals in 1973. Purchases in the United States between 1979 and 1981 placed Harrisons amongst the five largest chemical distributors in that country.

The diversifications were timely. Legislation within Asian countries limiting foreign ownership was to bring an end to Harrisons' involvement with most of the tea and rubber estate companies by the 1980s. The timber concession in Sabah (North Borneo) lapsed in 1982. Eventually it was decided that the firm's future lay with chemicals and all other interests were sold off. Harrisons and Crosfield was liquidated in 1998 and a new company, Elementis, was floated to takeover the chemical interests.

'Diversification strategies of British trading companies: Harrisons & Crosfield, *c.*1900-*c.*1980.' By Geoffrey Jones and Judith Wale. ***Business history*** (London), Vol. 41, No. 2 (April 1999), pp. 69-101.

Great enterprise: a history of Harrisons & Crosfield. By Peter Pugh *et al.*; edited by Guy Nickalls. [London:] The Company, 1990. 272p., ill.

One hundred years as East India merchants: Harrisons & Crosfield 1844-1943. London: [The Company,] 1943. 69p.
[British Library of Political and Economic Science.]

609 P. HENDERSON AND COMPANY

Patrick Henderson was only 25 when he founded the firm of P. Henderson and Company in 1834. He had already had experience in buying and selling goods and took advantage of the fact that two of his brothers had moved to Leghorn to work for the general merchants, Peter Senn and Company, while another brother was a ship's captain who partly owned his own vessel. Senns were particularly involved in the export of Italian marble and were anxious to import British goods (mainly textiles). In 1835 Senns made Patrick Henderson their official agent in Scotland. From that time Henderson showed energy, foresight and a meticulous attention to detail which enabled him to build up the business from practically nothing. He did not confine operations to Senns but established connections with firms in Germany, Switzerland and the Netherlands. This was fortunate as Hendersons were thereby cushioned from a slump in the demand for marble that began in 1835. Some time in 1840 the other three Henderson brothers gave up their own careers and joined Patrick's firm.

Hendersons would probably have remained a trading company but for Patrick's early death in 1841. The partnership then came under the control of George, the second brother, who was the seaman. The firm did not immediately abandon trading but increasing emphasis was placed on shipping. By the mid-1850s one of George's ships was sailing as far as India, Burma and Australia. After the Crimean War another of the brothers independently established the 'European and Australian Royal Mail Company' which won the Admiralty contract for the delivery of mail to Australia. This turned out to be a costly failure but it did direct attention to Australasia. Paddy Hendersons became very involved in the transport of emigrants to New Zealand in ships of the 'Albion Line' which it set-up in 1864. This operation was to last until 1882 when the Albion Line merged with the Shaw Savill Line.

The firm's connection with Burma began because of difficulties in finding homeward cargoes from New Zealand and because of the friendship of one of the partners with T.D. Finlay, a Glasgow merchant who had interests in Burma. By the end of the 1850s Henderson ships were returning via Burma having taken on cargoes of teak and rice. In 1863 the company started regular packet services between Britain and Rangoon and in 1870 it began a monthly direct steamer service to Burma via the Suez Canal. During 1874 the 'British and Burmese Navigation Company' was set-up to takeover Paddy Hendersons' Burmese steamer fleet with Hendersons remaining as managing agents. Hendersons were closely connected with the Irrawaddy Flotilla Company **(610)** from the start and acted as the flotilla's Glasgow agents.

Up to the first world war there was a steady development of trade with Burma, Henderson ships carrying out cargoes of steel, machinery, cotton goods and whisky while rice remained the mainstay of the homeward-bound trade. In 1889 the Bibby Line **(601)** entered into competition with the Henderson Line and henceforth trade was shared under shipping conference rules. By 1914 the two concerns were providing a weekly joint service to Burma.

The line lost three of its vessels in the first world war but was able to work normally up to 1916. It was only in the following year that the British government requisitioned its ships. Between the wars the Henderson Line engaged in a considerable re-building programme although the number of passengers carried tended to decline. Burma remained the principal focus of activity but it delivered a good deal of cargo and passengers to stops in the Middle East. After the Japanese blockaded the China coast in the late 1930s, Henderson vessels carried supplies for China, the items being off-loaded in Rangoon and taken on by river and road.

The line was dealt harshly by the second world war. It lost eight ships while trade with Burma was completely disrupted. After the war, sailings to Rangoon were resumed as soon as possible but it was not until 1948 that, in conjunction with the Bibby Line, a regular scheduled service was in operation. Henderson vessels sailed every 28 days for Rangoon from Birkenhead. In 1952 the British and Burmese Navigation Company was acquired by the Elder Dempster Lines and Hendersons were to find their management functions considerably reduced. During 1961 the Burmese Government-owned 'Burma Five Star Line' was set-up. Necessarily, it had to be admitted to the shipping conference, soon acquiring half the trade. In 1965 the Henderson Line was acquired by the Ocean Steam Ship Company **(112)** as part of their takeover of Liner Holdings. Two years later P. Henderson and Company was merged with Oceans' Glasgow subsidiary to become Roxburgh, Henderson and Company. During 1969 both the Henderson Line and the Bibby Line discontinued their services to Burma.

The Burma boats: Henderson and Bibby. By Duncan Haws. [Uckfield: The Author,] 1995. (Merchant fleets; No. 29.) 203p., ill.
[Cambridge University Library.]

Paddy Henderson: a history of the Scottish shipping firm* P. Henderson & Company *and other enterprises which sprang from their initiative and spirit of maritime adventure, 1834-1961. By Dorothy Laird. Glasgow: George Outram & Co., 1961. 230p., ill.
[The British Library copy has a typescript insert of five pages at end with the heading: '"Paddy Henderson: a short account of the final years 1962-67." By A.G. McCrae, the last senior partner.']

610. IRRAWADDY FLOTILLA COMPANY

After the end of the Second Burmese War (1852-3), the Governor-General of India, Lord Dalhousie, arranged for a small flotilla to be sent from Calcutta to Burma for use on the Irrawaddy. When Sir Arthur Phayre became Chief Commissioner he decided the service was better run by private enterprise. The Rangoon teak and rice merchants Todd, Findlay and Company won the contract which involved two monthly sailings from Rangoon to synchronise with the incoming mails. The Irrawaddy Flotilla and Burmese Steam Navigation Company was floated in January 1865 to carry out the operation but no dividends were paid in the second and third years of its existence as high repair costs had to be met on the boats which had been taken over. In 1871 George Swann, who had been sent out from Paddy Hendersons **(609)** in Glasgow, became manager of operations in Rangoon and he drafted a three year plan of expansion. By 1872 the company was running services in stages from Rangoon to Bhamo near the Chinese border (about a thousand miles) and had a lease on a dockyard in Rangoon. A fresh call for capital was made and in 1876 a new company took over with the name of the 'Irrawaddy Flotilla Company'. Following Frederick Kennedy's appointment as Rangoon Manager in 1880, the company opened up the Chindwin River and Irrawaddy Delta to steamer navigation and began a service from Rangoon through the delta to Bassein (for the Bay of Bengal).

The company became heavily involved in the Third Burmese War of 1885. As there was no British representation in Mandalay, Captain Cooper of the company's flotilla had the task of delivering the British ultimatum to King Thibaw. When this was rejected, the company transported about 10,000 soldiers, 7,000 followers and 500 mules up-river. It used 26 steamers for this work. After the war there was considerable expansion in the size of the flotilla. Special vessels were built to carry rice and petroleum. In the years up to 1920 profits were high (apart from many years in the 1890s) and dividends rarely below 15 per cent. 89 vessels were requisitioned for use in the Mesopotamia campaign.

The company reached its highest point of success in the 1920s. These were years of peak prosperity and the concern had become one of the greatest ever inland water transportation enterprises. In 1929 it carried nine million passengers. Throughout the decade dividends remained at 15 per cent annually but in the difficult 1930s they were reduced to 6 per cent. In 1934 the company founded the 'Irrawaddy Flotilla and Airways Limited' to operate flying boats within Burma using three planes but this was not a success and was wound up in 1937. During the early years of the second world war the flotilla played a big part in moving goods to China. With the Japanese invasion of Burma the fleet was used to evacuate refugees and supplies to the north. Eventually, as the Japanese moved up-country, almost all the fleet was scuttled. In 1945 the company returned and drew up plans for re-building the flotilla. However this was overtaken by Burmese independence and by the nationalisation of the company in 1948. It was finally wound up in 1957.

'The Irrawaddy Flotilla.' By Alister McCrae. ***Business history*** (London), Vol. 22, No.1 (January 1980), pp. 87-99.

Irrawaddy Flotilla. By Alister McCrae and Alan Prentice. Paisley: James Paxton, 1978. 195p., ill. Bibliog. Index.

'Irrawaddy Flotilla', 'War on the Irrawaddy', 'Growth of the Irrawaddy Company, Limited' and 'Tragedy of the Irrawaddy Flotilla Company, Limited' being Chapters 8, 9, 10 and 15 (pp. 113-57, 199-215) of ***Paddy Henderson: a history of the Scottish shipping firm* P. Henderson & Company *and other enterprises which sprang from their initiative and spirit of maritime adventure, 1834-1961.*** By Dorothy Laird. Glasgow: George Outram & Co., 1961.

The Irrawaddy Flotilla Company Limited 1865-1950. By Captain H.J. Chubb (late of the Company) and C.L.D. Duckworth. London: National Maritime Museum, 1973. (Maritime monographs and reports. (No. 7, 1973).) 177p., ill.

[A history and technical listing and description of vessels operated by the Company.]

611. LEWIS AND PEAT

Robert Lewis, a spice broker, began trading from Walbrook, London in 1775. His son and grandson were joined in the business by William Henry Peat in 1846 and the foundations of the later firm were laid. By the1900s rubber had begun to dominate the business and in 1918 Lewis and Peat opened an office in Singapore.

The new office established close relations with the Borneo Company **(603)** and this latter company kept the local accounts and made advances to the rubber estates. Lewis and Peat's job was to market the rubber. Since there was no trading floor the firm, in competition with other brokers, had to carry rubber samples around Singapore to the various merchant houses. Within a few years Lewis and Peat had taken back the bookwork and finance from the Borneo Company and, following a boom year in 1925, the Singapore office was floated as a separate limited company in 1926. The 1930s were difficult for the firm as its staff were paid by commission and these were years of depression in the rubber trade. However it did extremely well in the years immediately after the second world war and by the early 1950s was contributing the bulk of the parent firm's profits. In contrast the London concern did not pay a dividend on ordinary shares between 1929 and 1951.

During 1950 Lewis and Peat effectively came under the control of Harry Kissin's company, G.H. Kay. By 1953 the board of Kays were seeking to move Lewis and Peat into new activities. The three Singapore directors were not in agreement with this policy and resigned in order to start their own business. Then Sandy Pratt was sent out from London to re-establish Lewis and Peat's Singapore operation and he rapidly assembled a high quality team. Profits were unaffected by the changes and in 1955 the Singapore concern increased its capital and capitalised its reserves. The parent company entered the insurance and banking businesses while the Singapore subsidiary continued to thrive.

Two centuries of Lewis & Peat (now the Guinness Peat Group) 1775-1975. [By Leith McGrandle.] London: The Company, 1975. 64p., ill.

612. MANSFIELD AND COMPANY

The origins of the firm go back to 1861 when George Mansfield set-up a business in Singapore as a commission agent and auctioneer. On his death two years later, his brother Walter took over the firm and he was joined in 1865 by George's son, George John Mansfield, at the time no more than fifteen years old. Unfortunately by the mid-1860s trade was becoming very slack and in November 1866 letters were sent out to the firm's creditors with a view to its being wound-up. At this moment the new Ocean Steam Ship Company **(112)**, owner of the Blue Funnel Line, informally told their masters to use Mansfields for their supplies. Ocean were dissatisfied with their existing Singapore agents and by 1868 Mansfields had taken over the agency. When Walter Mansfield died in 1873, George John became senior partner of the firm and remained as such until his retirement in 1883 aged 33. Mansfields was joined in 1872 by Theodore Cornelius Bogaardt, a Dutchman with Javanese experience who had been shipping clerk in the Europe Hotel, Singapore. He was to serve as senior partner between 1883 and 1895.

The opening of the Suez Canal brought great importance to Singapore as a staging post and entrepôt. Mansfields' business increased enormously. Until the 1930s it chiefly acted for the Ocean Steam Ship Company and related concerns. However Bogaardt in particular was anxious to develop the significance of Singapore for Oceans' operations. Under his guidance Singapore became much more than a stopping place for the Blue Funnel ships on their way to China. He made the port into the hub of Ocean trade throughout South-East Asia. Feeder services were arranged to Sumatra, Bangkok and Borneo. The Straits Steamship Company **(617)** added the Malayan ports to this list. Mansfields itself set-up a branch office in Penang in 1878 and another at Sandakan, British North Borneo in 1890. By the turn of the century Mansfields were also managing a Singapore-Australia steamship service; a Spanish service from Singapore to the Philippines; and were organising the carriage of pilgrims from the Straits to Mecca.

A.P Adams retired as last senior partner of Mansfields in 1903 after which it was turned into a limited company. Ocean then acquired 135 of the 200 shares issued. However the directors of the Ocean Company were most anxious to leave Mansfields to its own management and rarely intervened. In 1922 Mansfields became agents for the Straits Steamship Company and the office staffs of the two companies were brought together and integrated within the same building. From this point the chairmen of Straits seem also to have held concurrently the chairmanship of Mansfields. So Mansfields was run by men of the calibre of H.E. Somerville and C.E. Wurtzberg. In 1933 Mansfields became general agents for Imperial Airways and shortly afterwards they took on the sales agency for Quantas. In 1940 they became agent to Pan American. At the beginning of the second world war (up to the Japanese occupation) Mansfields had the work of managing the Straits' vessels requisitioned by the Royal Navy. This was in addition to their usual work for Blue Funnel.

Mansfields held their first post-war board meeting in March 1946. It was to mark the beginning of a period of considerable diversification for the concern. For ten years from April 1947 Mansfields managed Malayan Airways which attracted considerable traffic as the Malayan emergency encouraged air travel. In the 1950s and 1960s Mansfields moved into travel agency work and it now held shipping agencies for a wider number of firms including P. & O. Mansfields acquired a considerable property portfolio. It serviced certain joint ventures it had entered into with Ocean and other companies. These included: Overseas Containers (OCL), Panocean Shipping and Terminals; and the Blue Sea Line. At the end of 1973 the Straits Steamship Company acquired the entire equity capital of Mansfields from Ocean Transport and Trading.

The history of Mansfield and Company: Part I, 1868-1924. By A. Jackson and C.E. Wurtzburg. [?Singapore:] [?The Company,] 1952. 8p. [Merseyside Maritime Museum.]

The history of Mansfield and Company: Part II, 1920-1953. By A. McLellan. [?Singapore:] [?The Company,] 1953. 12p. [Merseyside Maritime Museum.]

Mansfields: transport and distribution in South-East Asia. By Eric Jennings. Singapore: Meridian Communications, [?1973]. 48p., ill. [School of Oriental and African Studies, University of London.]

613. PAHANG CONSOLIDATED COMPANY

The origins of this company go back to 1883 when a Pahang Company was set-up in Malaya to work a tin and minerals concession covering 2, 500 square miles in the eastern state of Pahang. The people behind the venture were Towkay Lim Assam of Billiton and two businessmen from Singapore. In 1886 a Pahang Mining Company was formed in Britain to buy up the concession but it found difficulty raising capital and the concession apparently lapsed. The following year a new Pahang Corporation was set-up, again in Britain, through the initiative of William Fraser, and in September 1888 the Sultan granted a fresh concession of 2,000 square miles to this corporation for 80 years.

Work began immediately and by 1890 the corporation had a labour force of about 460. The first mining below adit level was begun in 1892. The corporation faced considerable difficulties in obtaining supplies and exporting its ores as the interval between ships calling at the local port could be as long as four months. The corporation's agents were forced to charter vessels and at one point purchased a steamer. By 1905 much work had been done. Nearly 8,500 tons of black tin had been mined yielding an income of more than half a million pounds. Wharves and warehouses had been built.

At this stage, however, it became clear that additional capital was needed. The mines were now less productive and would need to be extended and deepened if the venture was to be profitable. So the corporation was liquidated in October 1906, its assets being taken over by a new Pahang Consolidated Company which had been registered the previous July. The Borneo Company **(603)** was immediately appointed managing agents and took over the running of all the properties and business of the company in the East.

Pahang Consolidated had a difficult start. Formation costs were heavy and the tin reserves were not as good as expected. However two mining engineers considered there were favourable long-term prospects so the company's capital was doubled in 1910 to £500,000. From 1911 profits began to rise and over the long period from 1911-65 eight million tons of ore were found and mined. The company early on diversified into rubber and tobacco-growing.

In 1926 the company was affected by serious flooding in its mines and work had to be suspended for three months. It also suffered badly under the terms of the 1931 International Tin Agreement. Only high-grade ores could be mined and more than half the labour force had to be dismissed. When quotas were raised in the late 1930s, the company was able to increase its production. Overall in the period 1929-41, some 27,000 tons of black tin were produced at a profit of more than £1.5 million. In a report prepared at the suggestion of the British Colonial Secretary in 1939, Pahang Consolidated was credited as running 'the most thoroughly efficient tin-mining in Malaya'.

During the second world war the company's mines were flooded as a denial measure before the advancing Japanese. The occupying forces nonetheless made some use of the workings to extract copper. This resulted in their leaving the available mine machinery intact which was of great value after the war when Pahang Consolidated returned. It did, however, take until July 1949 to empty the mines of water. About half a million pounds was spent in rehabilitating the workings. The company faced great operating difficulties during the Malayan emergency and two of the senior staff of an associated rubber company were killed. As the end of the concession neared, Pahang Consolidated investigated other mining possibilities (including one in Thailand) without finding any which would repay exploitation. In 1965 it was granted a new lease for a further 21 years.

A history of the Pahang Consolidated Company Limited 1906-1966. London: The Company, 1966. p.70, ill.
[British Library of Political and Economic Science.]

614. SIME DARBY

William Middleton Sime was a young Scotsman who went East at the beginning of the twentieth century to seek his fortune. He started-up an export/import business and moved on to coffee-planting but both ventures failed. Sime then turned to rubber cultivation feeling it had great commercial potential. (At the time there was a boom in rubber shares.) He gave up his job as a mercantile assistant in Singapore and tramped through the jungles of Malaya looking for suitable land but encountered much hostility. However in due course he met up with Henry Darby, a wealthy English banker who owned property in northern Malaya. Darby sold off some of his land to provide capital and together the two established the Sime Darby Company in 1910 which was to manage 500 acres of rubber estates in Malacca.

The new company faced many problems in its early days and it was the local Chinese community in Malacca which bailed it out financially. Sime and Darby took into the firm as an associate Tun Tan Cheng Lock who was to become one of the first Chinese non-executive directors of the concern. He was to play a key role in the future of Sime Darby and was a prominent leader of Malaya's independence movement. The company became managing agent for a number of plantation companies and in 1915 established a branch in Singapore. This was followed soon after by the establishment of a London office to market Sime Darby rubber.

Sime Darby moved into agency work representing various western firms and supplying a wide range of consumer and other products. In 1929 the company acquired the Sarawak Trading Company which held the franchise for Caterpillar equipment. In due course Sime Darby was to become one of the largest distributors for Caterpillar products in the world. In 1936 the head office was moved to Singapore. (It was to return to Malaysia in 1979 when it was established in Kuala Lumpur.) By 1954 Sime Darby had 80,000 acres of rubber plantations and 18 branch offices in Singapore, Malaysia and Brunei.

During the 1970s Sime Darby became a major force in the plantation industry through the takeover of Seafield Estate and the incorporation of Consolidated Plantations Berhad. The company began planting oil palm and cocoa in addition to rubber. Sime Darby also diversified into engineering, manufacturing, insurance, shipping, motor franchises and banking. In the mid-1970s the Malaysian state trading corporation, Pernas, acquired a majority shareholding in Sime Darby through share purchases in the London market. The majority of the remaining shares were held by Asian investors thus making Sime Darby a predominantly Asian company. With operations in the ASEAN region, Hong Kong, Australia, the United Kingdom and the United States, Sime Darby had become Malaysia's multinational company.

Story of Sime Darby: Sime Darby 75th anniversary. Kuala Lumpur: The Company, [1985]. 12p., ill.
[Seen by courtesy of Sime Darby Berhad.]

615. SMITH, BELL AND COMPANY

James Adam Smith, a young Scot, was sent to Manila by his employers, Jardine Matheson **(307)**, in October 1838. His task was to try to recoup moneys owed by the firm of E. de Otadui and Company and for this purpose Smith was made an associate of the Manila firm. The arrangement was not satisfactory but Smith remained with Otaduis until 1844 when he returned to Liverpool. Smith never went back to the Philippines but he did become involved in business partnerships which started to trade with the country and opened a Manila office for the purpose. The representative sent out bought rice and unrefined sugar which were exchanged for cotton goods, iron sheets and machinery from Britain as well as sundry items purchased in the Chinese treaty ports. The partners' attention was soon drawn to the sales potential of Philippines' hemp for rope-making and it was probably so that this product could be traded that the American, Lawrence R. Bell, joined them. (Bell had much experience of the commodity and hemp was to become a major revenue earner for the firm.) In 1853 the partnership was re-named Smith, Bell and Company – although in this case the 'Smith' was probably John Knox Smith about whom little is known.

Bell left Manila and the company in 1862. His place was taken by George Rainy Young who was to play a central role over the next forty years. Under his influence an extensive branch network was established throughout the Philippines and there was a gradual but steady increase in the firm's activities. It became involved in banking, shipping and fire and marine insurance and was the predominant influence in the establishment in the 1870s and 1880s of the Luzon Rice Mills Limited and the Luzon Sugar Company. It entered the desiccated coconut trade and managed a fleet of inter-island steamers.

The twentieth century was to prove difficult for the firm. In 1905 it came close to liquidation as a result of having too large holdings in sugar in New York during a falling market. For the next four years vital aspects of the company's affairs were run by its creditors. Between 1929 and 1931 it made extremely heavy losses and its bankers ordered drastic cuts in overheads and staff. During the Japanese occupation of the Philippines, practically the entire assets of the company were lost so it ended the war with nothing except a two million pesos' debt to the banks. It was only restarted because both HSBC **(106)** and the Chartered Bank **(102)** foresaw a future for the firm. Smith, Bell and Company was able to re-enter the desiccated coconut and hemp trades and did well, despite difficult conditions, because there was a very considerable demand for these products. In 1959, in order to conform with Filipino legislation requiring companies trading in the country to be owned by Filipino nationals, a controlling interest in the company was taken by Aboitiz and Company.

Under four flags: the story of Smith, Bell & Company in the Philippines. Bristol: Printed by J. Arrowsmith Ltd. [?1973]. xi, 68p., ill.

616. STEEL BROTHERS AND COMPANY

William Strang Steel set-up his own business in Rangoon in 1870. By that time he had had almost twenty years' experience as a trader in the East. In 1851, aged only nineteen, he had been sent to Java to work for the firm of Martin Dyes and Company. He returned to Glasgow in 1856 with the aim of starting-up a business but presumably this did not prosper because the following year he took a post in Rangoon as a manager for the consignment house of Gladstone, Wylie and Company. In 1859 he became a partner in that firm and remained with it until 1870. Steel left Burma in 1873 and that year, with his older brother James, set-up a London arm of his business with the name 'Steel Brothers and Company'. In 1890 the Rangoon concern was merged with the London house.

Like many other British concerns in Asia, Steels' first activity was the importing of foreign manufactures, particularly British piece-goods, and ironically this was the last department of the firm to be closed down in Burma in 1963. Steels soon became involved in a variety of other operations which included agency work for shipping and insurance companies; tin-mining; cement production; and cotton procurement and ginning (the firm came to control some 60 per cent of the Burmese cotton crop). However Steels' reputation was made with three particular commodities: rice, timber and oil. Brief details of the firm's involvement with these commodities are given separately.

Rice. Steels' first mill, located near Rangoon, was opened in 1871 and a white milling plant was added in 1888. The whole complex was re-built in 1906. Steels' rice operations expanded considerably in the first world war when it acquired the German-owned 'Burma Rice and Trading Company'. By 1939 Steel Brothers were the world's largest millers and shippers of rice. Its twelve mills handled 44 per cent of the Burmese crop. Until about 1930 brokers brought the raw product to Steels' mills but then the firm set-up its own chain of jungle-buying stations. In 1937 these stations purchased 31 million baskets of rice.

Timber. Steels entered the teak business at a fairly early stage but until 1900 its interests were confined to selling and shipping the product. However it became involved in extraction when it bought up the forests leases and elephant herds of the established firm of J.W. Darwood and Company. Figures for the areas held by the company in 1939 are not available but at that time it had an elephant herd of about 700 out of a working population in Burma of around 5,000. Steels never achieved the significance in the teak trade which was attained by the Bombay Burmah Trading Corporation **(602)**.

Oil. Steels started-up the Indo-Burma Petroleum Company in 1908 to take a 50 per cent interest in the oil business developed by the local entrepreneur, A.K.A.S. Jamal. He had sunk two wells in the Yenangyaung Field and had built a small refinery. IBP immediately began investing in distributive installations in Bombay, Calcutta and Chittagong, the first of which was opened in 1912. In 1922-3 IBP bought out the Jamal family interests and during the inter-war years it invested large sums in oil-prospecting in Burma. However all installations in the country were destroyed in 1942 as part of the policy of denying them to the advancing Japanese. Besides IBP, Steels had another oil interest as managers for the Attock Oil Company in the Punjab. This company had been established in 1913 and struck substantial amounts of oil in the province. Steels never rivalled Burma Oil **(606)** in the oil industry.

During and after the second world war Steels' expertise in food procurement was in particular demand. In 1940 Steels was asked by the Government of Palestine to act as its agent for receiving, storing and distributing foodstuffs. Steels' staff was increased for the purpose from three to almost a thousand. By the end of the British mandate in 1948 more than two million tons of food had been handled. In Assam the firm was commissioned to take delivery of rice from the mills in Lower Assam and arrange for its despatch to the tea gardens of Upper Assam. This operation lasted from 1943 to 1968.

Steel Brothers never effectively resumed its core operations in Burma after the second world war and soon started to look elsewhere for business. During the 1950s it was largely kept going by its oil interests. (Indo-Burma Petroleum was now simply a distributor of other firms' oil in northern India.) Steels became much involved in the Middle East. In 1948 it took a 50 per cent interest in Spinneys, a firm which had a number of trading posts throughout the region and which was beginning to specialise in the provision of 'oilmen's stores'. (In 1967 Steels completely took over

Spinneys.) During the 1950s Steels entered Canada and purchased interests in the cement and building materials sector. In 1968 it became involved in the haulage and construction business in Australia. Within the U.K. the firm moved into insurance and various types of light industry. Steels remains in existence although it is understood to have much reduced the extent of its overseas activities.

Calling to mind: being some account of the first hundred years (1870 to 1970) of Steel Brothers and Company Limited. Compiled by H.E.W. Braund. Oxford: Pergamon Press, 1975. 151p., ill. Bibliog. Index.

617. STRAITS STEAMSHIP COMPANY

The company was floated in 1890 by a Dutchman, Theodore Cornelius Bogaardt, who at the time was senior partner of Mansfield and Company **(612)** in Singapore. The new company was the outcome of collaboration between European and Chinese shipping interests – there were three prominent Straits Chinese among the original seven directors. The object of the concern was to provide feeder lines and a coastal shipping service. While the big intercontinental shipping lines had been serving Singapore since 1845, it was felt there were inadequate local routes which linked up with the long-distance sailings. For its first twenty-five years, therefore, the Straits Steamship Company was very much a local concern and its operations were mainly confined to the west coast of Malaya. Here it transported all the primary products of the peninsula (including rubber) and became much involved in carrying tin and labourers for the Straits Trading Company **(618)**. By 1908 it was carrying all STC tin.

In 1914 the Ocean Steam Ship Company **(112)** became the major shareholder in the Straits Steamship Company. This came about because, with the outbreak of war, Ocean had lost the collaboration of the North German Lloyd Line which had provided feeder services to its ships in Singapore from other South-East Asian ports. In return for three new ships to be supplied by Ocean, the Straits Company agreed to takeover most of the North German Lloyd services. The years from 1914 to 1939 were, therefore, a period of considerable expansion for the Straits Company particularly under the management of H.E. Somerville who was managing director or chairman between 1914 and 1932. Besides the services for Ocean, the company expanded by acquiring controlling interests in the Eastern Shipping Company (1922), the Sarawak Steamship Company

(1931) and the Ho Hong Steamship Company (1932). The effect of all these developments was to considerably extend the Straits Steamship Company's operating area. In addition to the Malay peninsula, its ships now also served Borneo, Burma, Indonesia, South China and Thailand. In 1932 Straits ships called at 78 ports in South-East Asia. In the late 1930s trade based on Singapore contracted but, because of the skilful management of C.E. Wurtzburg (Somerville's successor), the profits of the company actually increased.

During the second world war the company's ships were requisitioned for government service. It lost 30 of its fleet of 51 vessels. The Straits Company was made solely responsible by South-East Asia Command for the supply of all small cargo vessels needed for the liberation of the region. The period after 1945 was one of some difficulty. There were fluctuations and eventually decline in the company's shipping operations with Indonesia, Burma, Thailand, Indo-China and Malaya. By 1960 the subsidiaries taken over in the 1920s and 1930s had either been sold off or wound down. Only with Borneo was there sustained growth and the company in the 1960s had two main emphases – trade to and from Sabah and the provision of tankers for the carriage of mineral and palm oils. By the end of 1973, as well as traditional shipping, the Straits Group (of which the Straits Steamship Company was now a part) was engaged in engineering, oilfield services, property development, data processing, road haulage and insurance-broking.

Home port Singapore: a history of Straits Steamship Company Limited 1890-1965. By K.G. Tregonning. Singapore: Published by Oxford University Press for Straits Steamship Company Limited, 1967. xii, 321p., ill. Bibliog. Index.

Malay waters: the story of little ships coasting out of Singapore and Penang in peace and war. By H.M. Tomlinson. London: Hodder and Stoughton, 1950. 199p.

[A popular account of events in the history of the Straits Steamship Company.]

'The origin of the Straits Steamship Company.' By K.G. Tregonning. ***Journal of the Malaysian Branch of the Royal Asiatic Society*** (Singapore), Vol. 38, Part 2 (December 1965), pp. 274-89.

The Straits Steamship Fleet 1890-1975. [By W.A. Laxon.] Singapore: Straits Steamship Company Limited, 1976. i, 72p., ill. Index.

[Includes a brief history of the company.]

[British Library of Political and Economic Science.]

618. STRAITS TRADING COMPANY

The Company owed its origins to a German, Herman Muhlinghaus, who had worked for two Singapore merchant houses. In 1886 he persuaded a reluctant Scot, James Sword, to join him in a venture to bring western methods of production to tin-smelting in Malaya. The two partners bought a second-hand smelter at Teluk Anson near the mouth of the Perak River and through generous loans from the Chartered Bank **(102)** were able to pay the Chinese prospectors in cash for their tin-ore (unlike existing European firms). The operation came close to bankruptcy as the Teluk Anson smelter was not efficient and the two entreprencurs were only saved by discovering considerable quantities of processed tin in the ground under the smelter – probably including tin smelted by the previous owner. By this time two of the Malay states had removed their ban on tin-ore exports. This allowed Muhlinghaus and Sword to move their business away from the Malayan jungle. They chose to set-up a more modern plant in a disused dry dock belonging to the Tanjong Pagar Dock Company **(619)** in Singapore. This called for considerable amounts of additional capital and for this purpose a Straits Trading Company was floated in Singapore during 1887. The new company was to be allowed to engage in a wide range of possible activities beyond simply tin-smelting.

From the flotation of the company up to the first world war, the history of the Straits Trading Company is one of successful expansion. Using ores from Malaya and the Dutch East Indies, the company's tin was recognised as being of the purest quality in the world. Indeed the company became the world's leading tin producer. It invested in a substantial branch network throughout Malaya to procure the ore and in 1901 opened a second smelting plant at Butterworth on a stretch of the Malayan coastline opposite Penang. After the first world war the company encountered considerable difficulties. In 1921-2 the managing director of the day caused huge losses by stockpiling tin-ore when the market was falling. During the 1930s the company suffered from the international tin regulation schemes which favoured high-cost producers. It was forced to make large reductions in staff and close the Butterworth smelter (although this was to re-open at the beginning of the second world war). It also diversified into tin-mining and rubber plantations in the latter case by taking over a substantial area of jungle land in Kedah.

The company's plant suffered considerable destruction during the Japanese occupation of Malaya and Singapore in the second world war. The support of the Chartered Bank was crucial in the re-establishment of the Straits Trading Company. With the help of retired staff and by canabalising plant, it was possible to resume smelting in a small way late in 1946 and five of the Singapore smelters were operating by April 1947. However it took until 1955 for the modernised Butterworth plant to be completed and re-commissioned. Long before this the company had returned to profit in 1948. From the 1950s there was a major change in the composition of the Straits Trading Company with very substantial shareholdings being acquired by Malay Chinese.

Straits tin: a brief account of the first seventy-five years of The Straits Trading Company, Limited 1887-1962. By K.G. Tregonning. [Singapore]: Printed by The Straits Times Press, [1962]. xii, 84p., ill.

619. TANJONG PAGAR DOCK COMPANY

For its first forty years Singapore did not have a proper dockyard and goods were unloaded from ships by lighter at the mouth of the Singapore River. Around 1860 two dockyard schemes came to fruition. One was for a Patent Slip and Dock Company (re-named the New Harbour Dock Company in 1875). The other was for a large dock on the west side of Tanjong Pagar. The Tanjong Pagar Dock Company was registered in September 1864 and its Victoria Dock was opened in October 1868.

In its first years the dock was not profitable and it was the wharves which kept the company going. However the opening of the Suez Canal changed things. Whereas dock revenues were only Singapore $22,700 in 1870, they had risen to $54,000 by 1876. A second dock became necessary and the Albert Dock, as it was named, opened in 1879. Dock profits fell again in the 1880s but by the 1890s they were close to the $300,000 mark each year. The company was wound up in 1899 and a new one was incorporated with a larger capital. In 1900 it merged with the New Harbour Company and what amounted to a dockyard monopoly came into existence in Singapore.

The Tanjong Pagar Company aimed to do as much business as was possible with the big ocean ships. This class of shipping held much more cargo proportionate to the wharf space occupied than did small coasters. The trade also involved two visits from the ships – on their way out to the Far East and on their return. The company at its start used Malay labour but soon switched to Chinese. It did however face considerable difficulties with its labour force. There was much pilferage and sympathy strikes often occurred.

The Tanjong Pagar Company's main operational problem was the funding of adequate development projects. Its shareholders were vociferous in demanding high dividends and a scheme existed to enhance directors' incomes if profits were over 10 per cent. In addition, directors were paid substantial 'contributory payments' if they brought business to the company. After 1870 (with only three exceptions) dividends were never below 10 per cent annually and after 1894 they did not go below 14 per cent. By 1904 they were effectively 52 per cent. These levels did not allow adequate resources to be put into the business for development. The establishment of a London Consulting Committee of European shareholders in 1883 further accentuated the difficulties as these individuals were apt to go behind the backs of the Singapore board directly to the chairman and staff.

Between 1885 and 1900 the company's facilities remained unaltered largely because negotiations were taking place with the Admiralty for the building of a naval yard which would have brought subsidies. However these negotiations fell through in 1899 and the company then started serious planning. By this time the situation was already grave. There was considerable congestion and delays in the Singapore docks. It was not entirely the company's fault that it took until 1904 before it adopted a development scheme. As this involved expenditure of some twelve million Singapore dollars, the directors applied to the Government of the Federated Malay States for a loan. In November 1904 the British Colonial Secretary decided that he favoured the expropriation of the company – an early example of nationalisation. The necessary legislation was passed in 1905 and the company ceased to exist. In 1906 an arbitrator awarded the shareholders Singapore $761.76 for each $100 share.

The Tanjong Pagar Dock Company, 1864-1905. By George Bogaars. Singapore: Printed at the Government Printing Office, 1956. (Memoirs of the Raffles Museum, No. 3, December 1956.) pp. 117-244, ill.

CHAPTER 7

Histories of British multinationals and other British companies which had branches, subsidiaries or networks in parts of Asia

701. BARCLAYS BANK (DOMINION, COLONIAL AND OVERSEAS)

Barclays DCO was set-up by Barclays Bank in 1925 as the bank felt a need for an overseas presence. Barclays DCO was an independent operation and was formed by the amalgamation of the Colonial Bank (largely active in the West Indies and East Africa), the National Bank of South Africa and the Anglo-Egyptian Bank. It is the later bank (originally acquired by Barclays in 1920) and the subsequent history of operations which are of concern to this bibliography.

The Anglo-Egyptian Bank was established in 1864 with its first branch being opened in Alexandria. The original sponsors were the Agra and Masterman's Bank and a French finance company belonging to Samuel Laing. The bank attracted commercial business on a modest scale but its main operations were with the Egyptian government in discounting treasury bills. It also participated in syndicates providing the government with long-term loans. In 1878 it opened a branch in Cairo; in 1913 it extended activities to Khartoum; while in 1919 a further branch was established in Port Sudan. In 1918 the bank moved into Palestine after General Allenby called for the extension of banking services in the British-administered territory. Here the Anglo-Egyptian Bank helped to shore up local banks and worked for the Palestine Currency Board.

The new Barclays DCO therefore found itself in 1925 with some 12 branches in Egypt, 5 branches in Palestine and 4 in the Sudan as well as a presence in Malta and Gibraltar. It rapidly implemented a local control system with the branches being run from Alexandria. However the Palestine branches were separated off in 1934 and thereafter were controlled from Jerusalem. The first years in the region for Barclays DCO were extremely difficult. The financial state of the Anglo-Egyptian branches was extremely serious and many bad debts came to light. None of the Sudan branches was making a profit and matters were exacerbated by the very weak cotton market throughout the 1930s. Just before the second world war, Barclays DCO was anxious to expand in the Middle East but it judged it unwise to open branches in other countries. Instead it acquired a considerable shareholding in the Eastern Bank.

The second world war brought heavy allied expenditure in the Middle East and large numbers of military accounts were opened with the bank. Barclays DCO was also agent for the British Secretary of State for War in Egypt. Turnover in Cairo in 1939 was £6 million. During the next four years this rose to almost £300 million. Taking all Middle East branches together, turnover in 1940-3 was nearly £600 million. The bank's most difficult period occurred after the fall of Tobruk in June 1942. There was a run on the Egyptian branches and in a single week £7 million was paid out in cash and £4.5 million was remitted abroad. However the steadfast action of the staff (mostly non-British) stemmed the crisis. In April 1943 the bank opened a branch in Tripoli at the request of the British military authorities. This branch was much used by *haj* pilgrims amongst others.

The post-war history of Barclays DCO in the Middle East region was a sad and difficult one. There were big operational problems when Egypt left the sterling area in June 1947 while in 1947 and 1948 the Palestinian branches suffered from raids by Jewish nationalists seeking cash. In January 1952 the principal Cairo office was set on fire by Egyptian nationalists rioting against the British and eleven members of staff were killed. During the 1956 Suez invasion, the bank's Egyptian branches were sequestrated by the Egyptian government and expatriate staff were dismissed. In the 1960s the bank was unwilling to stake much additional capital in Libya because it feared its operations in the country might suffer a similar fate to those in Egypt. These forebodings proved justified when its 19 offices in Libya were nationalised in 1969. The 24 offices in Sudan were also to be nationalised in 1970.

Barclays DCO therefore ended 1970 with its main Middle Eastern presence confined to Israel. However the Isreali branch network was considered too small to be viable and in 1972 it merged with a subsidiary of the Discount Bank to form Barclays Discount Bank. The new bank had 48 offices in the country. By this time, however, Barclays DCO had ceased to exist. In October 1971 it was reconstituted as Barclays Bank International and became a wholly-owned subsidiary of Barclays Bank.

A bank in battledress: being the story of Barclays Bank (Dominion, Colonial and Overseas) during the second world war 1939-45. [London:] The Bank, 1948. viii, 212p., ill.

A banking centenary: Barclay's Bank (Dominion, Colonial and Overseas) 1836-1936. [London: The Bank, ?1938.] 270p., ill. Index.
['For private circulation' – Title page.]

Barclays: the business of banking 1690-1996. By Margaret Ackrill and Leslie Hannah. Cambridge: Cambridge University Press, 2001. xxi, 481p., ill. Index.
[Chapters 2 and 6 contain material on the history of Barclays DCO.]

The DCO story: a history of banking in many countries 1925-71. By Sir Julian Crossley and John Blandford. London: Barclays Bank International, 1975. xxvii, 339p., ill. Index.

702. BRITISH AMERICAN TOBACCO COMPANY

The British American Tobacco Company was established in 1902 as part of a settlement between the warring American Tobacco Company and the U.K. Imperial Tobacco Company. BAT was to handle the tobacco interests of the two concerns in overseas markets. In 1911 the American Tobacco Company was broken up as a result of the anti-trust legislation in the United States. It was required to sell its holdings in BAT and by 1914 about 70 per cent of the company's shares were owned by investors with British addresses. *For the operations of BAT in India see* Imperial Tobacco Company of India **(513)**.

East Asia

The new BAT inherited two main plants in East Asia from its founding companies. In Japan there was an operation based on Kyoto while in China BAT took over the Wills plant in Shanghai. In addition BAT continued to distribute its cigarettes in the Shanghai region through the merchant house of Mustard and Company in which it gained a controlling interest. There was not a great deal of further direct investment in the region before the first world war. However in 1904 the Japanese government nationalised its tobacco industry. Consequently BAT relocated to China where it built a factory in Hankow and increased facilities at Shanghai. An import branch was operated from Hong Kong.

The company's early operations in China were directed by James Thomas. In 1914 he divided China into five marketing regions which in due course (with the exception of Hong Kong) were to be supplied by their own factories. In 1919 BAT was employing (in one form or another) almost 10,000 people in China. The company utilised local Chinese merchant networks to sell its cigarettes and also created two joint ventures with prominent Chinese entrepreneurs. One of these, with the Wing Tai Vo organisation, resulted in a separate and parallel operation for the sale of BAT products and marketed its own distinctive brands of cigarettes.

BAT suffered considerably from the troubled state of China in the 1920s. There were strikes at its factories and boycotts of its products. Some of these actions were financed by BAT's competitors. The company was forced to shut down its factories in Hankow and Shanghai for a time in 1926 and 1927. Things improved after 1928 with the rise of the Chiang Kai-shek government and BAT was sympathetic to Chiang's attempts to impose his administration throughout China. In particular the firm made advance payments of its cigarette taxes to provide him with revenue. From 1928 BAT's sales boomed despite increasing competition from the Japanese. The high watermark was 1937 when 5.5 billion sticks were sold. Thereafter sales went into sharp decline and by 1939 all of BAT's productive capacity was in areas of China controlled by the Japanese. Following Pearl Harbor, Japanese officials took command of the factories and by 1943 they were in full operational control. Immediately after the war BAT resumed operations in China but sales reached little more than a third of their pre-war peak. Except in Hong Kong, operations came to an end with the communist takeover.

Middle East

In 1905 BAT purchased the Cairo-based manufacturer, Maspero Frères and in 1911 this firm opened a cigarette factory in Jaffa (which was closed during the first world war). BAT also purchased the African Cigarette Company during 1906. In making these purchases, BAT was driven more by the need to supply the European and Indian markets with Turkish cigarettes than a desire to develop sales in the Middle East. However when BAT purchased control of two further Middle Eastern cigarette firms after 1918, it was with the intention of expanding its business in the region. By 1923 the reopened Maspero Frères' factory in Jaffa was said to be producing 4 million cigarettes a month. In Egypt, BAT faced a fiercely competitive market and it took over a number of firms. The most important development was the merger in 1927 of BAT's Egyptian interests with those of the Matossian Company. A holding company was set-up, the Eastern Company, in which BAT and the Matossian brothers had equal shares. The joint venture had four factories in Egypt and at the end of the 1920s was achieving sales of nearly 5 billion sticks in the country. This was claimed to represent 90 per cent of the market. However the cigarette industry in Egypt was badly hit by the 1930s depression and the joint venture suffered heavy losses. There was an attempt to rationalise the operation in 1938 when manufacture of all the Eastern Company's brands was concentrated at a single factory.

South-East Asia

Shortly after its formation, BAT set-up its own office in Singapore to handle the import and sales of its cigarettes. As in China, the firm used Chinese merchant networks to undertake distribution. Sales suffered considerably during the first world war because of shipping shortages and after the war BAT had to cope with several sharp rises in Singapore excise duties on imported cigarettes. It responded by buying out a major British competitor and also by setting-up its own manufacturing facility in 1926. However in the early 1930s the Singapore authorities imposed heavy duties on imported tobacco leaf. This led BAT to cease production in Singapore and return to importing cigarettes.

In Indonesia, the company purchased a Dutch competitor, Anton Justman, in 1908. Then in the mid-1920s it constructed a factory in Cirebon and opened a further factory at Surabaya soon afterwards. By 1931 BAT was probably supplying about 70 per cent of western-style cigarettes in Java. Government action thereafter favoured the production of the local variety and, although BAT's production continued, possibilities for growth were constrained. During the 1930s BAT began manufacturing cigarettes in Indo-China and around 1936 the firm set-up a factory in Bangkok.

Big business in China: Sino-foreign rivalry in the cigarette industry 1890-1930. By Sherman Cochran. Cambridge, Mass.: Harvard University Press, 1980. (Harvard studies in business history; 33.) x, 332p., ill. Bibliog. Index. [A history of the growth of BAT in China as well as the Nanyang Brothers Tobacco Company (a local competitor).]

'British-American Tobacco Company.' Being pp. 44-69 of ***Encountering Chinese networks: Western, Japanese and Chinese corporations in China, 1880-1937.*** By Sherman Cochran. Berkeley: University of California Press, 2000.

Creating a distribution network for cigarettes in China, 1900-1941. By Howard Cox. Reading, University of Reading, Department of Economics 1995. (Discussion papers in international investment and business studies. Series B; Vol. 8 (1995/96).) 49p.

The global cigarette: origins and evolution of British American Tobacco 1880-1945. By Howard Cox. Oxford: Oxford University Press, 2000. xxii, 401p., ill. Bibliog. Index.

'Growth and ownership in the international tobacco industry: BAT 1902-27.' By Howard Cox. ***Business history*** (London), Vol. 31, No. 1 (January 1989), pp. 44-67.

'Learning to do business in China: the evolution of BAT's cigarette distribution network 1902-41.' By Howard Cox. ***Business history*** (London), Vol. 39, No. 3 (July 1997), pp. 30-64.

A pioneer tobacco merchant in the Orient. By James A. Thomas. Durham, N.C.: Duke University Press, 1928. 339p., ill. Index.
[Account of the early history of BAT's operations in China and elsewhere in Asia.]
[Bodleian Library, Oxford.]

703. BROOKE BOND AND COMPANY

Arthur Brooke was the son of a tea-wholesaler and in 1869 he set-up his own retail business, Brooke Bond and Company, in Manchester selling tea, coffee and sugar for cash. (There was no 'Bond'; the name was added for appearance.) By 1900 the firm had had its ups and downs and had become mainly a tea-blender and supplier of bulk and packet tea to the British trade. It was registered as a public company in 1892.

In 1900 the firm sent John McKay to investigate the position in Calcutta. He was to see whether it was possible to buy suitable teas in the Calcutta auctions more cheaply than in London. He was also to say whether Brooke Bond could create and make pay a packet and blended tea business in India. McKay reported favourably and in 1901 he returned to Calcutta to run the Brooke Bond operation in India. He had an early success in supplying tea to the Delhi Durbar of 1903 but in 1905, on instructions from London, he bought tea heavily on the market early in the season before the price collapsed. There were substantial losses and the firm's dividend was reduced that year. Thereafter McKay was given total responsibility for purchasing in Calcutta. McKay introduced three of the Brooke Bond blends of tea to the Indian market and sold them in tins which weighed a quarter of a pound. He also added a local brand named 'Kora' – the Urdu word for 'pure'. When political boycotts of British goods took place many products were affected but 'Kora' thrived. In 1912 the Indian part of the firm was incorporated as 'Brooke Bond and Company (India) Limited'. It had 96 people on the payroll and monthly sales of tea were of the order of 68,000 lbs. The firm was to take on agencies for biscuits, coffee, safety matches and tinned milk.

Immediately after the first world war the company bought its first tea estate in Assam to be followed by a further estate in India and two in Sri

Lanka. A tea warehouse in the Calcutta docks at Kidderpore was started-up and 16 new depots were opened. In Sri Lanka, Brooke Bond purchased Websters' Automatic Packing Factory in 1919 (taking it into that country's market) and in 1927 it built the Assambrook Mills for blending and packing. By the 1930s all Brooke Bond branches in India were managed by Indians and at the end of the 1930s 'little red vans' were in use, on the British model, to distribute tea to local markets and sell the 'Hotel Blend' to hot tea shops. (In India the 'vans' were pushed by hand.)

After independence separate Brooke Bond companies began operating in India, Pakistan and Sri Lanka. In 1953 in India the company had 2,200 depots and sub-depots, 7,000 acres of tea gardens, filled 30 million packets each week and serviced half a million dealers. It was estimated that 65 million cups of Brooke Bond tea were drunk each day. In Pakistan a modern blending and packing factory was provided in Karachi during 1948. The tea was brought by sea round the coast from Chittagong. In Sri Lanka times were difficult but in 1955 the company took over the Galaha Tea Company with a further three estates. Tea distribution was entrusted to E.B. Creasy and Company.

The Brooke Bond Group was taken over by Unilever **(724)** in October 1984.

Brooke Bond: a hundred years. Written by David Wainwright. [London:] Newman Neame Limited [for the Company], [1969]. 58, [16]p., ill.

704. CABLE AND WIRELESS

The company traces its origins to 1868 when the Anglo-Mediterranean Telegraph Company was set-up to lay a direct submarine cable between Malta and Alexandria. By that time there were already partly submarine and partly land telegraph connections between the U.K and India but they were unreliable, particularly where the lines went over Turkish and Persian territory. So it occurred to Sir John Pender, a wealthy British textile merchant, that a better service could be provided if telegrams were sent mainly by submarine cables under British control. With this aim in view he set-up two further companies to lay cable between Bombay and Suez and Porthcurno (in Cornwall) and Malta. (Suez and Alexandria were linked by land line.) The work of laying the cables was undertaken in the first half of 1870 and the chain was opened for public service in June of that year. In 1872 the three companies were amalgamated into the Eastern Telegraph Company.

In 1869 and 1870 Pender set-up another three companies to link India with Penang and Singapore; Singapore with Java and Australia; and Singapore with Hong Kong via Saigon. Work on all these cables was completed by the end of 1871. In due course the whole conglomerate became known as the Eastern and Associated Companies. The story of the concern up to the 1920s is basically one of geographical expansion of lines and duplication to take increased traffic. In 1880 Hong Kong was linked with Manila; in 1884 Foochow was linked with Macau via Shanghai and Hong Kong; and in 1894 Borneo was linked with Hong Kong and Singapore. The network was extended through North China in 1900 and an Aden-Colombo-Penang cable was introduced in 1913-14.

In the 1920s the Eastern Companies were much affected by the introduction of short-wave radio transmission. Marconi's Wireless Telegraph Company (set-up under a different name in 1897) was given a contract in 1924 by the British Post Office to build short-wave radio stations and these were beaming messages to Canada, Australia, South Africa and India by 1926 and 1927. Radio messages were cheaper and speech could also be transmitted. In 1928 an Imperial Wireless and Cable Conference was convened to examine the position. It recommended merging the overseas cable and wireless resources of the British empire. This was duly done in 1929. 'Cable and Wireless' was the name given to the company which was to acquire the shares of the affected companies while the new operating company had the title 'Imperial and International Communications'. This latter name was considered cumbersome and was changed to 'Cable and Wireless' in 1934.

The new concern came into operation at a difficult time. The 1930s depression reduced receipts by about 30 per cent. Consequently there were reductions in staff and much rationalisation of the structure. A new agreement with the British government in 1938 lessened some of the burdens on the company and lowered the standard revenue which was required of it but also enforced a reduction in the cost of telegrams. During the second world war Cable and Wireless faced a great number of difficulties. It was busy keeping bombed wireless stations going and mending submarine cables which had been cut. The loss of the Singapore station in February 1942 was a particularly heavy blow as it was the main base for traffic to the Far East and Australasia. Signals had to be re-routed via Canada and the Pacific and via West Africa and the Cocos Islands. Eleven of the company's stations and 18,000 miles of cable routes remained in Japanese hands until 1945. There was an immense increase in traffic. Over the entire system 231 million words were handled in 1938. This had risen to 705 million words in 1944. Cable and Wireless was nationalised in 1946 and was not returned to the private sector until 1981.

A century of service: a brief history of Cable and Wireless Ltd. 1868-1968. By K.C. Baglehole. Welwyn Garden City: Bournehall Press [for the Company], 1969. 54p., ill. Index.

Girdle round the earth: the story of Cable and Wireless and its predecessors to mark the group's jubilee 1929-1979. By Hugh Barty-King. London: William Heinemann, 1979. xvi, 413p., ill. Index.

The thin red lines. By Charles Graves. London: Standard Art Book Company, [?1946]. 183p., ill.
[A history of Cable and Wireless during the second world war.]

705. COMMERCIAL UNION ASSURANCE COMPANY

The Commercial Union was founded in the wake of the 'Great Tooley Street Fire' in London of 1861. As a consequence of the fire (largest in the city since 1666), the existing insurance companies raised their premiums to an extremely high level. So a sizeable group of London merchants and others decided to set-up their own Commercial Union Fire Insurance Company. The new company became involved in Asia almost immediately and by 1890 its net profits from fire insurance throughout the continent amounted to almost £16,000. Ten years later these exceeded £26,000.

East and South-East Asia

External agencies were established in Rangoon in 1862 and in Batavia, Manila and Shanghai in 1863. Good progress was made and in 1894 the CU acquired the Straits Fire Insurance Company of Singapore which it then converted into a Far Eastern branch. A sub-branch was founded at Hong Kong at this time which took on typhoon risks. At the start of the twentieth century a Japanese branch was established at Yokohama in 1901 and a Shanghai branch was set-up in 1908. The Shanghai branch suffered considerably from the troubled conditions of the 1920s in China but until 1928 it undertook extensive underwriting for British American Tobacco **(702)**. A sub-branch was set-up in Harbin in 1926. After the second world war, CU re-established branches in Djakarta, Kuala Lumpur, Singapore and Hong Kong. It was a member of the British Insurance Group in Japan.

Middle East

The CU considerably extended its activities here after the first world war. It became represented in Basra, Baghdad and Jaffa and revived pre-war agencies in Constantinople and Smyrna. However the Group left Turkey in 1923 following the Turkish occupation of Smyrna which gave rise to a very large volume of claims.

South Asia

The CU soon realised the importance of having its own branches in South Asia and one was opened in Calcutta in 1870. This suffered from some diminution of business in the early 1890s but it began to show excellent results around the turn of the century. A branch established in Madras in 1870 was closed after a year but was resurrected in 1897 and made headway underwriting fire risks in Mysore and the south. A branch was established in Bombay in 1893. In Ceylon the CU benefited from its acquisition in 1894 of part of the business of the British-based Economic Fire Office. This company had underwritten insurance risks on many tea estates. After independence the CU retained branches in Calcutta, Colombo and Karachi and there was a network of offices throughout South Asia.

In 1959 the CU merged with the North British and Mercantile Insurance Company. The latter concern had opened a branch in Shanghai in 1911. It also had a sizeable operation in India before 1914 with a central office and board of directors in Calcutta and branches in Bombay, Calcutta and Colombo.

A century of insurance: the Commercial Union Group of insurance companies, 1861-1961. A centenary history. By Edward Liveing. London: H.F. & G. Witherby, 1961. 320p., ill. Bibliog. Index.

706. THOMAS COOK AND SON

Thomas Cook was an enthusiastic supporter of the early Victorian temperance movement and the first excursion he organised was a return train journey in 1841 from Leicester to Loughborough where the party attended a temperance meeting. Out of this the famous travel business developed although it was barely profitable in the early years. In 1855 Cook took large numbers of people to Calais en route for the Paris Exhibition of that year. By 1868 Cook claimed to have organised the travel of some two million people in Britain and western Europe. Cook's son, John Mason Cook, was an important force in the firm from the 1860s. He became a partner in 1871 and sole partner from 1879 when Thomas retired. John Cook was more businesslike than his father and transformed Cooks into a profitable organisation.

Cook's first tours to Egypt and the Holy Land took place in 1869 and by 1873 these tours had become commercially very important for the firm which opened an office in Cairo and an agency in Jaffa. During 1875 John was allowed by the Khedive of Egypt to start a regular passenger service on the Nile between Aswan and Wadi Halfa. The following year Cook opened a hotel in Luxor. In 1880 he signed a ten-year contract with the Khedive which gave him complete control of the Nile steamers. During 1882 Thomas Cook and Sons conveyed from Cairo to Alexandria (at cost price) the British troops wounded during Arabi Pasha's nationalist revolt. The following year Cooks again were used in the evacuation of troops and civilians from Khartoum following the Mahdi's uprising. Later the firm transported the relief operation of some 18,000 British and Egyptian troops (with stores) from Alexandria to Wadi Halfa. This wore out the steamers and John Cook built a replacement fleet, the first vessel of which sailed in December 1886. Cooks were to transport British troops once more during the 1897-8 conquest of the Sudan although their role was more limited on that occasion. It was estimated that nearly half the firm's revenues in 1894 came from the Nile steamers and they played a very significant part in the net profits of £82,000 earned in 1900.

Cooks became involved in India as a result of an initiative of the Italian government. It wanted passengers to travel on the European land route via Brindisi and it offered Cook a commission on all passages booked from India to Brindisi. In 1881 John Cook visited India and set-up a Bombay office. Two years later a Calcutta office was established. In 1887, following a request from the Government of India, Cooks began conveying pilgrims on the annual *haj* to Mecca. Special pilgrim offices were opened in Bombay and Jeddah. Cooks greatly improved travelling conditions but the contract was ended in 1893 by which time 25,000 Muslims had been conveyed. During the 1890s Cooks set-up a special department to handle the travel arrangements of Indian Princes and the department remained in existence well beyond 1947. By the turn of the century Cooks had established offices in Rangoon, Colombo and Yokohama. There were more than 50 Cook's offices worldwide.

John Cook died in 1899 shortly after organising a visit to the Holy Land by Kaiser Wilhelm II. Two of Cook's sons took over the business and although they started new initiatives they lacked their father's entrepreneurial flair. The firm suffered considerably during the first world war when its total losses amounted to some £250,000. However most of its foreign offices remained open during the hostilities and the shipping and forwarding department grew considerably. After the war there was a resurgence in foreign travel and the Nile cruises really began again from 1923. In February 1928 the Cooks sold the business to the Compagnie Internationale des Wagons-Lits of Belgium for £3,500,000. In 1940 Cooks was taken over by the British Custodian of Enemy Property. It was rescued from near bankruptcy in 1941 by the British railway companies and a quarter of the overseas assets were assigned to Wagons-Lits after the war. Cooks remained with the British Transport Commission Holding Company from 1948 to 1972 when it was sold to a group led by the Midland Bank. In 1992 the Midland Bank sold the business to a German firm.

The romantic journey: the story of Thomas Cook and Victorian travel. By Edmund Swinglehurst. London: Pica Editions, 1974. 208p., ill. Bibliog. Index.

Thomas Cook: 150 years of popular tourism. By Piers Brendon. London: Secker & Warburg, 1991. xii, 372p., ill. Bibliog. Index.

The Thomas Cook story. By John Pudney. London: Michael Joseph, 1953. 264p., ill. Index.

707. DUNLOP RUBBER COMPANY

Dunlop traces its origins to a small venture launched in Dublin in 1889 to exploit John Boyd Dunlop's re-discovery of the pneumatic tyre principle. The concern was floated on the London Stock Exchange in 1896 as the Dunlop Pneumatic Company. In the early 1900s Dunlop acquired a rubber-goods business and a rubber-mills. These were organised in a subsidiary called the Dunlop Rubber Company. In 1912 all Dunlops' trading activities were vested in the Dunlop Rubber Company. Dunlop began developing its own rubber plantations at an early stage. Initially, possibilities in Brazil and West Africa were examined but these were not considered attractive. Then, following a visit to Ceylon by Sir Arthur Du Cros in 1910, the Dunlop board decided to purchase its first estate on the island. Du Cros' next visit to Asia also took in Malaya and it was there that the company was to develop most of its plantations. By 1919 Dunlop owned 50,000 acres of planted rubber estates in Malaya.

Dunlop was interested in the Japanese market from the early 1900s and rumours in 1906 that a competitor was starting-up caused Dunlop to launch a company in the country to which it provided technology in return for part of the equity. In 1909 a factory in Kobe began production, apparently specialising in tyres for rickshaws. The Japanese company came under full Dunlop control in 1928 and, although profits and turnover were expanding by the mid-1930s, the growth of warlike policies in Japan made the market less attractive to Dunlop in London. Attempts were made to sell-off a controlling part of the Japanese company to local interests but it did not prove possible to organise a sale before 1941.

Dunlop set-up a local company in India during the inter-war years as an alternative to using an agency house to sell its products. It was felt that a local company would be more attractive to Indian nationalist opinion and, in addition, the Government of India preferred giving contracts to Indian-registered companies. In 1936 Dunlop opened a factory in Calcutta. This was in response to reports that a competitor, probably Goodyear, was about to begin production in the country. By 1939 the Dunlop plant was employing 1,200 workers and was turning out annually 200,000 truck and car covers and tubes and a million cycle covers and tubes. The factory played a major part in the war effort and by 1945 its output was nearly four times that of 1939.

After the war Dunlop opened further tyre factories in Ambattur, India (1959); Nagaya, Japan (1962); and Malaysia (1963). Although Dunlop was manufacturing sophisticated rubber products of all types in Japan, its market share in the country fell from the pre-war level of 26 per cent to 7 per cent in 1960. It failed to take up a suggestion that it should invest £12 million in its plant there. Instead, during 1960, it entered into an agreement with the Sumitomo Corporation for the establishment of a new firm called Sumitomo Rubber Industries. The company was 45 per cent owned by Sumitomo and 40 per cent owned by Dunlop. As it happened Dunlop was in serious difficulties by the 1980s and during 1983 it was Sumitomo Rubber Industries which acquired Dunlops' tyre operations in much of the world for £112 million. (The Indian and United States' tyre operations were sold off separately in 1984.) The remainder of the Dunlop concern was to be taken over by the British conglomerate BTR.

Dunlop in war and peace. By Sir Ronald Storrs. London: Hutchison and Company, [1947]. xii,147p., ill.

The Dunlop story: the life, death and re-birth of a multi-national. By James McMillan. London: Weidenfeld and Nicolson, 1989. vii, 215p., ill. Index.

'The growth and performance of British multinational firms before 1939: the case of Dunlop.' By Geoffrey Jones. ***Economic History Review*** (Kendal), Second series, Vol. XXXVII, No. 1 (February 1984), pp. 35-53.

'The multinational expansion of Dunlop, 1890-1939.' By Geoffrey Jones. Being pp. 24-42 of ***British multinationals: origins, management and performance.*** Edited by Geoffrey Jones. Aldershot: Gower, 1986.

Wheels of fortune: a salute to pioneers. By Sir Arthur Du Cros. London: Chapman & Hall, 1938. xiii, 316p., ill. Index.

708. GENERAL ACCIDENT FIRE AND LIFE ASSURANCE CORPORATION

The 'General Accident & Employers' Liability Assurance Association' was established at Perth in 1885 by four members of the Highland and Agricultural Society of Scotland. The new concern became actively involved in Asia in the early years of the twentieth century.

East and South-East Asia

General Accident opened a Far Eastern Branch in Shanghai in 1903. The same year a presence was established in Japan and three years later in Hong Kong. Following the Japanese incursion into China in the late 1930s, the Far Eastern Branch was transferred to Singapore. General Accident ceased operations in China in 1949 and after the second world war the Singapore Branch controlled operations in the 'tiger' economies of Brunei, Hong Kong, Malaysia, Singapore and Thailand. These provided an ever-growing proportion of General Accidents' Pacific area business. The corporation re-opened representative offices in Beijing and Shanghai in the mid-1990s. General Accident was a member of the British Insurance Group in Japan after the second world war. It withdrew from the Group in 1993 as it had been unable to develop an acceptable market share and level of profitability in Japan.

Middle East

General Accident was represented in Cairo from 1903; in Alexandria from 1905; and in Iraq from 1930. The corporation had ceased operations in Aden by the mid-1960s and left Iran in 1979 following the overthrow of the Shah.

South Asia and Burma

General Accident appointed external agents in Bombay in 1902 and in Burma and Ceylon in 1904. The corporation acquired the Indian Guarantee and General Company in 1922 and this continued as a subsidiary with its own board in Bombay. General Accident withdrew from Pakistan in 1954 and India in 1955. It returned to India in the mid-1990s to participate in a joint venture with the Wadia Group.

A premium business: a history of General Accident. By Peter Young. Cambridge: Granta Editions, 1999. viii, 294p., ill. Index.

709. GLAXO LABORATORIES

Glaxo originated from the trading activities of Joseph Nathan. A Londoner, who settled in New Zealand in 1857, Nathan set-up an international merchandising business. In the 1900s it was realised that a new process for making dried milk-powder (suitable for babies and invalids) would help use-up the firm's surpluses from its New Zealand creameries. 'Glaxo Powder', as the product was called, was launched in 1908. After the first world war the business moved also into the manufacture of vitamins and pharmaceuticals. Glaxo Laboratories was registered as a separate company in 1935.

'Glaxo' powder was imported into India fairly soon after its development and H.J. Foster was appointed agent in India for the product in 1914. Although Foster died in 1925 and his business was taken over by the Nathans, the Foster name was retained for operations in India for the next 25 years. In 1933 the firm began packing 'Glaxo' powder from bulk in Bombay and in 1939 a new packing factory was opened at Worli.

After the second world war Glaxo decided to begin local manufacturing in India and a consultancy agreement was signed with Fosters in 1947. By 1952 antibiotic filling capacity in India had reached one million vials and the following year this had increased to 2.2 million vials. However during the mid-1950s Glaxo began to suffer from increased competition (including from a government-owned plant) and its share of the Indian penicillin market dropped to 31 per cent. At that point it had 65 per cent of the market in milk-foods and over 50 per cent of the market in vitamin B12. Glaxo then took the decision to expand operations in food products and pharmaceuticals other than penicillin. A new factory was erected in Aligarh in the late 1950s which manufactured 1,500 tons of milk-powder in its first season. A plant opened at Thana near Bombay in 1962 was designed to produce corticosteroids, laxatives and vitamin A.

Glaxo already had plants in Chittagong and Lahore in Pakistan when the country became independent. In 1948 it decided to move its Pakistan head office from Lahore to Karachi where it built new manufacturing and packing facilities in 1950. Glaxo set-up a new subsidiary in Pakistan in 1948 and five years later this was converted into a local private company. Primary production was begun in Pakistan in 1963 at the Renala milk factory.

The first fifty years: an account of the early life of Joseph Edward Nathan and the first fifty years of his merchandise business that eventually became the Glaxo Group. Compiled by Sir Harry Jephcott. [Wellington: Glaxo Group, 1969.] 118p., ill.
[British Library of Political and Economic Science.]

Glaxo: a history to 1962. By R.P.T. Davenport-Hines and Judy Slinn. Cambridge: Cambridge University Press, 1992. xiv, 406p., ill. Bibliog. Index.

'Glaxo as a multinational before 1963.' By R.P.T. Davenport-Hines. Being pp. 137-163 of ***British multinationals: origins, management and performance.*** Edited by Geoffrey Jones. Aldershot: Gower, 1986.

710. GUEST, KEEN AND NETTLEFOLDS (GUEST, KEEN, WILLIAMS)

The firm of Guest, Keen and Nettlefolds was created between 1899 and 1902 through two mergers in the British engineering industry. By 1930 the concern was a major producer of steel and dominated the UK market in fasteners (nuts, bolts, rivets, screws and hooks). It also had an established export trade with India but as far as sales of nuts and bolts were concerned, GKN was in competition with the local firm of Henry Williams India. This had been set-up in October 1922 by a Darlington railway and signal manufacturer and soon opened two works in Calcutta for the manufacture of steel-sleepers, fish-bolts, crossing-bolts and dog-spikes. Henry Williams was also to lay down three re-rolling mills.

After extensive discussions, GKN took a 51 per cent interest in Henry Williams India during 1934. A new company, Guest, Keen, Williams, was set-up and Owen R. Williams, who had run Henry Williams India, stayed on as chairman of the new company. GKN put in capital which allowed new nuts and bolts mills to be constructed but it is uncertain how profitable the company was before the second world war. It seems that Owen Williams did not run the new concern to GKN's satisfaction and in 1936 he resigned. GKN was not able, however, to purchase his share of the business until 1946 when it took on the name GKW.

There was a considerable increase in nut and bolt production in India during the war and in 1943 Guest, Keen, Williams bought a site at Bhandup near Bombay for further expansion. These works were completed in 1945 but in fact the plant purchased for Bombay was moved to Calcutta early in 1946. Bhandup was then used by GKN's constituent company, Sankey Electrical Stampings, which made cooking utensils, steel furniture and the like. At the end of the war GKN in India were poised to enter a period of expansion and commercial activity.

A history of GKN. By Edgar Jones.
Vol. 2: *The growth of a business, 1918-45.* Basingstoke: Macmillan Academic and Professional, 1990. xxxvii, 389p., ill. Bibliog. Index.

'Steel and engineering overseas: Guest, Keen and Nettlefolds' multinational growth, 1918-1965.' By Edgar Jones. Being pp. 164-83 of ***British multinationals: origins, management and performance.*** Edited by Geoffrey Jones. Aldershot: Gower, 1986.

711. IMPERIAL CHEMICAL INDUSTRIES

Imperial Chemical Industries was formed in 1926 by a merger of four companies: British Dyestuffs Corporation; Brunner Mond; United Alkali; and Nobel Industries. Although Nobel's explosives company sold small quantities of dynamite to Shanghai and Hong Kong in the 1880s, and although United Alkali had a presence in Japan in the 1910s and 1920s, it was Brunner Mond (set-up in 1873) which was the most important of the four companies in Asia before 1926. Brunner Mond supplied two main chemicals to the continent: soda-ash (used in industry and domestically) and ammonia-sulphate (an important fertiliser). In 1899 the company sent Henry Glendinning to China, Korea and Japan to investigate trading possibilities. As a result, the following year Brunner Mond appointed E.S. Little as its general manager in the Far East. Little established an office in Shanghai in 1903 and a branch network which in turn supported many individual agents. In India sales were achieved through agents initially and in 1911 the company opened its own office in Calcutta. It then opened a further branch office in Japan in 1918 to counteract profiteering by local dealers. By the 1920s Brunner Mond was itself acting as local agents for other British companies and in some years this provided considerably more than half its income in parts of Asia. During and after the first world war there was an immense increase in the value of Brunner Monds' trade with the area, particularly with Japan which became very important financially for the firm. In China profits were somewhat held back by the company's large European staff amounting to more than sixty people by 1926. Nonetheless between about 1918 and 1924 Brunner Monds' entire output of ammonia-sulphate was reserved for China. Sales jumped from 3,000 tons in 1924 to 69,000 tons in 1929.

After its formation, Imperial Chemical Industries found trading conditions in Asia much more difficult than those which had faced Brunner Mond. In China a local entrepreneur started manufacturing soda-ash and effectively was subsidised by the government. The whole region was subject to intense Japanese competition. Furthermore a major German company was able to supply fertiliser which was four times more efficient than ICI's. There was also competition from Germany in the area of dyestuffs. ICI did not favour local manufacturing but to try to reduce costs it decided in 1929 to send officials to both China and India to look at the possibilities of starting-up factories. Nothing resulted in China because of the Japanese entry into the country. However in India an alkali factory was set-up at Khewra in Jhelum District of the Punjab. ICI also established the largest sales network of any firm in the Indian subcontinent. By the mid-1930s it had 1,500 depots, 15,000 distributors and a staff of 2,500. The second world war provided some protection for the company as far as dyestuffs in India were concerned since the British naval blockade cut-off German imports. In response ICI started-up a local dyestuffs plant although this was later to cause the company some embarrassment. ICI continued trading in China until 1952 and its last European member of staff did not leave the country until 1956.

Crescent over Cathy: China and I.C.I., 1898 to 1956. By Patrick Brodie. Hong Kong: Oxford University Press, 1990. xi, 294p., ill. Index.

Imperial Chemical Industries: a history. By W.J. Reader.

Vol. I: ***The forerunners 1870-1926.*** London: Oxford University Press, 1970. xvi, 563p., ill. Bibliog. Index.

Vol. II. ***The first quarter-century 1926-1952.*** London: Oxford University Press, 1975. xvii, 569p., ill. Bibliog. Index.

712. LLOYDS BANK

The bank traces its origins to 1765 when the partnership between Taylors and Lloyds was established in Birmingham but it was not until February 1923 that Lloyds directly owned and ran an overseas bank. This occurred through the takeover (following British official pressure) of the ailing Indian banking firm of Cox and Company. Coxs had themselves been involved in a merger in October 1922 when Henry S. King and Company joined them.

It was owing to its position as an army agent (dating back to 1758) that Coxs set-up branches in India. In 1905 it opened its first office in Bombay to provide specialised services for regiments moving to India. Further branches were soon opened in Calcutta, Karachi, Rangoon, Rawalpindi and Srinagar. At first the army provided the mainstay of the business but gradually commercial connections were built up centred on the finance of India's overseas trade. Kings, which dated from 1816, had established branches in Bombay, Calcutta, Delhi and Simla. In 1919-20 it opened branches in Alexandria and Cairo to finance the cotton crop and general imports. It also owned two ginning factories in Egypt.

Lloyds found the Egyptian operation extremely unprofitable and, after examining the various alternatives, sold it off to the National Bank of Egypt **(407)** in September 1926. However Lloyds was to remain in South Asia until 1960 after an early offer to purchase the concern fell through. The bank which Lloyds took over was not profitable (losses amounted to £80,000 in 1924) and it was soon faced with a serious fraud in Bombay. However it re-organised both the Bombay and Calcutta operations and by the end of the 1920s it had opened further branches in Chowringhee, Lahore and New Delhi. By 1928 it was making a profit of £20,000 but then there was another fraud in Rangoon connected with the failure of a firm of rice-merchants. These difficulties were again surmounted and profits reached £100,000 in 1934. They then fluctuated and were just over £70,000 in 1939. Additional branches were opened in Amritsar, Darjeeling, Bombay and Peshawar.

The Rangoon branch was, of course, closed during the Japanese occupation and the staff left the country as best it could. In India there was increased activity. Deposits increased from £9.7 million in 1939 to over £38 million in 1945 and current accounts rose from 23,000 to 67,000 over the same period. Profits were more than £300,000 in 1945. Lloyds continued to run its eastern operation from Calcutta, even after the partition of India in 1947, but there were many new banking regulations to be adhered to and operations became more difficult. Lloyds found that the new governments did not look with favour at proposals that it should open new branches. Its own activities were hampered by a relatively small number of large borrowers and an inadequate branch network. Eastern affairs were taking a disproportionate amount of time in London. The business was therefore sold to National and Grindlays Bank **(516)** in 1960, Lloyds receiving about a quarter of the share capital of that bank in payment. By 1971 Lloyds had a 41.4 per cent share of National and

Grindlays' equity. Lloyds' decision to leave the East wisely anticipated a decision by the Burmese government in 1963 to nationalise banks.

Lloyds Bank 1918-1969. By J.R. Winton. Oxford: Oxford University Press, 1982. xi, 210p., ill. Index.

713. LONDON AND LANCASHIRE INSURANCE COMPANY

Like the Commercial Union **(705)**, the London and Lancashire was founded as a consequence of the 'Great Tooley Street Fire' of 1861. Alexander Gunn, a London merchant with some experience in company promotion, reasoned that a recurrence of the fire was possible not only in London but also in the crowded Liverpool docks. Gunn secured the support of influential figures in both cities and the new insurance company was operating by 1862. The same year external agents were appointed in Bombay and Calcutta. Further agencies were begun in Madras, Singapore, Hong Kong and Shanghai (1863); in Rangoon (1864); and in Batavia (1868).

The London and Lancashire established its own branch offices in Calcutta in 1888 and in Bombay in 1893. These offices were still in existence in the early 1960s. After Indian independence the company became associated with the British India General Insurance Company for the conduct of business in West Pakistan. A headquarters was set-up in Karachi in 1948.

London and Lancashire appointed Butterfield and Swire **(309)** as its agents in China from 1875 and this association continued until the communist takeover. (Swires then remained agents in Hong Kong.) Swires also acted as agents in parts of Japan until 1907. From that point, until the Pacific war, London and Lancashire had a succession of different agents. After 1951, Swires again became the company's agents in Japan.

London and Lancashire history: the history of the London and Lancashire Insurance Company Limited. By E.V. Francis. London: Privately published for the Company by Newman Neame, 1962. xi,171p., ill. Index.

714. MAY AND BAKER

John May, a manufacturing chemist, began a partnership with two others in 1834. That partnership came to an end in 1839 but May was then joined by the young William Baker who had managed his father's chemist business in London. By the time of the second world war, the firm of May and Baker was at the forefront of the production of sulphonamide drugs and was involved in the early commercial development of penicillin.

In March 1941 May and Baker established a subsidiary company in Singapore. Three years later the firm decided to set-up a similar company in Egypt. It had started a small-scale manufacturing plant in India (in rented premises) during 1943. By 1946 the London board had resolved to manufacture sulphonamides and ephedrine in India and in 1948 a factory was opened near Bombay. Branch offices of the firm were then opened throughout India.

In 1961 a new Indian factory began production at Bhandup and the range of products manufactured in the country was expanded. By 1965 the entire production staff was Indian and local production of drugs exceeded the firm's imports. In due course May and Baker retained only a 40 per cent interest in its Indian operations.

Until the 1960s May and Baker imported its products into Pakistan but at the end of the decade it built a factory in East Pakistan intending this to serve both halves of Pakistan. The creation of Bangladesh in 1971 left the firm with a plant larger than its needs but it maintained operations. In 1976 May and Baker took a 60 per cent shareholding in Wah Chemicals of Pakistan which gave it a factory near Rawalpindi.

A history of May and Baker 1834-1984. By Judy Slinn. Cambridge: Hobsons, 1984. 196p., ill. Bibliog. Index.

715. METAL BOX COMPANY

Metal Box came into existence late in 1921 through a merger of three firms: Hudson Scott; Atkins; and Barclay and Fry. (Two of these firms were much involved in printing on paper as well as printing and fabricating tinplate.) During the 1920s the new combine took over a number of related British firms and by the 1930s it was actively considering trading possibilities overseas. In 1933 a senior executive visited Asia. Prospects in China and Malaya were not considered attractive and an office which had been opened in Shanghai was closed. However it was felt that Metal Box could provide packaging in India for some of its existing UK customers like Brooke Bond **(703)**, Carreras and Glaxo **(709)**. The Metal Box Company of India was established in the spring of 1933 and in June a factory was set-up in Calcutta. Apart from a few senior British staff, the workforce was entirely Indian. Production soon expanded to take in the needs of makers of paints, polishes, confectionery and other goods. In 1935 a second factory was set-up in Bombay. By early 1939, turnover was around £67,000 or more than three times the 1933 figure.

The company further expanded in India during the second world war. By its close the turnover was around £4 million and it was employing 4,000 people. Management had come to the conclusion in 1944 that the Indian concern would in due course have Indian shareholders. Accordingly a 20-year consultancy agreement was signed between the British and Indian companies in 1946. The Metal Box Company of India prospered after independence. Sales of £4.3 million in 1956-7 had reached nearly £19 million in 1970. By the late 1960s Hindustan Lever (*see* Unilever **(724)**) was the biggest customer followed by Glaxo, Reckitt and Coleman and Esso. Management was gradually Indianised with the number of Europeans employed down to 19 in 1966. The last European chairman of the Indian company left in 1959. By 1970, the British Metal Box's holding in the Indian company was down to 60 per cent.

During the 1950s, Metal Box established local companies in Malaysia and Pakistan and in 1968 a company was established in Thailand. In the 1960s security printing (particularly of cheques) was begun in India and Malaysia.

Metal Box: a history. By W.J. Reader; research by Judy Slinn. London: Heinemann, 1976. xii, 256p., ill. Index.

716. PHOENIX ASSURANCE COMPANY

Phoenix Assurance was established as a result of meetings of a group of London sugar-bakers held late in 1781 with the aim of providing insurance amongst themselves. The operation was first known as 'The New Fire Office' but by 1785 it was calling itself 'The Phoenix'. The company entered Asia as early as 1827 when it appointed external agents in Calcutta and during the 1830s it was writing risks in China. At the time of the first world war, the Phoenix appears to have been the market leader of British insurance companies in East, South and South-East Asia.

East and South-East Asia

Agencies were established in Java (1852); Singapore (1855); Shanghai (1858); Penang (1861); Hong Kong (1862); Yokohama (1863); Manila

(1871); and Rangoon (1883). As in India, there was a sharp downturn in premium receipts during the late nineteenth century depression. In 1906 the Phoenix opened a branch in Shanghai with responsibility for all of East and South-East Asia. Thereafter there was a considerable growth of business. The Phoenix was particularly skilled at tapping local markets through the appointment of many sub-agents. In 1910, with takings of nearly £49,000, Japan was the Phoenix's best performer throughout the Far East and India. During the inter-war period, the insurer suffered heavily from the unsettled situation in China while in Japan it was effectively frozen out of the market by government policy. In 1968 the company retained branches or subsidiary companies in Malaya, the Philippines and Singapore and was a member of the British Insurance Group in Japan.

Middle East

External agents were appointed in Alexandria (1864) and Constantinople (1870) with many sub-agencies in the region. An agency was opened in Iraq in 1912 and lasted for almost 50 years while one in the Lebanon set-up in 1920 came to an end in 1963. Operations in Turkey ceased in 1922 following the hostilities in Smyrna. The Phoenix established many agencies in the Middle East (including the Persian Gulf) at the close of the second world war but most lasted for only relatively short periods. The Egyptian agencies were closed in 1956 and an agency at Aden was in existence between 1948 and 1967. In 1949 the Phoenix joined with the Israel Discount Bank to form Israel Phoenix.

South Asia

As well as the Calcutta agency, the Phoenix appointed agents in Madras and Bombay (1858) and Karachi (1864). From 1903 the Phoenix maintained a Branch in India (at Bombay) with managerial powers over a large part of the subcontinent but not Calcutta or Madras where it was evidently satisfied with existing arrangements. Premium income fell heavily during the depression from 1875 to 1890 but recovered strongly thereafter. There was a brief surge in receipts around the end of the first world war but, in the inter-war period, the Phoenix suffered from not having sufficiently large firms as its agents and sub-agents. Consequently the insurer was not able to compete effectively with rising Indian-registered companies. (The situation was not as bleak in Ceylon or Burma.) An Indian branch (covering the whole country) was established at Calcutta in 1922 and the company continued to maintain a presence there in 1968.

Phoenix Assurance and the development of British insurance. By Clive Trebilcock.
Vol. 1: 1782-1870. Cambridge: Cambridge University Press, 1985. xx, 792p., ill. Bibliog. Index.
Vol. 2: ***The era of the insurance giants, 1870-1984.*** Cambridge: Cambridge University Press, 1998. xxiv, 1064p., ill. Bibliog. Index.

Phoenix renascent: a history of the Phoenix Assurance Company Limited 1782-1968 and of the Pelican Life Insurance Office 1797-1907. By George Hurren. [London:] Phoenix Assurance Company Limited, 1973. 173, xviii, ill. Index.

717. PILKINGTON BROTHERS

Pilkingtons, established at St. Helens in Lancashire in 1826, had become the sole British manufacturer of plate glass by the twentieth century and was also a major producer of sheet- (window-) glass. The firm was reluctant to become directly involved in overseas manufacturing as it preferred to use its British plant as intensively as possible. However it did open an agency in China for a brief time during the 1920s.

In 1950 Pilkingtons took up a suggestion from the Hindusthan Development Corporation that it should provide know-how and finance for a joint venture in India. The firm contributed 48 per cent of the capital of Hindusthan Pilkington Glassworks which opened at Asansol in Bengal in 1954. Pilkingtons encountered considerable problems with the management of the new business and with the remittance of payments. However the works were rebuilt and extended in the early 1960s as the market for glass was expanding in India. Pilkingtons then became majority shareholder in the concern. It also took up an interest in a new fibreglass business. From that point on the company faced considerable labour problems in the sheet-glass works and by the later 1970s it was seeking to reduce its stake in the business. In 1982 Pilkingtons' holding was reduced to 28 per cent of the ordinary shares and 41 per cent of the preference shares. The following year all remaining shares were sold and Pilkingtons' interests in India were confined to a 40 per cent holding in the fibreglass operation.

Pilkingtons granted a float-glass manufacturing licence to Japan's second major glass maker, Nippon Sheet Glass (NSG), in 1966. Relations between the two firms were to become much closer in the 1980s

The glassmakers. Pilkington the rise of an international company 1826-1976. By T.C. Barker. London: Weidenfeld and Nicolson, 1977. xxxi, 557p., ill. Index.

Pilkington: an age of glass. The illustrated history. By T.C. Barker. London: Boxtree, 1994. 144p., ill. Index.

'Pilkington, the reluctant multinational.' By Theo Barker. Being pp. 184-201 of ***British multinationals: origins, management and performance.*** Edited by Geoffrey Jones. Aldershot: Gower, 1986.

718. PROVINCIAL INSURANCE COMPANY

The Bolton-based 'Provincial Fire Insurance Company' was formally inaugurated in October 1903. It was the outcome of an initiative by James William Scott who was the son of an early nineteenth century immigrant from Frankfurt. The company appears to have become interested in insurance possibilities in Asia after the first world war. However it took until 1938 for an external agency to become established in Bombay. By that time the company was also represented in Singapore. In 1929 the Provincial persuaded a local agent in Alexandria to takeover its fire business and establish a branch for it in Egypt. Offices were opened in Alexandria and Cairo. It was hoped the branch would develop a profitable fire business from the Egyptian cotton trade. Unfortunately the inter-war depression affected results and the business did not take off as quickly as had been expected. Although the branch provided the company's largest direct source of overseas fire business in the 1930s (about a third of all overseas fire receipts), it never managed to cover its costs. This would probably explain why the Provincial gave no thought to opening further branches in Asia.

The Provincial Insurance Company 1903-38: family, markets and competitive growth. By Oliver M. Westall. Manchester: Manchester University Press, 1992. xiv, 465p., ill. Bibliog. Index.

719. PRUDENTIAL ASSURANCE COMPANY

India and Ceylon

The 'Prudential Mutual Assurance, Investment and Loan Association' was registered in London in 1848. After the first world war the Prudential entered the Indian market and during 1923 it appointed Gillanders, Arbuthnot **(509)** as its chief life representatives in the country. Prudential organisations were set-up in the main Indian cities and in 1927 the first moves were taken to create a field-staff. The following year a manager for India and Ceylon was appointed with a headquarters in Gillanders' Calcutta building. New business for 1929 exceeded £1 million. By 1932 control of the field-staff was entirely in the Prudential's own hands and it was the company's policy to employ Indian staff as far as possible. Business continued to grow; in 1937 administration of the Burma business was transferred to the Prudential's Rangoon office. The company faced great difficulties during the second world war partly because of the fall of Burma and partly because of the need to move its entire Calcutta staff to Lucknow. However operations expanded during the war and by 1945 new business totalled more than £2 million. After independence the Prudential's operations initially prospered in the region but in 1956 the Government of India nationalised its life assurance industry. Ceylon also created a nationalised insurance corporation in 1961 with Pakistan similarly nationalising insurance operations ten years' later.

Middle East

By 1921 the Prudential was writing insurance in Egypt through the agency of an Alexandria cotton company. In 1934 the Prudential established its own office in Cairo to provide life assurance and it also appointed general agents in Palestine. The company suffered considerably from the political turmoil in the Middle East and, although progress was initially made in Palestine, considerable difficulties were encountered in Egypt where it was unable to find good field-agents. Eventually, in 1943, the Prudential decided to employ part-time agents in Egypt (outside Cairo and Alexandria). The Prudential benefited from the elimination of Italian competition in the area following that country's entrance into the second world war in June 1940. Total sums assured in Middle East countries exceeded a million Egyptian pounds by 1941. After the war there was renewed political discontent in the Middle East. As a result the Prudential had decided to stop writing new life assurance in Palestine by 1950 and in Egypt and the Sudan by 1955. In 1957 the company's assets in Egypt were seized and the Prudential was not compensated for them until 1964.

South-East Asia

The Prudential was transacting fire business in Singapore and Malaya through an agency house as early as 1924. In 1931 the company established a branch in Singapore which supplied most of the usual classes of insurance. Progress was most rapid in the life assurance field. Although employing agents from all communities, the company was able to secure particularly able Chinese businessmen as its representatives. The Prudential established sub-offices during the 1930s in Kuala Lumpur, Ipoh, Malacca and Penang. In 1935 operations were extended to Borneo. The Prudential re-entered the region at the end of the Japanese War and accepted new business from August 1946. Thereafter there was steady growth with good results on the life assurance side but profits on general insurance fluctuated considerably. By the 1990s the Prudential was operating in Singapore, Hong Kong, Malaysia, Thailand, Indonesia and the Philippines. Offices had been set-up in China and Vietnam and the company was re-establishing itself in India.

A century of service: the story of the Prudential 1848-1948. Compiled by R.W. Barnard. [London: The Company, 1948.] viii, 139p., ill.

Salute to service: the Prudential in the second world war. Compiled by G.L. Hosking. London: The Company, 1947. xii, 146p., ill.

A sense of security: 150 years of Prudential. By Laurie Dennett. Cambridge: Granta Editions, 1998. ix, 438p., ill. Bibliog. Index.

720. ROYAL EXCHANGE ASSURANCE CORPORATION

Royal Exchange Assurance was established in June 1720 at the height of the South Sea Bubble speculation in Britain. Throughout the eighteenth century the corporation had a sizeable proportion of its investments in East India Company paper. The corporation's great expansion overseas occurred late in the nineteenth century after which overseas premiums and profits became very important for it. In addition some of REA's subsidiaries established in due course their own overseas networks. These included such companies as: The Motor Union Insurance Company, National Plate Glass Insurance Company and The State Assurance Company.

REA established its own agencies in Egypt (1890); Ceylon, Turkey, the Philippines and Burma (1891); Java (1892); Japan (1895); Singapore (1896); and India (1900). In China the corporation used other firms as agents, the most famous being Butterfield and Swire (**309**). By the time of the first world war, net annual marine premiums in India were of the order of £40,000 while annual fire premiums in India, Burma and Malaya came to £35,000.

After the war, REA was one of the first companies to re-establish itself in the Middle East. In 1920 a Levant Branch was established which covered the Balkans, Asia Minor and the Middle East. However these arrangements lasted only until 1923 after which the Egyptian Branch resumed its independence with responsibility for Egypt, Sudan, Syria, Palestine, Cyprus and Malta. The corporation's income was badly affected in Malaya during the great depression because of the reduction in commodity prices. It is estimated that between 1930 and 1931 revenues were reduced by 25 per cent. Throughout the inter-war period the corporation suffered considerably from fluctuating exchange rates.

The Royal Exchange Assurance: a history of British insurance 1720-1970. By Barry Supple. Cambridge: Cambridge University Press, 1970. xxii, 584p., ill. Bibliog. Index.

721. SHELL TRANSPORT AND TRADING COMPANY

The Samuel family business in the mid-Victorian period centred on general trade with the Middle East and Orient including the import into Britain of shells and shell-boxes which were much in vogue at the time. On the death of their father in 1870, Marcus and Samuel took over the business, Samuel in particular becoming very involved with Far Eastern trade. Around 1890 the brothers looked into a proposal for transporting oil from the Russian oilfields in Baku, via Batum, to Asia where the oil would be sold. The Baku fields and the rail link to Batum were under the control of the Paris Rothschilds and the proposal involved a commercial war with the American Standard Oil Company which was seeking a world monopoly in oil sales.

The Samuels decided that the proposal would be viable but only if the oil was shipped in bulk tankers rather than in drums packed in cases which was the main mode of transporting oil at the time. They had a fleet of tankers built – eleven were in use by the end of 1893 – which were so safe and clean that the Suez authorities allowed them to go through the Canal. The Samuels used a network of seven famous Eastern agency houses to sell the oil. Tanks and associated unloading facilities were constructed throughout Asia mainly under the supervision of Mark Abrahams, Marcus Samuel's nephew. The oil was sold under the name 'Shell Oil' and when it was found that it sold best in cans, the Samuels had tin-plated cans produced locally in a bright red colour which became famous.

In 1893 the Samuels felt that there was a need to formalise the selling arrangements and a 'Tank Syndicate' was set-up consisting of themselves, the agency houses and a ship-broker. The Syndicate owned all the tanks and unloading facilities in the Far East. Members shared profits and losses and all transactions were done on a joint basis. In 1897 these arrangements were taken a stage further when the 'Shell Transport and Trading Company' was registered. It consisted of the members of the Tank Syndicate but the new company also controlled the Samuels' tanker fleet.

The original agreement with the Rothschilds for the supply of oil lasted until 1899 and Marcus Samuel became concerned when Standard Oil and the Rothschilds came to an agreement over oil pricing in 1895. Samuel feared his oil supply might become too costly and the tankers be unemployed. He therefore decided that Shell should prospect for oil itself in Borneo. The operations were not very well organised although Mark Abrahams (who was placed in charge) undoubtedly prevented complete catastrophe. By 1898 the concession was producing 130 barrels of oil a day but it was of a heavy type. This was not of much use for illumination but was excellent as a fuel-oil. In 1899, as it happened, the Rothschild agreement was renewed.

Marcus Samuel decided that the way forward in the circumstances was to maximise sales of fuel-oil. Considerable expenditure was incurred in 1899 with this aim and at first it brought substantial profits. The situation was also helped by an agreement with the Royal Dutch Petroleum Company not to undercut each other in Eastern markets. However the new century was to bring a series of misfortunes for the Shell company. From 1900 the price of fuel-oil tumbled; tests in 1902 using fuel-oil to power British naval vessels proved unsuccessful; and the same year the Suez Canal was closed to Shell tankers following a disastrous fire on one ship. Somewhat reluctantly Marcus Samuel agreed to join with Royal Dutch and the Rothschilds to form the Asiatic Petroleum Company. This concern was to market the oil of the three partners in Asia as a joint operation.

The Samuels undoubtedly hoped that the new Asiatic Petroleum Company would use Shell tankers to transport its oil. It was however not bound to do so and the Royal Dutch persuaded it to use cheaper tankers whenever it could. The result was that half of the Shell vessels were unemployed. It was a time which called for high management skills on the part of the Samuels but regrettably Marcus's attention became dominated by civic and other responsibilities. (He was the first Jewish Lord Mayor of London in 1902-3.) By 1906 Shell was face-to-face with ruin. The non-Asian interests were sold to the Deutsche Bank and Marcus was forced to come to an accommodation with the Royal Dutch as far as the remaining business was concerned. The outcome of these negotiations was that Royal

Dutch and Shell would stay separate entities but would unite their interests and would share risks and rewards on the basis of 60 per cent to the Royal Dutch and 40 per cent to Shell. The new arrangements came into effect on 1 January 1907 and from that date, although the 'Shell Transport and Trading Company' continued to exist, its destinies were controlled by the Royal Dutch Shell Group which is not a majority British-owned concern. Consequently consideration of its history in this bibliography must conclude at this point.

A century in oil: the "Shell" Transport and Trading Company 1897-1997. By Stephen Howarth. London: Weidenfeld & Nicolson, 1997. 397p., ill. Index.

Marcus Samuel: first Viscount Bearsted and founder of the 'Shell' Transport and Trading Company 1853-1927. By Robert Henriques. London: Barrie and Rockliff, 1960. xi, 676p., ill. Bibliog. Index.

The technical development of the Royal Dutch/Shell 1890-1940. By R.J. Forbes and D.R. O'Beirne. Leiden: E.J. Brill, 1957. ix, 670p., ill. Bibliog. Index.

722. STANDARD LIFE ASSURANCE COMPANY

Standard Life was established in 1825 under the auspices of the Insurance Company of Scotland which was a fire office. By the 1840s the directors of Standard Life became anxious to attract life assurance business from professionals in the British colonies. Rather than take on the business itself, Standard Life floated a new company for the purpose, the 'Colonial Life Assurance Company', which held its first board meeting in January 1846. During 1847 the new concern appointed agents in India, Ceylon and Shanghai but its early years in Asia were difficult. Some of the houses representing it soon collapsed while its life assurance rates were considered uncompetitive. However in the years before 1857, the agents in Madras and Colombo were producing as much new business for the company as it was receiving from the whole of Canada. In the mid-1860s, following a visit by its inspector, Colonial Life came to the conclusion that possibilities in northern India were too important to be left to agents and decided to establish its own branch in Calcutta. This was set-up in 1869 but by this time Colonial Life had ceased to exist. In 1866 it was dissolved; its policies, risks and activities having been taken over by Standard Life.

There were considerable difficulties in India for Standard Life in the 1870s caused partly by the declining value of the rupee and also by the company's reluctance to insure native lives. However a Bombay branch was set-up in 1876 which oversaw operations in Madras and Ceylon. In

1877 the relatively small India Life Office was taken over. By the 1880s Standard Life dominated the Indian life assurance market and was doing nearly 2,500,000 rupees' new business a year. This success story continued until the mid-1890s but by the new century Standard Life faced a considerable decline in business in India. It responded by expanding elsewhere in Asia. Offices were opened in Shanghai in 1900 and Cairo in 1901. However the decline in the East continued largely because of poor management, outmoded sales techniques and uncompetitive rates. By 1915 drastic pruning of activities had been decided upon. The Singapore and Straits Settlement branch was replaced by an agency while the following year the Bombay branch was closed down. In 1922 the Shanghai branch was closed and for a time Calcutta took over responsibility for the whole of the Far East. (Standard Life was to continue business in China until the late 1940s.)

As it happened the Calcutta branch performed well after the first world war. In 1925 Standard Life celebrated its centenary by converting into a mutual society and by this time it enjoyed a virtual monopoly of business from Indian civil servants. Two years later the society took on record levels of new business in the subcontinent. However the 1930s brought fresh difficulties. The Cairo office was closed in 1930 as a consequence of the declining political situation. In India there were the effects of the depression and Gandhi's non-co-operation movement with its boycott of British firms. Matters were made worse by the setting-up of the new provincial ministries in 1937 and the passing of tough new insurance legislation. Operations in Bombay were wound up in 1939 and the Calcutta office was closed in 1946 when Standard Life's remaining business was transferred to the Gresham Life Assurance Company. Standard Life had therefore effectively left Asia before the years of Western decolonisation. It was to return to Shanghai in 1996.

The overseas history of the Standard Life Assurance Company. [Edinburgh: The Company, 1958.] 2 vols. (339p. continuously paged), ill. Indexes (in both vols.).

[Two chapters in Vol. 2 are relevant: Chapter XXI – 'Campaign in Egypt and the Mediterranean' and Chapter XXIV – 'The Standard under Oriental skies'.]

[Seen by courtesy of Standard Life Assurance Company.]

'The pattern of investment of the Standard Life Assurance Company 1875-1914.' By J.H. Treble. ***Business history*** (London), Vol. 22, No. 2 (July 1980), pp. 170-88.

Standard Life 1825-2000: the building of Europe's largest mutual life company.

By Michael Moss. Edinburgh: Mainstream Publishing, 2000. 431p., ill. Bibliog. Index.

The Standard Life Assurance Company 1825-1925. By Sir William Schooling. Edinburgh: William Blackwood and Sons, 1925. 122p., ill. Index.

723. SUN INSURANCE OFFICE

The Sun Insurance Office resulted from pioneering initiatives in the field of fire insurance by Charles Povey early in the eighteenth century. In March 1710, Povey transferred to the Company of London Insurers all his rights in the 'Exchange House alias Sun Fire Office'. The Sun became involved in Asia from the middle of the nineteenth century.

East Asia and South-East Asia

The Sun appointed external agents in Hong Kong, Shanghai and Canton in 1852; Singapore (1856); Batavia (1857); Yokohama (1864); Penang and Manila (1865); Saigon (1869); and Bangkok (1890). The company met considerable difficulties in Penang but in Java business was particularly good. An important development was the Office's acquisition of the Patriotic Assurance Company of Dublin in 1906 with its extensive Far Eastern connections. This came under the control of the Sun's newly established Far Eastern branch with its head office in Shanghai. As a consequence Java was divided into two for agency purposes. It was found that the area covered by the Far Eastern branch was too wide and, on his own initiative, the local general manager established a separate Japanese branch in 1911 with offices in Tokyo and Osaka.

Middle East

The Sun appointed a local solicitor as its agent in Smyrna in 1863. Four years later an agent was appointed in Constantinople and by the early 1880s there were external agents in Cyprus, Beirut, Jerusalem, Alexandria and Port Said.

South Asia

The Sun was re-insuring risks for the Bombay Fire Office as early as the 1840s. In 1852 it appointed external agents in Bombay, Madras and Calcutta and an agent in Colombo in 1857. By 1897 the Sun had decided that it wished to set-up its own branch in India. It was able to do this by taking over the Asiatic Company of Bombay and retained the Asiatic's general manager as its first manager for India.

After the first world war the Sun continued to expand its foreign commitments and built up an organisation of considerable complexity.

The Sun Insurance Office 1710-1960: the history of two and a half centuries of British insurance. By P.G.M. Dickson. London: Oxford University Press, 1960. xiv, 324p., ill. Bibliog. Index.

724. UNILEVER

Unilever came into existence in September 1929 through the merger of the Dutch Margarine Union and the British company, Lever Brothers. The Margarine Union consisted of the firms of Jurgens and Van den Bergh whose businesses, originally in butter, went well back into the nineteenth century and beyond. Lever Brothers, established around the mid-1880s, had a history in soap and margarine-making and had taken over a number of important, related businesses. Strictly speaking, therefore, Unilever is not a company which is wholly-owned by the British. It would however be impossible to exclude it from this bibliography. Inclusion of the company is also justified by the fact that very soon after the merger the effective headquarters of the new concern was established in London. Moreover in Asia, Unilever very largely built on the existing Lever Brothers' sales operations.

Details of Unilever's main operations in Asia are given below on a country basis.

China

Levers' exports of soap to China had reached about 3,000 tons in 1912 and the following year the company opened a soap factory at Kobe in Japan partly with the object of supplying the Chinese market. Over the next five years there were suggestions of a link up with either Brunner Mond, Crosfields or Gossages for the purpose of jointly constructing a soap factory in China but the project did not come about. However in 1923 Lord Leverhulme set-up a small soap-making factory in Shanghai and in 1932 a margarine factory also began operations in the city. The company faced considerable difficulties because of the Japanese invasion in the late 1930s. Notwithstanding this, 1939 sales were up by more than

25 per cent on 1937 (itself a good year). Unilever's factories were nationalised following the communist takeover in 1949 and the company did not return to China until 1986.

India

Levers was exporting soap to India from early in its existence and Lever (India) was set-up as a British registered company in 1913. In 1933 Unilever decided to manufacture soap locally and the first consignment was produced in Bombay in 1934. Meanwhile Van den Berghs had started making vegetable ghee (vanaspati) in Bombay in 1932. Both operations came about because of increasing Indian tariffs on imported goods. Up to the second world war, soap sales were good and there was spectacular growth in vanaspati production. However in the longer term vanaspati sales were checked while between 1947 and 1965 soap and detergent production increased about five times. After the war Unilever also went into toothpaste manufacture and other health-care products. However by the mid-1950s it was becoming crucial for the concern to find new opportunities in India. It turned to milk products, dried vegetables and animal feeds but only the latter could be counted a success. All told Unilever regarded India as a rewarding market. Between 1956 and 1965 it achieved 9.3 per cent average annual profits there compared with 9 per cent in Europe.

Indonesia

Until the mid-1930s Lever soaps had dominated the import market while on the edible fats side the Margarine Union companies had not found it feasible to manufacture locally. In 1933 the company decided to begin manufacturing soap at a factory in Jakarta. Three years later Unilever went into the production of margarine on the site in order to compete with cheap imports. Business was expanding when the Japanese invaded in 1942. Sales of edible fat products had risen over six times between 1936 and 1940.

After the war Unilever in Indonesia had twelve relatively successful years until 1957. There then followed ten very difficult years. Up to about 1953 the company was anxious to diversify and follow up opportunities and by 1957 soap sales were about six times the 1940 figure. However from the mid-1950s company executives were becoming increasingly concerned about the economic future of Indonesia and no fresh capital was remitted from Europe. By this time soap and edible products were ceasing to make a profit and the company was dependant on other health-care products to keep it in the black.

From 1957 Indonesia was effectively a quasi-dictatorship and although Sukarno respected the concern, Unilever faced import controls, licensing regulations and increased trade union power. In addition there were periods of hostility between Indonesia and the Dutch and then Indonesia and the British. During 1964 communist workers took control of the Unilever factories (relying on the help of local managers to run them) and government 'supervisors' were appointed. The London headquarters had lost control of its Indonesian operations and at one stage was prepared to press for compensation and disown responsibility for what was being done in its name. However in 1967 Unilever was allowed to resume control of the factories on its promise of fresh investment. Production was then only 15 per cent of the 1956 level but by 1973 it had returned to a little over the 1956 figures.

Pakistan

From about 1946 Unilever saw its future in the Pakistan area in terms of collaboration with the Ali family who were local entrepreneurs. The Alis owned (with others) a factory site at Rahim Yar Khan in Bahawalpur State on the Lahore-Karachi railway. It was decided to manufacture both vanaspati and soap at the factory. At first Unilever had only a minority interest in the concern but in 1955 it acquired 69.3 per cent of the voting rights. In fact the site and manufacturing capacity at Rahim Yar Khan were both unsuitable and between 1956 and 1965 average profits were only 3.6 per cent of average gross capital employed. In 1965 Unilever opened new factories in Karachi and Chittagong. The concern tried throughout the post-war years to diversify in Pakistan but down to 1970 had not found any suitable products.

Sri Lanka (Ceylon)

Unilever began production of soap in Ceylon in 1940 and vanaspati in 1941. The absence of American competition allowed the company to secure the major share of the soap and vanaspati markets. In 1951 and 1952 production began of talcum powder, toothpaste and other special products to avoid a punitive duty on the import of toilet preparations. Further attempts to diversify failed. From 1957 Ceylon elected quasi-Marxist governments which imposed stringent controls on foreign investment and the repatriation of funds. Unilever (which continued to make good profits in Ceylon well into the 1960s) responded by permitting little external capital inflow. In 1959 the company's operations were organised within a new holding company 'Ceylon Unilever' which was locally registered. By the middle of the 1960s there was little optimism within Unilever for future operations in Sri Lanka.

Turkey

Unilever had no established market in Turkey when it formed a company in the early 1950s to produce vanaspati and margarine. The 'Is' Bank took a 20 per cent stake in the company. Production began early in 1953 and considerable sales were achieved. Unilever benefited from very low overheads in Turkey and was able to use locally produced sunflower-oil. At the time butter prices were rising considerably because of shortages. Unilever was unable to diversify in Turkey. It never received licences to produce laundry-soap or detergents on any substantial scale because of the opposition of local soap-makers. Unilever produced about 72,000 tons of hard-soaps in Turkey during 1962.

Conclusion

The executives of Unilever were always conscious of their relative powerlessness when dealing with the governments of newly independent Asian countries. They showed great sensitivity in their relations with these governments and consistently refused to be associated with the hostile diplomacy of Western nations. Unilever was able to make a considerable contribution through training programmes and technological development. It was in general rewarded with the respect of the independent states and often treated more leniently than other Western businesses.

Fifty years of Unilever 1930-1980. By W.J. Reader. London: William Heinemann, 1980. xi, 148p., ill. Bibliog. Index.

The history of Unilever: a study in economic growth and social change. By Charles Wilson. London; Cassell, 1954.

Vol. 1: *Lever Brothers.* xx, 331p., ill. Index.

Vol. 2: *Jurgens' and Van den Bergh's.* 486p., ill. Bibliog. Index.

[The two volumes take the history of Unilever to the end of the second world war.]

Unilever 1945-1965: challenge and response in the post-war industrial revolution. By Charles Wilson. London: Cassell, 1968. xii, 290p. Index.
Unilever overseas: the anatomy of a multinational 1895-1965. By D.K. Fieldhouse. London: Croom Helm, 1978. (Hoover Institution publication, No. 205.) 620p. Index.

725. UNION COLD STORAGE

Samuel Vestey was a Liverpool provisions-broker trading in the 1870s. With his two sons he came to appreciate the considerable possibilities which nineteenth century developments in canning and refrigeration had opened up. Meat, butter and other products could be brought from all over the world, on a large-scale basis, to supply the British market. At first the family used a friend's cold store but in 1890 they had their own plant constructed and this was eventually to lead to the formation of the family company 'Union Cold Storage'. The Vesteys' first cold stores overseas were in Riga, Petrograd and Moscow and then they opened in China at Hangkow and Shanghai (where the business was named 'The Shanghai Ice and Cold Storage Company'). In 1909 the Vesteys purchased two second-hand refrigerated steamers and this was the start of their specialised shipping concern 'The Blue Star Line' (registered in 1911).

In China the Vesteys main interests were chickens, rabbits, sheep and particularly hen and duck eggs. The family sent their own manager to China to negotiate with the peasants through local warlords. Payment was often made on a barter basis (rice, paraffin and denim cloth were supplied). The Chinese egg supply was subject to considerable seasonal variation but the Vesteys solved this problem by manufacturing beaten egg and then transporting the frozen mixture in tins. Before the second world war, Britain was importing 40,000 tons of frozen egg each year from Russia and China and the value of egg imports from China was £3 million.

Operations in troubled inter-war China were not easy and in March 1927 the Vesteys' packing plant, warehouses and offices in Nanking were wrecked during riots. Compensation was subsequently paid. In 1945 the family were planning to build a dried-egg plant in China to meet anticipated American competition. However nothing came of this idea because of the communist takeover. The family's connection with China ended in the 1950s.

The Vestey affair. By Phillip Knightley. London: Macdonald Futura, 1981. 151p., ill.

(2nd edition published under the title: ***The rise and fall of the House of Vestey: the true story of how Britain's richest family beat the taxman - and came to grief.*** By Phillip Knightley. London: Warner Books, 1993. xi, 211p., ill. Index.)

726. VICKERS (VICKERS-ARMSTRONG)

The firm of Vickers, which began in the nineteenth century as a flour-milling business, had by the 1870s become a major civilian steel maker. In 1888 the firm entered the armaments field and soon ranked as one of Britain's leading manufacturers, with particular strength in naval armaments. After 1919 the firm made strenuous efforts to widen its activities beyond the armaments field. However, in 1927 Vickers absorbed the arms and other interests of its leading competitor, Armstrongs. While Vickers steel works merged with Cammell Laird to form the English Steel Corporation in 1929, the armaments side of the business now became the new concern of Vickers-Armstrong.

Japan

In 1907 Vickers and Armstrongs joined with a Japanese firm to establish Nihon Seikosho (the Japanese Steelworks). The two British firms each provided 37.5 per cent of the original capital of £1 million (later increased to £1.5 million). Unfortunately the new business was badly run and machinery was allowed to deteriorate. When the original agreements expired in 1917 they were renegotiated so that Seikosho became the sole Japanese agent for all armament and commercial products of the two British companies. By 1928 the value of Vickers-Armstrongs' combined holding in the company was only £1,50,000 – this meant a joint loss of over £6,00,000.

There was a reconstruction of Seikosho in the early 1930s and by December 1934 Vickers-Armstrong had recovered over £85,000 of the par value of the shares issued to them in 1919. By that time Seikosho was of minor significance to Vickers. The gross value of its direct arms exports to Japan in the years 1926-34 was a little over £1 million. In 1941 Vickers sold about a third of its shares in Seikosho and the remainder were seized on the outbreak of war. Vickers later received compensation of nearly 6 million yen. In 1952 Vickers declined an offer to have its holding in Seikosho restored to it. As a consequence of its holding in Seikosho, Vickers also held shares in Wanishi, originally a pig-iron producer. This company was liquidated by the Japanese government in 1944 and again Vickers received a compensation payment.

Turkey

Shortly before the first world war, Vickers and Armstrongs entered into a joint venture (called the Ottoman Dock Company) with the Turkish government for the regeneration of the Golden Horn arsenals. The two British companies each held 20 per cent of the venture capital with the Turkish government taking up the remainder. The agreement was for 30 years and involved putting the existing plant in order, installing a floating-dock and workshops, and training Turkish personnel. Unfortunately Turkey entered the war on the German side soon after the venture was agreed and seized the assets of the company. After the war the British companies recovered their rights in the dock company and in April 1920 they took it over. Profits were made until about the end of 1921 but after that there were losses. The British firms left Turkey in October 1923.

Post 1945

Vickers engaged in a number of collaborative projects in India. Jointly with Babcock and Wilcox and an Indian company, Vickers set-up a heavy engineering works near Calcutta which came into operation in 1962. Also in the 1960s, with the Government of India, the company started-up a factory to manufacture Vickers battle tanks. Vickers were additionally involved in a project to build Leander class frigates for the Indian Navy. This necessitated the expansion and modernisation of Mazagon Dock near Bombay. In the early 1970s, Vickers Australia entered into collaborative projects in both Indonesia and Singapore.

Vickers: a history. By J.D. Scott. London: Weidenfeld and Nicolson, 1962. xxiii, 416p., ill. Index.

Vickers against the odds, 1956-1977. By Harold Evans. London: Hodder and Stoughton, 1978. 287p., ill. Index.

'Vickers as a multinational before 1945.' By R.P.T. Davenport-Hines. Being pp. 43-74 of ***British multinationals: origins, management and performance.*** Edited by Geoffrey Jones. Aldershot: Gower, 1986.

The Vickers brothers: armaments and enterprise 1854-1914. By Clive Trebilcock. London: Europa Publications, 1977. xl, 181p., ill. Bibliog. Index.

APPENDIX 1

A select list of other British shipping companies and lines serving Asian ports where histories are known to exist

Company or Line	History
801. Albyn Line	*The thistle boats (the Albyn Line story).* By D.C.E. Burrell. Kendal: World Ship Society, 1987. 72p., ill.
802. Anchor Line (Henderson Brothers)	*Anchor Line 1856-1956.* By R.S. McLellan. Glasgow: The Company, 1956. 184p., ill. [British Library of Political and Economic Science.]
803. Bank Line	*Bank Line and Andrew Weir and Company.* By H.S. Appleyard. Kendal: World Ship Society, 1985. 176p., ill.
	Sixty adventurous years: story of the Bank Line 1885-1955. Liverpool: The Line, 1956. 136p., ill.
804. Brocklebanks	*Brocklebanks 1770-1950.* By John Frederic Gibson. Liverpool: Henry Young, 1953. 2 vols. (xvi, 287p.; 231p.) Index.
	From Cumberland to Cape Horn: the complete history of the sailing fleet of Thomas & John Brocklebank of Whitehaven and Liverpool – 'the world's oldest shipping company'. By D. Hollett. London: Fairplay Publications, 1984. 204p., ill. Bibliog. Indexes.
805. Charente Steamship Company	*Shipping enterprise and management 1830-1939: Harrisons of Liverpool.* By Francis E. Hyde with contributions from J.R. Harris and A.M. Bourn. Liverpool: Liverpool University Press, 1967. xx, 208p., ill. Index.

806. Clan Line — *A Victorian shipowner: a portrait of Sir Charles Cayzer, Baronet of Gartmore.* By Augustus Muir and Mair Davies. [London]: Published privately by Cayzer, Irvine and Company, 1978. 320p., ill. Index.

807. Den Line — *The Den Line.* By D.C.E. Burrell. Kendal: World Ship Society, 1990. 80p., ill.

808. George Gibson and Company — *George Gibson and Company.* By Graeme Somner. Kendal: World Ship Society, 1988. 80p., ill.

809. Hindustan Steam Shipping Company — *The trades increase: a centenary history of the 'Hindustan' Steam Shipping Company Limited managed by Common Brothers.* By John Lingwood and Kevin O'Donoghue. Kendal: World Ship Society, 1993. 200p., ill. Index. [Cambridge University Library.]

810. Houlder Brothers — *A record of the history of Houlder Brothers and Co. Ltd. from 1849-1950.* Compiled by Edward F. Stevens. [London]: The Company, [1951]. 101p., ill. Index.

811. King Line — *Idyll of the Kings 1889-1979: the story of the King Line, its ships and the men who sailed and managed them.* By Alan S. Mallett. Kendal: World Ship Society, 1980. 64p., ill.

812. Lamport and Holt — *Lamport and Holt.* By P.M. Heaton. Newport: Starling, 1986. 142p., ill.

Lamport & Holt and Booth. By Duncan Haws. Uckfield: TCL, 1998. (Merchant fleets; no. 34.) iv, 180p., ill. [Cambridge University Library.]

Sea transport: Lamport and Holt Line. London: Ed.J. Burrow and Co., 1936. 66p., ill.

813. Lyle Shipping Company — *From Cape to Cape: the history of the Lyle Shipping Company.* By John Orbell with Edwin Green and Michael Moss. Edinburgh: Paul Harris Publishing, 1978. xiii, 239p., ill. Index.

814. Orient Line — *Origins, Orient and Oriana.* By Charles F. Morris. Brighton: Teredo Books, 1980. xx, 491p., ill. Index.

Ships of the Orient Line. Edited by Colin Stewart. Southampton: Alard Coles, [1953]. 78p., ill.
[Includes a history of the Line from the 1870s.]

815. Reardon Smith Line — *Reardon Smith Line: the history of a South Wales shipping venture.* By P.M. Heaton. Newport, Gwent: Starling Press, 1984. 133p., ill.

816. Royal Mail Shipping Group — *A business of national importance: the Royal Mail Shipping Group 1902-1937.* By Edwin Green and Michael Moss. London: Methuen, 1982. xii, 291p., ill. Index.

Eight bells: Royal Mail Lines war story 1939-1945. By T.A. Bushell. London: Trade and Travel Publications, [1950]. xv, 207p., ill. Index.

'Lord Kylsant and the Royal Mail.' By P.N. Davies and A.M. Bourn. *Business history* (London), Vol. 14, No. 2 (July 1972), pp. 103-23.

"Royal Mail": a centenary history of the Royal Mail Line 1839-1939. By T.A. Bushell. London: Trade and Travel Publications, [1939]. xvi, 270p., ill.

817. Union Castle Line — *Race to the Cape: story of the Union Castle line 1857-1977.* By Norman Hodson. Ringwood: Navigator Books, 1995. 148p., ill.

The Union Castle and the War 1914-1919. By E.F. Knight. London: Union-Castle Mail Steamship Company, 1920. 63p., ill.

Union Castle chronicle 1853-1953. By Marischal Murray. London: Longmans, Green and Company, 1953. xvii, 392p., ill. Index.

APPENDIX 2

Histories of Indian railway companies which originated as British-controlled companies

Railway Company	History
901. Bengal-Nagpur	*The blue chip railway 1887-1987.* By R.R. Bhandari. [Calcutta:] C.P.R.O., S.E. Railway, [?1988]. 142p., ill. [Bodleian Library, Oxford.]
902. Delhi, Umballa, Kalka (including Kalka-Simla)	*Kalka-Simla and Kangra Valley Railways.* By R.R. Bhandari. New Delhi: Northern Railway, 1983. vi, 95p., ill.
903. East Indian	*The early history of the East Indian Railway 1845-1879.* By Hena Mukherjee. Calcutta: Firma KLM, 1994. xii, 195p. Bibliog. Index. [School of Oriental and African Studies.]
	History of the East Indian Railway. By George Huddlestone.
	Part I. Calcutta: Thacker, Spink and Co., 1906. ix, 281p., ill.
	Part II. Bristol: St. Stephen's Bristol Press, 1932. 95p., ill.
904. Great Indian Peninsula	*History of the Great Indian Peninsula Railway.* By S.N. Sharma. 2nd. ed.
	Part I, Vol. I: 1853-1869. New Delhi: Manohar, [1990]. vi, 117p., ill. Bibliog. [School of Oriental and African Studies.]
	Part I, Vol. II: 1870-1900. New Delhi, Manohar, [1990]. xxv, 457p. Bibliog. Index. [School of Oriental and African Studies.]

General Index

The references are to the numbers of the bibliographical entries

Index of Firms and Persons (Including Authors)

The references are to the numbers of the bibliographical entries